THE GENESIS OF POLITICAL CORRECTNESS

The Basis of a False Morality

Michael William

PREFACE

Political Correctness, like communism proper, is a resilient ideology. It has survived and continued to grow despite the hostility shown to it by most ordinary people and even a large number of politicians. Like communism proper, it has survived its obvious disasters. The politically correct even shrug off the various communist genocides as a nuisance.

Grappling with the issue of how to describe the evolution of political correctness is difficult due to the vast number of books, essays, articles etc. produced by the Left, and the Frankfurt School in particular. I have focused on key items to make sense of the creed and to explain the logic of it.

I am grateful for the essay, given as a speech, of William Lind for establishing a starting point of enquiry and highlighting the skeleton of the ideology.

This book is written as a sister book to *The Ponzi Class: Ponzi Economics, Globalization and Class Oppression in the 21st Century*, Amazon, Great Britain, 2015, which was published in December 2015. It is helpful for readers of this book to have read that one, but it is not necessary. I make references to that book as appropriate to minimize duplication.

The morality of the Ponzi Class is political correctness. Understanding that false morality and the damage done by it is the purpose of this book.

Micheal William

January 2016

Also by Michael William

Brexit Means Brexit: How the British Ponzi Class Survived the EU Referendum
The Ponzi Class: Ponzi Economics, Globalization and Class Oppression in the 21st Century
Multiculturalist Ideology (Part One): A Rationale For Race War Politics
Multiculturalist Ideology (Part Two): The Rising Tide of Race War Politics

Contents

INTRODUCTION

In his essay 'The Origins of Political Correctness' the American writer William Lind advances the case that political correctness is a Marxist offshoot originally developed by the Frankfurt School in the 1930s. William Lind concludes his essay by warning:

> 'America today is in the throws of the greatest and direst transformation in its history. We are becoming an ideological state, a country with an official state ideology enforced by the power of the state. In 'hate crimes' we now have people serving jail sentences for political thoughts. And the Congress is now moving to expand that category ever further. Affirmative action is part of it. The terror against anyone who dissents from Political Correctness on campus is part of it. It's exactly what we have seen happen in Russia, in Germany, in Italy, in China, and now it's coming here. And we don't recognize it because we call it Political Correctness and laugh it off. My message today is that it's not funny, it's here, it's growing and it will eventually destroy, as it seeks to destroy, everything that we have ever defined as our freedom and our culture.'

The purpose of this book is to add to the understanding of William Lind's thesis and to set out key aspects of political correctness that are particularly relevant. This examination will necessitate an understanding of that aspect of Marxism from which political correctness is drawn. The book will be written primarily from an English perspective. England is different from the USA as it has been a settled society for many centuries, whereas the USA has been a country that has encouraged large scale immigration and so has a more fluid cultural mix. With England, it is only relatively recently that mass immigration has been vigorously promoted.

William Lind defines political correctness as 'cultural Marxism'. This book will define it as being 'the mechanism for the enforcement of neo-Marxist ideology'. This neo-Marxist ideology is focused on culture and is fixated with race, feminism, and gay rights in particular. It is also firmly opposed to nationhood, at least as far as Western countries are concerned, and with regards to the English in particular.

The book will expand upon what William Lind has said; it will set out basic, relevant aspects of Marxist ideology, and it will examine three key works in the evolution of political correctness: *The Authoritarian*

1

Personality; 'Repressive Tolerance', and 'Citizenship and National Identity: Some Reflections on the Future of Europe' (Citizenship and National Identity). The latter item, unlike the two others, is focused on Europe (not the USA), although the matters raised are relevant to the USA. Furthermore, the latter item involves an ideological battle, the outcome of which is still uncertain, whereas the other two items have generally been an outright victory for the politically correct, and the thrust of the arguments contained within them are now accepted as being the norm – that is to say that, in as much as there was a battle between conservatives and the politically correct over the ideology in the first two items, the conservatives lost. In the latter item, the conservatives are losing (one could argue that the politically correct are wiping the floor with the conservatives), but the battle is not yet over; the reason for this is that the adverse economic and social consequences of what is being imposed on European countries (not least the mass unemployment, insolvent banks, teetering national defaults, and the anger at the harm done by mass immigration) is impacting so quickly and so devastatingly that an outright victory for the politically correct has not yet been possible. A key part of this is the drive towards an EU superstate. It is not that the conservative viewpoint has been successful in combating the drive to establish an EU superstate; it is more that the superstatist drive has run into a hostile public opinion. This hostility is due, in part, to the democratic deficit of the EU and its manipulation of referendum results (people have to keep on voting until they vote in favour of whatever EU proposal is being proposed), which obviously renders the EU governing class detached from the people. It is also due, in part, to the damage done to ordinary peoples' lives by the superstate agenda and its attempted enforcement. It is often overlooked, or not understood, that the looming EU superstate is at least as much a product of political correctness as it is an issue in its own right. The desire to destroy nations and nation states has been a key, integral part of communist ideology since that creed's inception.

Marxism rejects the idea that Western society is good and rejects capitalism. Neo-Marxism likewise rejects Western society but instead focuses on culture and condemns the West for the supposed oppression of non-Western peoples. This leads to the supposed oppression of ethnic and other minorities in Western countries and the supposed need for political correctness as a solution to this alleged oppression. England is different from the USA in this important aspect as the USA did treat its black population as slaves and then discriminated against them. Consequently, political correctness can exploit this historical fact (however, this does not apply to all ethnic minorities nor all immigrants,

2

who were not all affected by the USA's slavery). In England, there was no substantial ethnic minority population until after World War II (WWII), when mass immigration began. So the promotion of ethnic minorities and so-called positive discrimination, or affirmative action as it is described in the USA, is a mechanism for the promotion of the interests of immigrants ahead of the indigenous population. In England, the English are to be treated as second class citizens and discriminated against. The English now find, for example, that they are denied social housing, that schools and the NHS are under strain, and that their job prospects are more difficult, all because the ruling class have deliberately opened Britain's borders and allowed uncontrolled mass immigration. If mass immigration continues, then the English will become a minority in England in around 40-50 years. There is almost no discussion of this.

This combination of the drive towards a European superstate and political correctness has had a profound effect on English society. Political correctness, it will be argued, has had the effect of enforcing an anti-English culture in England itself (with the English being portrayed as racist, colonialist, etc.), suppressing legitimate English concerns, and is an obstruction to the reassertion of English rights and interests. William Lind's assessment is correct. Political correctness is a threat to our way of life and even the existence of the English nation itself. The advocacy of multiculturalism and the attendant mass immigration, this book will argue, is to the detriment of the English, and is intended to be so.

This book will begin with an overview of the classical understanding of civilization and how it has developed. It will focus on the philosophers JS Mill (1806-1873) and RG Collingwood (1889-1943). An understanding of the development of civilization is relevant as political correctness is a rejection of it, portraying what had hitherto been regarded as civilized values as prejudiced and something bad. It further portrays less developed peoples as being victims and as being oppressed. Thus the relationship between civilized and less civilized peoples is important.

Next, the genesis of political correctness will be explored. This will involve examining the French Revolution, which bore all the bloody hallmarks of the subsequent communist revolutions and which was inspired by the ideology of Jean-Jacques Rousseau (1712-1778) that was also influential on communism, and then the basic tenets of Marxism and the establishment of the Frankfurt School. The book will analyse three key works of the Frankfurt School: *The Authoritarian Personality*; 'Repressive Tolerance', and 'Citizenship and National Identity'. The first of these is a report, written in 1950; the second two are essays written in 1965 and 1995, respectively. 'Citizenship and National Identity' leads on to the issues of constitutional patriotism, a variant term for civic nationalism, and multiculturalism, which will also be examined in respect to the essay.

Finally, there will be an examination of the current impact of political correctness. This will include some practical examples as well as an ideological dimension to reveal its malign manifestation, which is more pervasive than many appreciate.

For ease of understanding, the book prefers to use the terms Tory and Tories rather than Conservative and Conservatives. The term Tory has been informally used as an alternative to Conservative in Britain for a very long time. The Tories and the Conservatives are seen as one and the same. The Conservative Party ceased to be conservative politically some time in the 1980s. Margaret Thatcher could be more accurately described as a classical liberal (with a philosophy focused on free trade and free markets) rather than a conservative. By 2015, the Tories had forcefully adopted the ideology of political correctness, which is totally incompatible with conservative philosophy. However, historically, Tory and Conservative are interchangeable terms.

CIVILIZATION

I n his essay 'Civilization', JS Mill identifies two different meanings of the term 'civilization'. First, he identifies the meaning as a description of human improvement and states that a country is thought of as being more civilized. He describes it as being 'farther down the road to perfection; happier, nobler, wiser'.[1] Second, he identifies civilization as those factors which distinguish a country from barbarianism and describes it as 'that kind of improvement only, which distinguishes a wealthy and powerful nation from savages or barbarians'.[2] It is this second meaning that Mill concentrates on in his analysis. This book will concentrate, as did Mill, on the second meaning.

Mill defines civilization as being the opposite of a savage life. He identifies a savage tribe as one which consists of a small group of individuals scattered thinly or wandering across a large area. By contrast, civilization has a dense population of settled people in fixed dwellings, forming villages or towns.[3] Savage life does not have manufacturing or agriculture, whereas civilization does.[4] According to Mill, a savage way of life involves little, if any, cooperation, and the savages act as individuals without society or coordination. They do not have any laws, justice, or true administration of society.[5] By contrast, a civilized society does cooperate. Members of a civilized society cooperate for the common good, to improve the effectiveness of their efforts (e.g. in work practices), and to rely upon the law and justice to protect them and their property. A civilized society has meaningful social intercourse.[6] Mill believes these attributes of civilization tend to co-exist and grow alongside development in wealth and population. He further regards Europe, Great Britain in particular, as having all of the elements of civilization.

Mill cites two ingredients as being the key characteristics of a civilization: the spread of property ownership and the willingness to cooperate.[7] Mill regards the willingness to cooperate as being the limiting factor in the savage lifestyle. He resolutely states that it was the inability of savages to cooperate which was the primary reason for their savagery; only civilized people can cooperate because they are able and willing to sacrifice some of their individuality for a common purpose.[8] One aspect of cooperation is the establishment of law and justice, which Mill identifies as one of the differences between a savage tribe and a civilized society. The legal possession of property requires law. Mill particularly highlights the issue of war, where discipline counts for more than numbers, referring specifically to Spain and its inability to unite in the war against Napoleon.[9] Mill further regards the ability to cooperate as being something difficult which has to be learnt. He highlights the division of labour, which he says is central to 'the great school of cooperation'.[10] Mill sees the effect of the growth of newspapers, arguing that newspapers allow the masses to be better able to participate in the democratic process. This participation betters the masses as a result of their being better educated and informed. In this way, there is the formation of a public opinion, and that public opinion has its own collective influence. Mill believes that one of the benefits of this is the integration of the individual into society, that the individual would be then concerned not simply with himself, but with the society as a whole.

However, Mill believes that civilization was prone to decay, that over time there would be an accumulation of factors that would pose a threat to the continuity of the civilization itself. Mill highlights the softening effects of civilization: 'There has crept over the refined classes, over the whole class of gentlemen in England, moral effeminacy, an inaptitude for every kind of struggle'. Mill sees such people as being capable of stoicism but differentiated that from heroism – heroism requiring an active rather than passive response.[11] Mill is also concerned that the influence of the masses would hold back a civilization in mediocrity and conformity.[12] This is why he believes education is so important and that it should concentrate on promoting free thought and an enquiring mind.[13]

Having set out the problems of civilization, Mill then advocates the importance of education. He fastens upon Oxford, Cambridge, Eton, and Westminster as being the leading educational establishments of their day (and arguably still today). He also defends the teaching of classics and logic, in preference to physics,[14] as a means to building character and intellect and is dismissive of mathematics.[15] Mill condemns the English educational establishment. He believes they produce disciples and not individuals or enquirers.[16] Even those who are recognized as being learned, Mill asserts, are spoiled: 'They give him an income, not for continuing to learn, but for having learnt; not for doing anything, but for what he has already done'.[17]

To understand Mill on this issue, it must be born in mind that he is attacking religious influence on education, which he believes should be secularized. Nevertheless, his condemnation of mathematics, physics, and 'the business of the world'[18] are important. Given that Britain was then undergoing the industrial revolution, the importance of physics (and the production of engineers), for example, cannot be underestimated. 'The business of the world' is important.

Of Mill's argument, the philosopher, Alexander Bain (1818-1903) makes the following criticism:

'I never felt quite satisfied with the article on Civilization. The definition given at the outset seems inadequate; and the remainder of the article is one of his many attacks on the vicious tendencies of the time. He regards as consequences of our civilization, the decay of individual energy, the weakening of the influence of superior minds, the growth of *charlatanerie*, and the diminished efficacy of public opinion, and insists on some remedies for the evils; winding up with an attack on the Universities. To my mind, these topics should have been detached from any theory of Civilization, or any attempt, to extol the past at the cost of the present.'[19]

In his criticism of Mill's Civilization, Bain importantly highlights the essay's context and that Mill was influenced by contemporaneous events and a fixation with the educational establishment. Mill had ulterior motives; his angst with education was revealed when, speaking of himself and his wife, he said, 'We were now much less democrats than I had been, because so long as education continued to be so wretchedly imperfect, we dreaded the ignorance and especially the selfishness and brutality of the mass.'[20]

An important influence on Mill was the French Revolution, which he had fully studied.[21] Mob rule had been a feature of that revolution,[22] which Mill regarded as an aberration.[23] Given the revolution's bloody aftermath, Mill's concerns are understandable. Underlying this aspect is the philosophical difference between Mill, an individualist, and Rousseau, who was held to have inspired the French Revolution and who asserted the supremacy of what he termed the general will and hence the state.[24]

Professor Beate Jahn's analysis of Mill's philosophy sets out the process of civilization as Mill believed it: 'savagism, slavery, barbarism and civilization'.[25] Mill did not believe that this process was automatic, and he believed that it could fail due to stagnation if not decline, citing China in particular.[26] To Mill, the nurturing of individuality, including in education, is an important antidote to stagnation and decline.[27] History was important to Mill.[28] The historical context is further complicated by the British Empire and its rule over other peoples, and Mill concentrates on the distinction between savages and civilization.

To put Mill's argument into context, the development of civilization does require cooperation, the rule of law, and some form of government legitimacy – even an absolute monarchy. The rule of law allows property rights which, for example, the World Bank includes as a part of its good governance criteria.[29] Property rights allow the ownership of land and, hence, farming. The first steps in the creation of civilization were the move away from hunter-gathering and towards agriculture. It is an historical fact that the Roman Empire first conquered and then prevailed against far greater numbers of barbarians for many centuries because of their disciplined military capability.[30] But the Roman Empire fell. The reasons cited for that are many, but they include the gradual loss of martial spirit and military discipline, including the abandonment of the wearing of helmets and breastplate by the infantry.[31] The loss of cooperation went much further, not only with the struggle for power between the Christians and Pagans at the time of the barbarian invasions,[32] but with the division of the Empire between East and West, and even by outright civil wars in the Western Empire.[33] The Romans lacked the resolve to unite against the enemy,[34] as did the British Empire.[35] This feebleness and lack of resolve and cooperation proved fatal.

Mill places an emphasis on the classics in his analysis of the importance of education. He is dismissive of mathematics and the sciences. This tended to be the prevailing view of the English educational establishment in the 19th century,[36] and some would argue well into the 20th century, although Britain did respond to the industrial challenges posed by Germany and the USA.[37] Mill's criticism of Oxford and Cambridge was pertinent to its day, but those universities did soon change the religious tests for undergraduates[38] and even went so far as to embrace the modernity of the industrial revolution by introducing new chairs for sciences. This was not what Mill had in mind in his criticisms of those two universities.

Yet one of the problems which science encountered was the difficulty in attracting funds and jobs for its graduates,[39] with the British industrial culture still relying on the cult of the 'practical man'.[40] Britain's industrial decline, hence the decline of its wealth and power and, consequently, its position as the leading world civilization, was partly the result of the failure to embrace modern education when compared to its primary competitors.[41] Mill went further in that he positively rejected the importance of science and even mathematics.

Mill's analysis of the differences between civilization and savagery is well founded. His emphasis on the necessity for cooperation in order to establish a civilized society is correct. Civilization is preferable to savagery; through civilization, a more fulfilling and a more prosperous lifestyle is made possible. Civilizations do decline, and many are overthrown – often by invasion. But the underlying weakness of the civilization itself is a key factor. This was true of the Roman Empire and was true of the British Empire. Mill's dismissal of the importance of mathematics and science in education is a failing. The classics could not and did not allow Britain to maintain her world position. Mill's emphasis on the classics was the product of its day, and he wrote 'Civilization' while influenced by contemporaneous factors and history. Mill did not see that the British industrial economy needed more, not less, importance attached to those sciences in order to maintain Britain's position as an industrial and world power.

Like Mill, in his book the *New Leviathan*, RG Collingwood examines the different meanings of civilization, the variety of civilizations, and civilization's relationship to more backward peoples. He identifies those who reject and wish to destroy civilization as 'barbarists' who seek to barbarize society. Collingwood's view is that the barbarists cannot succeed as 'there is no such thing as civilization' and that it therefore cannot be destroyed. Like Mill and Rousseau, Collingwood was concerned with civilization's potential demise. In the *New Leviathan*, Collingwood begins his examination of civilization by identifying the term to mean the act of civilizing and progressing a society towards civilization and away from barbarism.[42] Collingwood asserts that there is no clear distinction between civilization and barbarism.[43] The term is relative and changes over time as all societies progress. He therefore regards civilization as 'a process which has no absolute beginning and no absolute end',[44] and states that there are two meanings relating to the relationship between the terms civilization and barbarism:

> 'First, they may be used absolutely. As so used they are 'contraries': names for the two ends of a scale, between which there are many intermediate terms. But these two ends are not really existing conditions of society. No society is or even has been in this absolute sense civilized or barbarous.
>
> Second, they have a relative meaning. Any given society at any given time stands somewhere on the scale between the infinity of absolute civilization and the zero of absolute barbarism. But although in an absolute sense it is neither civilized nor barbarous, in a relative sense it is civilized as compared with one lower down in the scale, and barbarous as compared with one higher up.'[45]

Collingwood accepts that civilization is also used to denote a particular entity of society, such as the Chinese civilization, European civilization, or Roman civilization.[46] Collingwood believes that this distinction between different entities of civilization means that each tries to be civilized in different ways, so that a Chinaman will attempt to be civilized in a way that might be regarded barbarous to a European and vice versa.[47] Collingwood rejects historical relativism[48] but does believe that civilization underlies every society and that it is realized in different ways. He divides the concept of civilization into three orders, with the third order being the universal ideal shared by all, and the source of the other two ideals.[49] To Collingwood, 'civilization and advancement of civilization are one and the same',[50] and he identifies three senses of civilizing: economic, social, and legal. The economic definition of being civilized is the ability to generate wealth by more advanced means than pure effort alone. The social definition is the manner in which people treat one another with civility, not force, and 'proper and seemly' behaviour. The legal definition means a society governed by law, in particular civil law.[51]

Collingwood differentiates between barbarism and savagery. Savagery is not being civilized, and there is no such thing as absolute savagery.[52] A savage people have a limited sense of being civilized relative to more civilized peoples. Barbarism is defined as either conscious or unconscious hostility to civilization.[53] It is a force to become less civilized and to promote others also to do likewise.[54] Collingwood describes this process as one to barbarize civilization. 'To barbarize' is the opposite of 'to civilize'. In a conflict between civilization and barbarism, Collingwood believes that it is only civilization that can be the product of unconscious action, unlike barbarism:

> 'Barbarism can never be in this sense unconscious. The barbarist, as I will call the man who imitates the conditions of an uncivilized world cannot afford to forget what it is that he is trying to bring about; he is trying to bring about, not anything positive, but something negative, the destruction of civilization; and he must remember, if not what civilization is, at least what the destruction of civilization is.
> Concentrating his mind on this question as he must do, the barbarist feels himself to be in one sense at least the intellectual superior of his enemy, and prides himself upon it.'[55]

Collingwood believes that the barbarist, holding the initiative, has the advantage over his target initially. His victims are unprepared.[56] But he needs to maintain a fluid situation in order to keep momentum in his attack. Collingwood believes that, in the long term, the barbarist will lose and can only win temporary engagements. Collingwood's rationale is that the barbarist must lose because:

> 'There is no such thing as civilization. If there were, it could be exterminated, and the barbarist would have won; but in fact there   are   only   innumerable   and   variously   distant

approximations to it, a kaleidoscope of patterns all more or less akin to the ideal ... what ensures the defeat of barbarism is not so much the enormous diversity of existing civilizations, too numerous for any conqueror to dream of overcoming; it is the literally infinite possibility of varying the nature of the thing called civilization, leaving it recognizable in this diversity; a possibility which will be exploited as soon as success in a barbarian attack stimulates the inventive powers of civilization to look for new channels of development.[57]

This assertion makes two assumptions. First, that civilization is not distinct and that it is a process that will triumph in the end. Second, that the barbarist seeks to destroy the process of civilization and not a civilization as an entity. The assertion further overlooks the civilized status of the barbarist, who will himself be civilized, according to Collingwood's own logic, to some extent. It does not follow that the barbarist seeks to destroy the extent of his own degree of civilization, nor does it follow that he will not seek to benefit from, for example, the increased power that more advanced economic civilization brings, nor seek to use the law to legitimize and fasten any gains won. The various invading barbarians of the Western Roman Empire sought to hold and defend their territorial conquests once they had settled down, rather than live in a lawless wasteland under threat from imperial forces.[58] Collingwood's assertion that 'there is no such thing as civilization' and that it is the variety of civilization which guarantees its ability to defeat the barbarist assumes that the barbarist is at war with civilization as a whole and that civilization as a whole is opposed to the objectives of the barbarist. However, the barbarist may only be attacking one entity of civilization, and other civilizations may choose not to get involved, or may seek to support the barbarist for their own reasons (the Eastern Roman Empire did not fully mobilize in support of the West,[59] and the barbarians were able to play one half of the empire off against the other).[60] Collingwood believes that barbarism involves conflict with civilization and between one barbarist and another.[61]

Collingwood picks four historical examples. The Saracens are cited as being the first barbarism[62] and Collingwood contrasts them with the other barbarians who overran the Western Roman Empire and who were less hostile – Collingwood asserts – to Roman civilization.[63] However, the Muslims were hostile to Christianity, whereas the northern barbarians were not, although they adopted the 'Arian heresy'.[64] The Muslim invasion of the Byzantine Empire (the surviving Eastern Roman Empire) resulted in the conquest of Arabia, Syria, and Egypt before the first attack on Constantinople itself. The defeat of the Saracens at

Constantinople,[65] and the defeat at Tours, halted their advance.[66] Collingwood asserts that they were disgusted with the wealth and peaceful state of civilization and were responsible for the destruction of civilization in North Africa.[67] It is important that Collingwood recognizes the role of the disunity within civilization which assisted the Saracens in their conquests.[68] Disunity is something which both Mill and Rousseau fastened upon. Collingwood points out that the French victory at Tours was 'carefully prepared' and involved 'the entire strength of Europe'.[69] He attributes desire of minority religions in the Empire to seek protection from the dominant religion as being a factor in the initial success of Islam.[70] He regards the destruction of Africa as being the principle achievement of the Saracens.[71] Collingwood regards Islam as being only half barbarous, having abandoned barbarism after the defeats at Constantinople and in France.[72]

Collingwood identifies the 'Albigensian heresy' as being the second barbarism.[73] Collingwood describes this as an anti-Christian aberration of Manichaeism (a belief that the world is a battleground between good and evil) practised by believers who lived like hermits.[74] The Manichees attracted hostility from both Christians and pagans,[75] and the Albigenses regarded everything corporeal as Satanic and regarded churches as being inhabited by evil spirits.[76] Collingwood regards the creed as a megalomania[77] and incompatible with a Christian society and values.[78] The Albigensian heresy was 'stamped out' in the thirteenth century.[79]

The third barbarism is the Turks. Collingwood distinguishes between the Seljuk and Ottoman Turks.[80] Gibbon described the Seljuks as being a 'pastoral and predatory caste'[81] who invaded the Byzantine Empire in l050 and eventually conquered part of Asia Minor and Jerusalem in 1076. Asia Minor went into decline following the incursion by the Seljuks, which continued when they were succeeded by the Ottoman Turks. Asia Minor fell to the Ottomans in 1340.[82] Subsequently, the Ottomans proceeded to conquer Greece and the Balkans, forcing the European powers to unite against them.[83] Nevertheless, the Turks steadily advanced, defeating the Christian armies.[84] Collingwood highlights the complacency, lack of unity, and even treachery amongst the Christians. The fall of Constantinople in 1453 was aided by the gunnery of a treacherous Hungarian.[85] Collingwood portrays the Turks as cruel, untrustworthy,[86] and piratical.[87] He describes the Turks' failure to conquer Europe as a failure of barbarism and the success of civilization, although he overlooks the Turks' retention of their conquests. Collingwood describes the Turks as having turned away from barbarism.[88]

Collingwood's fourth barbarism is the Germans.[89] With the Germans, Collingwood believes that barbarism was not innate, stating that barbarism in the German 'seems to have grown in him as his reaction to a peculiar situation in which a certain element in him, his nationality, was involved at a certain time'.[90] He describes the Germans as having always been 'bad neighbours', a form of latent barbarism.[91] He believes that German barbarism emerged gradually, possibly starting with Bismarck, if not before, sweeping away the civilized elements of society.[92] He cites the Nazi concept of 'thinking with your blood' rather than 'the old-fashioned way of doing it with your brains.'[93] He condemns the Germans for their evil national vanity.[94] He describes Bismarck's Germany as 'displaying barbarism in an ambiguous form'.[95] He believes that the benefit of hindsight reveals that the German attitude to England at the time of the Boer War was barbarist.[96] He asserts that German barbarism relied upon using diplomacy to divide opposition to it[97] and that there are no allies or loyalty for the barbarists; it is 'all fight against all'.[98] He reiterates that the barbarists exploit the slowness of civilization to recognize its threat.[99] He identifies with Germans the tendency to 'herd-worship' and regards this as a symptom of a lack of civilization, stating that the Germans are insufficiently civilized and suffer from 'a defect in civilization where more civilization is needed'.[100] And while Germany was an advanced European country, civilized in many respects, Collingwood condemns them for 'incivility'.[101] This lack of civility was a key missing factor.

Collingwood sums up his account of the four arch-barbarists by saying that they were all defeated, or withered away, for a variety of reasons, not for one single reason.[102] That Collingwood was writing during WWII[103] is pertinent and explains the case he is making. Collingwood's optimistic conclusion that barbarists will always be defeated is understandable, especially as Britain's victory was by no means assured, and defeat would have resulted in a definite victory for barbarism, given Nazi ideology.

Of the four barbarisms cited by Collingwood, two were relatively backward peoples living on the edges of civilization, the Saracens and the Turks, one, the Albigensian heresy, was internal to civilization itself, and the fourth, the Germans, was a civilization technologically and economically advanced but lacking the necessary civility to act responsibly. Three of the examples waged aggressive wars against civilization, and the fourth, the Albigenses, who were plundering in southern France and who were described by Pope Innocent III as being 'worse than the Saracens', were vanquished in a crusade when peaceful means failed.[104] All four examples have in common a strident ideology.

Rousseau also was alert to the potential friction within society that could be caused by different parts of the civic society,[105] and he believed that decay would set in when people were motivated by private interests rather than the common good.[106] For Rousseau, this would lead to a failure of the general will and a breakdown in the proper functioning of the state. Rousseau asks the question: 'If Sparta and Rome perished, what state can hope to endure forever?'[107] He continues:

> 'The body politic, as well as the human body, begins to die as soon as it is born, and carries in itself the causes of its destruction ... it is for [men] to prolong as much as possible the life of the state, by giving it the best possible constitution.'[108]

Collingwood was himself concerned as to the potential decay of civilization, as were other inter-war writers,[109] and he did not regard the barbarians as being the chief cause of the collapse of the Roman Empire.[110] However, the Western Roman Empire fell 1,000 years before the Eastern Roman Empire did.[111] Whatever failings the empire had, it was only in the West where those failings proved fatal. The Western Empire had twice the length of frontier to defend against the barbarians, while the Eastern Empire was strategically stronger, which meant the barbarians headed west.[112] The late 19th and early 20th centuries witnessed a sense of alarm at Britain's decline,[113] and the lead up to WWII was dominated by the threat of the rise of Nazism, and these factors undoubtedly influenced the concerns of Collingwood and the other inter-war writers.

If civilizations can fall, then it does not follow that barbarism must be defeated. Barbarism may be quite likely to triumph over a declining civilization, not only as a result of the aggressiveness and opportunism of the barbarism, but also as a result of civilization's weakness. Collingwood, however, is optimistic that civilization will always triumph. This statement is dependent upon what meaning is conferred upon the term civilization. Collingwood identifies three categories of civilization: first, civilization as a process of civilizing; second, civilization as distinct from savagery or barbarism; and third, civilization as an entity, such as the Roman civilization.

The Roman civilization no longer exists. It was overrun by various barbarian tribes in the west, and the surviving Byzantine Empire was eventually completely overrun too. Constantinople was conquered by the Turks. In this instance, the barbarists, as Collingwood describes the Turks, succeeded to destroy the Byzantine Empire. That they subsequently failed to conquer the rest of Europe may be true, but that does not help the Byzantines. Civilization as distinct from savage, or less civilized, peoples is a relative phenomenon which can change. China, as Mill highlighted,[114] was once more advanced than many other

14

civilizations but was surpassed by the European powers as it slid into decline. In this sense too, civilization can cease.

Civilization as a process may be more difficult to destroy. But the process stems from the civilization as an entity and is dependent upon it. If the entity is destroyed, then so is the process. The Eastern Roman Empire was wealthier than the Western,[115] yet the eastern Mediterranean countries are not so now. Furthermore, to cite the failure of the barbarists to be able to destroy the process assumes that that is their intention. In fact, they are certainly keen on the wealth created by the process, as the Saracens, Turks, and all the other barbarians who overran the Roman Empire were keen to plunder and take whatever booty they could find. Mohammad told one of his commanders: 'May God keep you safe and bring you much booty.'[116] The Visigoths, who had been accepted into the Roman Empire, rebelled in a prolonged campaign of plunder, including the plundering of Rome, supported by various disaffected locals, slaves and bandits,[117] before finally settling down in Aquitaine. Collingwood cites Alaric's successor, Ataulf, as a barbarian who accepted Roman civilization.[118] Ataulf did adopt a friendlier stance towards Rome,[119] although this was after the Visigoths had plundered Greece, Illyricum, Italy (including Rome), and southern Gaul. Burdened with booty, holding the Western Roman emperor's sister hostage after plundering Rome – a woman who Ataulf later married – and settling down on some of the richest land in Gaul, it was only then that Ataulf was happy to adopt friendly relations with Rome, and legitimacy. The Visigoths subsequently reverted to a more hostile and warlike stance.[120]

The Vandals (from whom the term vandalism originates)[121] plundered their way through Gaul[122] and Spain (Spain being plundered by both Visigoths and Vandals in a war between them in the years 416-418),[123] before crossing into Africa and plundering that previously unplundered province, capturing Carthage and the Roman fleet facilities.[124] Having settled in North Africa, they used their new navy to invade and plunder much of the Mediterranean, including an undefended Rome.[125] The war to conquer Africa was bitterly fought, partly because of the religious hostility between the Arian Vandals and the Catholic North Africans. Saint Augustine, the highly influential theologian and bishop of Hippo, died while besieged in that city.[126] Collingwood distinguishes between the Saracens and those barbarians who overran the Western Roman Empire.[127] This distinction should not facilitate a revisionist history. The Vandals, Goths, Huns, and others were capable of being just as destructive as the Saracens, despite a policy of appeasement from the Romans. (e.g. Alaric, the Gothic leader, who was appointed master-general of Eastern Illyricum, despite his plundering of Greece, used the post to access Roman munitions[128] before invading and plundering Italy and Rome;[129] the Huns' sacking of Naissus left the city almost deserted save for the stench of corpses, and the nearby riverbanks were full of human bones;[130] and the city of Aquileia was so totally devastated that 'the succeeding generation could scarcely discover the ruins.')[131] Mecca, although outside the Roman Empire, grew wealthy through trade.[132] The combination of religious zeal and desire for booty may have motivated Saracen expansionist conquests of the Persian and Byzantine empires, aided by a pragmatic governance of recently conquered territories,[133] but there is no reason to dismiss them as being more backward than the northern barbarians. Where the Saracens and Turks were distinguishable is that they were Muslim, and their destruction of Byzantine civilization was more complete. Constantinople was plundered, its inhabitants were taken for, or sold into, slavery,[134] and the city was renamed and has remained an Ottoman city.

Mill's assertion that savages are unwilling to cooperate is a factor in their failure to become civilized[135] perhaps explaining their determination to conquer and plunder instead. However, as Collingwood himself points out, the concepts of civilization and savagery are relative.[136] Germany was an advanced country even under the Nazis, who were unlikely to balk at more effective industrial production methods or more advanced weaponry. Their barbarity stemmed from their bloody ideology. Their defeat was uncertain, and Britain would have become bankrupt were it not for US assistance.[137] Collingwood avers that Germany was barbarist as far back as Bismarck.[138] Germany was united under Prussian dominance by Bismarck, using subterfuge and military action against other powers, including France, Denmark, and the Austro-Hungarian Empire.[139] It was duplicitous in its aggressive participation in the scramble for Africa.[140] It industrialized, overtaking Britain,[141] and introduced the world's most advanced welfare system.[142] Although nationally arrogant, it was Hitler and the Nazis who took Germany into outright barbarism with a series of invasions seeking plunder, Lebensraum,[143] and genocide. Nazism entailed an aggressive rejection of Western Civilization as had, to a lesser extent, the French Revolution, which led to the Napoleonic wars and the attendant revolutionary zeal, plunder,[144] and bloodshed, including the Terror, when those deemed to be enemies of the revolution were persecuted and tens of thousands were summarily executed.[145]

Barbarists do not necessarily set out to destroy the process of civilization, although their actions may harm and set back the process. They are more interested in the destruction of civilization as an entity, either for territorial conquest or booty. Had Germany triumphed in war, then it might eventually have become bored[146] with Nazism, and a more

16

civilized culture might have developed. But that would have been no use to the exterminated Jews and Slavs, and the emerging civilization would have been very different. Barbarists internal to a civilization are more motivated by a hatred of established values, and Collingwood's analysis is more pertinent to them as they do seek to destroy the process of civilization identified with the host society's culture. Barbarist ideology is important and, when combined with the desire to plunder, poses a major threat to civilization.

Collingwood develops the understanding of the relationship between civilization and barbarism with his attention to the barbarist. His definition of civilization and his appreciation of its many forms is complete, as is his analysis of barbarism and his concept of barbarization, being the goal of the barbarist. Ideology is important. However, Collingwood's writing was influenced by WWII, and his optimistic assertion that the barbarist will fail because there is no such thing as civilization is incomplete. Collingwood does not fully explore the impact of barbarists on civilization in all its forms, and he does not properly take into account that barbarists may not set out to destroy civilization in all its forms. Often, as with the Nazis and the Turks, barbarists are interested in territorial conquest and loot. They do not reject the process of civilization but seek to destroy an entity of civilization. They can succeed in doing so. The Roman Empire was destroyed. The Byzantines were exterminated. Both have ceased to exist as entities. Even the process of civilization reflected in the Byzantine Empire ended, superseded by that of the Turks. The eastern Mediterranean is now far poorer and more backward than the western. Civilization as a relative distinction from savagery can change and be destroyed as different entities of civilizations rise and fall. The northern barbarians were as destructive as the Saracens, and they did destroy the Western Roman Empire. The Byzantine Empire survived another 1,000 years. Barbarists can destroy civilization, and Collingwood's assertion is not a complete explanation. However, his development of the understanding of civilization is important. The concept of the barbarist who wishes to barbarize civilization is crucial.

SUMMARY

Civilization is complex, involving moral, social, and economic advancement. Civilization can also be a nation and its culture. Economic advancement is important as it creates the wealth necessary to provide a higher standard of living. Civilization requires cooperation, the rule of law, and property rights. It needs to be defended.

There is a danger that a civilized people takes its wealth and advancement for granted and becomes too soft and effete to defend itself. Society can become fragmented with vested interests. Civilization can decay.

Civilization is a relative term that distinguishes a more advanced people from those less advanced, who may be described as savages or barbarians. Collingwood identifies the barbarist as someone, either from outside a civilization or from within it, who rejects the values of civilization and seeks to destroy it. A barbarist may be motivated by hatred, a desire for plunder, or both.

THE GENESIS AND DEVELOPMENT
OF POLITICAL CORRECTNESS

To begin with, it is necessary to define political correctness. There are those who deny it exists, who say that it is just a term of abuse used by right-wing people. There are those who define the concept very broadly to include health and safety legislation, for example, or who use the term to apply to any intolerance by authority of views disapproved of. Much of this denial is mischief-making to cover up the true politically-correct agenda. William Lind fastens upon 'the victim feminism, the gay rights movement, the invented statistics, the rewritten history, the lies, the demands, all the rest of it' and describes it as 'cultural Marxism' and 'Marxism translated from economic into cultural terms'.[147] For the purposes of this book, political correctness will be defined as 'the mechanism for the enforcement of neo-Marxist ideology'. This definition splits political correctness into two parts. First, the ideology, and second, the manner in which that ideology is imposed. The ideology is restricted to neo-Marxism and does not include such matters as health and safety, nor any other intolerance such as religion.

This begs the question as to what is neo-Marxism? Classical Marxism was concerned primarily with economics and was an attack upon the capitalist system. It was fixated with class division and advocated the ultimate triumph of the proletariat and the destruction of the bourgeoisie. However, the excitement that Marx generated with his theory that communism was an historical inevitability was not matched by reality. Communism failed to conquer the world and stalled in Russia after World War I (WWI). This led many to question Marx's writing and to seek to explain the failure of worldwide revolution. The theorists of the Frankfurt School were at the forefront of this. Eventually, despite the spread of communism after WWII to include China, much of Indo-China, many African countries, and Eastern Europe, the communist system collapsed, and only China today might be described as a communist state – albeit one which has embraced capitalism! When communism did spread, it did so by force of arms and war. China became communist as a result of a communist victory in a civil war, Eastern Europe did so as a result of Russian invasion following the defeat of Nazi Germany, and many other Third World countries as a result of the collapse of the various European empires, allowing for coups, one-man-one-vote once 'democracies', and also invasion and conquest, such as in South Vietnam.

In the West, Marxism took a different form and, following the analysis of the Frankfurt School and others, it infiltrated into public institutions and sought to take over and undermine Western society from within. Multiculturalism and victim feminism are examples of this. However, even Marx drew his ideology from others such as Hegel (1770-1831) and Rousseau.

So what might be best described as the genesis of political correctness? When did classical Marxism become neo-Marxism? This book will argue that a good starting point in understanding an answer to that question is the French Revolution and the ideology of Rousseau. The French Revolution was an exceptionally bloody affair motivated by a non-religious ideology feeding off an incompetently run defective constitution, which, despite its high ideals, degenerated into bloodshed. Rousseau did not advocate regicide, or bloody revolution, yet that is the outcome of what was inspired in his name. The French Revolution led to anarchy, regicide, the Terror, and ultimately the Napoleonic wars. Rousseau's thinking is appealing to many Marxists and became more fashionable with the rise of political correctness.

In its analysis, this book will begin with the French Revolution, then examine the basic tenets of Marxism and its reworking in the inter-war years, including the work of the Frankfurt School.

THE FRENCH REVOLUTION

Rousseau wrote the *Social Contract* against the background of the failings of the French government and its inability to reduce the oppressive taxation on ordinary French citizens.[148] For Rousseau, society should reflect the general will of the people. The interpretation of the general will is to be aided by a 'legislator' who helps draft laws.[149] For Rousseau, sovereignty is the exercise of the general will,[150] and he intends this to explain the role of the state and that of ordinary people.[151]

Rousseau's rationale is at odds with Mill, who believes in protecting the freedoms of the individual. Mill had studied the French Revolution[152] and learnt from the failings of Rousseau's theories when put into practice. Mob rule had been one result.[153] For Mill, as with other classical liberal philosophers,[154] the concept of the general will is a route to the loss of freedom, if not tyranny. Mill warns about the danger of the tyranny of the majority.[155] For Mill, the freedom of the individual is necessary for the development of society, the betterment of mankind, and to counteract the decay of civilization.[156] To increase the power of the state over the individual should be avoided. Its legitimization is potentially dangerous if used to reduce the freedom of the individual. Mill is dismissive of 'abstract and metaphysical' political thought and regards men as 'historical human beings, already shaped, and made what they are, by human society' and 'by the accumulated influence of past generations over the present'.[157]

By comparison, the English philosopher Bernard Bosanquet (1848-1923) is very sympathetic to Rousseau, although he does not accept the need for a legislator.[158] For Bosanquet, the general will is a part of an individual's unconsciousness.[159] Bosanquet goes further than Rousseau in the development of the general will and sees it as evolving as a result of social interchange within civil society, as Rousseau himself sees morality developing, although not the general will.[160] For Rousseau, civil institutions are likely to have their own interests and so will not reflect the general will,[161] whereas Bosanquet believes that such institutions are manifestations of the general will.[162] They are a forum for interchange and the evolution of ideas[163] and reflect the general will, and hence, it finds its own expression in the decisions of the state, which is a composition of all of society. Both Bosanquet and Rousseau believe that the general will is the main embodiment of liberty.[164] Bosanquet emphasizes the importance of the role of the state: 'We profit at every turn by institutions, rules, traditions, researches, made by minds at their best, which, through State action are now in a form to operate as extensions of our own minds.'[165] The state enables a greater scope of consciousness than individuals by themselves. Bosanquet, like other idealist liberals, takes a more collectivist approach than classical liberals such as Mill,[166] believing that self-realization is best obtained within society as a whole.[167] Like Rousseau, Bosanquet believes that society is necessary to enable the individual to achieve the best life, justice, and freedom:[168] 'It is from the State that our first distinct notions of justice and injustice are derived. For the law is anterior to Justice, not Justice to the Law.'[169]

In reference to his *Second Discourse*, Rousseau wrote: 'I dared to strip man's nature naked. I compared man as he made himself with natural man, and showed that his supposed improvement was the true fount of all his miseries.'[170] The two Discourses were an attack on the philosophe movement and provoked hostility from its members, who would normally have been respectful of Rousseau's work. The philosopher Voltaire wrote to Rousseau: 'I have received, Monsieur, your new book against the human race and I thank you. Never has so much intelligence been seen to try to turn men into beasts.'[171] The Church was angry with Rousseau's rejection of the doctrine of original sin.[172] The controversy

Rousseau had caused eventually resulted in him breaking with his philosophe colleagues and, in 1756, flouncing off to live a solitary life in the countryside in a 'hermitage' (his philosophe critics pictured him on all fours eating grass).[173]

Rousseau's well known peroration, 'Man was born free but is everywhere in chains',[174] was a cry for freedom for the oppressed and overtaxed French peasant. His theory of the General Will and his *Social Contract,* written in 1762, was followed by his sentimental novel *Emile,* which, although fiction, was political and sought to demonstrate how a child could retain the natural goodness of man from the influences of a corrupt society. It was widely read to great acclaim by many and condemned by others, including the Archbishop of Paris. Despite it becoming a bestseller, Rousseau only escaped arrest and imprisonment by fleeing France in the middle of the night. *Emile* contained a heretical discussion about religion, and the Archbishop of Paris in particular was angered by Rousseau's advocacy that mankind was naturally good but was corrupted by society.[175] Rousseau, despite his own prejudices, tended to support the view that more primitive societies had a natural virtue[176] and described towns as 'the abyss of the human race[177]'.

Rousseau achieved adulation upon his death. A statue was erected in Geneva. It was claimed that 'half of France has transported itself to Ermenonville to visit the little island consecrated to him where the friends of his morals and his doctrine each year renew their little philosophical journey'.[178] To pay homage to the great man involved a three to four hour walk which began at a little hamlet, described as being 'inhabited by faithful lovers' by Thiery.[179] Visitors would be taken to Rousseau's cabin. The walk would venture into a forest in which there was a little temple consecrated to Nature before venturing onto a plain where another monument to Philosophy could be found. Next, the walk would cross a wilderness before arriving at a lake. In the middle of the lake was the Isle of Poplars where Rousseau's tomb was located. A monument read:

> *Among these poplars, beneath their peaceful shade*
> *Rests Jean-Jacques Rousseau*
> *Mothers, old men, children, true hearts and feeling souls*
> *Your friend sleeps in this tomb*[180]

At the tomb, the visitors were encouraged to weep freely: 'Never will you have spilled such delicious or such well-merited teardrops.'[181] Rousseau's works, in particular his *Social Contract*, his draft constitution, and *Emile*, contributed to the development of a particular doctrine which was inimical to the French establishment and which contributed to the revolution. French literature abounded with the idea of man's lost innocence corrupted by the wickedness of society.[182] His *Social Contract* influenced the revolutionary government in its attempt to re-order society.

When put into practice, Rousseau's ideas had disastrous consequences. To be fair to Rousseau, he died before he could witness the outcome of what he had inspired, and it is highly likely that he would have balked at what happened. Maximilien Robespierre (1758-1794), a major figure in the French Revolution, was influenced by Rousseau and believed that it was the role of the revolution to educate a population reluctant to embrace revolutionary virtues – 'to recall men to nature and to truth'.[183] Robespierre was also swayed by Rousseau's definition of patriotism: 'There can be no patriotism without liberty; no liberty without virtue; no virtue without citizens. Create citizens and you have everything you need; without them you have nothing but debased slaves, from the rulers of the state downwards.'[184] It was even rumoured that Robespierre slept with a copy of Rousseau's Social Contract under his pillow, so influenced was he by it and so often did he refer to it in his speeches.[185] The talk of liberty and of a virtuous constitution, the protested horror of the injustices of the previous government, were used to justify bloodshed and the Terror. Of the so-called September massacres, when those deemed counter-revolutionaries, including prison inmates (half the prison population of Paris was killed), were butchered and even mutilated, Robespierre said:

> 'It is certain that an innocent Person perished [an alleged victim of mistaken identity]; the numbers have been exaggerated, but one [innocent], without doubt [perished]. We should weep, citizens, at this cruel mistake, and we have wept over it for a long time. He was said to be a good citizen, and was therefore one of our friends. We should weep also for the guilty victims, reserved for vengeance of the laws, who fell beneath the blade of popular justice; but let this grief have an end, like all mortal things. Keep back some tears for more touching calamities; weep instead for the hundred thousand victims of tyranny.'[186]

The irony of the General Will is that it was vested in a revolutionary government which sought to impose its own view on the population, condemning dissenters and even the disinterested to death. The revolutionary and member of the Committee of Public Safety, Saint-Just (1767-1794) said:

'There is no prosperity to hope for so long as the last enemy of liberty breathes. You have to punish not only the traitors, but even those who are indifferent; you have to punish whoever is passive in the republic, and who does nothing for it. For, since the French people has manifested its will, everything opposed to it is outside the sovereign; all that is outside the sovereign is the enemy.'[187]

Robespierre took a similar line and said: 'Whoever trembles is guilty.'[188] The Surveillance Committee pronounced that 'indifference is a crime' and condemned one suspect as 'a dangerous aristocrat' because he spoke three languages.[189] The determination to put down a rebellion in the Vendee region of France resulted in the following order:

'All brigands taken under arms, or convicted of having taken them up, are to be run through with bayonets. One will act likewise with women, girls and children ... Those merely suspected are not to be spared. All villages, settlements, heathlands and all that can burn are to be put to flames.'[190]

This policy was implemented by hell columns. The orders to kill all captured rebels, including women and children, were repeatedly issued. A hell column descended upon the village of Montbert on 11th February 1794 and killed 72, including 49 women. Another column passed through on the 24th February and killed another 20, including 14 women. Throughout the spring the surviving villagers were picked off by roving patrols. More than 175 were killed with an equal number dying of disease. A fifth of the Vendee's population died, almost a quarter of a million people.[191] Robespierre said:

'If the mainspring of popular government in peacetime is virtue, amid revolution it is at the same time both virtue and terror: virtue, without which terror is fatal; terror, without which virtue is impotent. Terror is nothing but prompt, severe, inflexible justice; it is therefore an emanation of virtue.'[192]

Claude Payan (national agent of the Paris Commune) wrote:

'Commissions charged with punishing conspirators bear absolutely no comparison with the tribunals of the old Regime or even with those of the new. There must not be any forms; the judge's conscience is there to replace them. It does not matter whether an accused has been interrogated in such or such a manner ... in a word these commissions are revolutionary commissions ... they should also be political tribunals; they should remember that everyone who has not been for the Revolution has been by that very fact against it because he has not done anything for the patrie.'[193]

Underlying the Terror and the determination of the revolution to subdue its perceived opponents was the determination to cut France off from its past, to reinvent a new society uncorrupted by history. This was in part reflected by the introduction of a new calendar and the invention of a new 10-day week, as well as settling scores with those deemed to be 'oppressors'.[194] Between the months of March and July 1794, the monthly total of those sent to the guillotine by the Revolutionary Tribunal rose from l00 to more than 900.[195]

The determination to subdue the public by means of terror was one of the practices of communists – although they adopted the policy on an industrial scale. More than 100 million people were killed by the various communist revolutions in the 20th century. Rousseau's ideology found favour amongst communists. Rousseau's idea that more primitive societies, and peoples, had a natural virtue that was corrupted by civilization reinforced the notion that minorities and immigrants were to be considered victims and were morally superior. The concept that civilized society was bad and to be held responsible for the world's ills was highly appealing to the communists. However, whereas Rousseau had an idealistic outlook, communism, from its very inception, was imbued with hatred of and contempt for society that was unconcealed.

THE BASIC TENETS OF MARXISM

With Friedrich Englels, Karl Marx wrote *The Communist Manifesto* in 1848, and *Das Kapital*, which Marx wrote between the 1850s and his death in 1883, was completed by Engels. It should be noted that it was not the case, as is often assumed and implied, that Marx wrote *Das Kapital* in order to understand capitalism and arrived at his communist views as a result of a scientific study in depth. His views were set out in *The Communist Manifesto*, and he then set out to justify his views afterwards – *and he failed to do so*, leaving Engels to eventually complete and publish *Das Kapital* many years after his death (the first volume however had been published in 1867).

The 19th century was a period of rapid social change arising out of the French Revolution with the Napoleonic wars and the abolition of feudalism throughout many European countries, as well as the industrial revolution, which led to more people working in factories rather than in agriculture or as craftsmen.[196] At the University of Berlin, Marx was a prominent member of the Young Hegelians, an association which led to him having to seek work as a journalist rather than as an academic.[197] After working for radical newspapers and journals, he became influenced by anarchists while in Paris. *The Communist Manifesto* was published by the Communist League in 1848. In 1849 Marx moved to London having been expelled from France, Belgium, and Prussia because of his revolutionary views. He died in London before completing *Das Kapital*; Engels took 11 years to complete the final volumes.[198]

Marx was influenced by Hegel, in particular Hegel's concept that change is the result of conflict between opposing movements. This change had three stages: thesis – the original idea; antithesis – the opposing view; and synthesis – the compromise between the two opposing views. Marx applied this idea of the dialectic to the development of society and economics.[199] Marx further developed Hegel's view of alienation.

Marx regarded capitalism as unique because it turned labour into a commodity to be bought and sold and because of the capital needed to buy the factories and machinery, which meant that all production was the production of commodities. All products under capitalism are commodities. Marx's theory of surplus value held that workers were exploited as the capitalist was able to retain the surplus value produced by the workers. Capitalism also entailed a division of labour which meant that workers were employed to do repetitive tasks. Marx believed that capitalism was in crisis and that its internal contradictions would ultimately lead to its collapse. The main problems he foresaw were:

- Workers' wages would fall to subsistence level
- Profits would tend to fall
- Smaller companies would be taken over by larger ones
- More people would be forced into the working class
- Economic crises would become increasingly severe
- The workers would eventually rise up and overthrow the system[200]

Marx believed that communism was the only solution. He believed that a communist society would manage the economy better and avoid what he saw as the damage caused by competition. Marx believed that society was corrupted by three types of fetishism: money fetishism was a desire for money for its own sake; capital fetishism was a belief that capital was itself valuable and a means to increase productivity rather than the labour of workers; and commodity fetishism was a belief that some commodities had a premium value above their market value. To Marx, these fetishisms prevented people from understanding and changing society and were illusions.[201]

Marx believed that both capitalists and workers were alienated, although the capitalists were happy with their alienation due to their wealth and privilege. The workers were alienated as they were exploited by the capitalists but did not realize it. They were denied the satisfaction of the product of their labours. Additionally, consumers were seduced by false needs to work for more money to consume more goods and pursue money for its own sake; they were trapped into a cycle that enslaved them.[202]

Marx believed that the capitalist economy was divided into 'two great hostile camps, into two great classes directly facing each other':[203] the bourgeoisie, who owned the means of production, and the proletariat, who were compelled to sell their labour in order to live. He believed that this was a new phenomena brought about by the rise of capitalism and that the proletariat had been created by capitalism and would eventually rise up and destroy capitalism. The proletariat and the bourgeoisie were in conflict, which would lead to class struggle and eventually revolution.[204]

Marx predicted that as profits under capitalism fell, then the capitalists would try to compensate for this by resorting to new overseas markets. Marx was of course writing when the British Empire was a growing and major force. Marx believed that capitalism would lead to colonialism and the alienation of the proletariat in the new developing countries. This was a necessary step on the path to worldwide revolution.

For Marx, world history was a history of class warfare, one in which classes were always in competition with those above or below them. He believed that each type of society, whether based on slavery, feudalism, or capitalism, contains contradictions that would cause conflict. This conflict would ultimately lead to the destruction of that society and a new one would take its place:

> 'The history of all hitherto existing society is the history of class struggles. Freeman and slave, patrician and plebeian, lord and serf, guild-master and journeyman, in a word, oppressor and oppressed, stood in constant opposition to one another, carried on an uninterrupted, now hidden, now open fight, a fight that each time ended, either in a revolutionary reconstitution of

society at large, or in the common ruin of the contending classes ... The modern bourgeois society that has sprouted from the ruins of feudal society has not done away with class antagonisms. It has but established new classes, new conditions of oppression, new forms of struggle in place of the old ones. Our epoch, the epoch of the bourgeoisie, possesses, however, this distinct feature: it has simplified class antagonisms. Society as a whole is more and more splitting up into two great hostile camps, into two great classes directly facing each other – Bourgeoisie and Proletariat.'[205]

The original hunter-gatherer societies were deemed a form of 'primitive communism' and contained no real division of labour. They were classless societies, but they developed into slave-owning societies dependent upon warfare. They were unstable with economic pressures and collapsed due to their internal contradictions. Slavery was replaced with feudalism, which allowed people to develop skills under the patronage of the landed nobility. Feudalism was eventually overthrown, and the revolutions continued into the 19th century when capitalism emerged. To Marx, every society was a necessary phase that would eventually collapse. He regarded revolution as desirable and inevitable and rejected the moves of utopian socialists who believed that philanthropy, with model communities, could act as a beacon for change. For Marx, the economic system was wrong and had to be overthrown with force: 'The weapon of criticism obviously cannot replace the criticism of weapons. Material force must be overthrown by material force.'[206] Marx viewed the state as acting in the interests of the ruling class, the bourgeoisie in capitalist societies, and would try to block change: 'the executive of the modern state is but a committee for managing the common affairs of the whole bourgeoisie.'[207] Marx believed that revolution would begin in capitalist countries in Europe before spreading across the world due to the way countries had become economically dependent upon one another.[208]

Under communism, Marx believed that the state would wither away as there would no longer be a need for oppression because there would be no classes and no money. He believed that private property would disappear and that the means of production would be centrally controlled:

'The distinguishing feature of Communism is not the abolition of property generally, but the abolition of bourgeois property. But modern bourgeois private property is the final and most complete expression of the system of producing and

28

appropriating products, that is based on class antagonisms, on the exploitation of the many by the few. In this sense, the theory of the Communists may be summed up in the single sentence: Abolition of private property.'[209]

The difference between a capitalist society and a communist one was so great that there would have to be an intermediate phase known as socialism. This phase would consist of a dictatorship of the proletariat, and the communist party would be the vanguard of the proletariat since the majority of the population was still in the grip of alienation and false consciousness and would need to be led towards a true understanding of true communism.

Engels, on behalf of the Communist League, set out how a communist society was supposed to operate in *The Principles of Communism*. This involved:

- Limitation of private property via taxation, including inheritance tax, and abolition of family inheritance rights
- Capitalists to be expropriated
- Confiscation of possessions belonging to emigrants and rebels
- Competition between workers to be abolished and the introduction of central organization of wages
- Industrial armies to be formed
- Suppression of private banks and the introduction of national banks
- State-owned factories
- Education in state schools for all children
- Communal housing on waste land
- Destruction of insanitary housing
- Equal inheritance rights for children born out of wedlock
- Nationalization of transport[210]

The Communist Manifesto itself is hardline:

'The proletariat will use its political supremacy to wrest, by degree, all capital from the bourgeoisie, to centralise all instruments of production in the hands of the State, i.e. of the proletariat organised as the ruling class; and to increase the total productive forces as rapidly as possible. Of course, in the beginning, this cannot be effected except by means of despotic inroads on the rights of property, and on the conditions of bourgeois production; by means of measures, therefore, which appear economically insufficient and untenable, but which, in the course of the movement, outstrip themselves, necessitate further inroads upon the old social order, and are unavoidable as a means of entirely revolutionising the mode of production. These measures will, of course, be different in different countries. Nevertheless, in most advanced countries, the following will be pretty generally applicable.

1. Abolition of property in land and application of all rents of land to public purposes.
2. A heavy progressive or graduated income tax.
3. Abolition of all rights of inheritance.
4. Confiscation of the property of all emigrants and rebels.
5. Centralisation of credit in the hands of the state, by means of a national bank with State capital and an exclusive monopoly.
6. Centralisation of the means of communication and transport in the hands of the State
7. Extension of factories and instruments of production owned by the State; the bringing into cultivation of waste-lands, and the improvement of the soil generally in accordance with a common plan.
8. Equal liability of all to work. Establishment of industrial armies, especially for agriculture.
9. Combination of agriculture with manufacturing industries; gradual abolition of all the distinction between town and country by a more equable distribution of the populace over the country.
10. Free education for all children in public schools. Abolition of children's factory labour in its present form. Combination of education with industrial production, etc., etc.

When, in the course of development, class distinctions have disappeared, and all production has been concentrated in the hands of a vast association of the whole nation, the public power will lose its political character. Political power, properly so called, is merely the organised power of one class for oppressing another. If the proletariat during its contest with the bourgeoisie is compelled, by the force of circumstances, to organise itself as a class, if, by means of a revolution, it makes itself the ruling class, and, as such, sweeps away by force the old conditions of production, then it will, along with these conditions, have swept away the conditions for the existence of class antagonisms and of classes generally, and will thereby have abolished its own supremacy as a class. In place of the old bourgeois society, with its classes and class antagonisms, we shall have an association, in which the free development of each is the condition for the free development of all.'[211]

Marx insisted that the dominant ideas and laws in a country were of the ruling class. These beliefs developed from economic necessities and from the inherited beliefs of society, which meant that people were influenced by the economic system and the past in ways that they did not realize. This artificial construction of peoples' beliefs is false consciousness.[212] This was reinforced by capitalists controlling information, education, and entertainment. Marx believed that this needed to be challenged by a revolutionary workers party, which would highlight the exploitation and false consciousness which the workers were suffering from. For Marx, in order for true consciousness to exist, it is necessary not only for consciousness to understand reality, but for reality to be changed so that it no longer, through ideology, produces false consciousness.[213]

Marx stated that women would not be equals of men so long as men were considered to be the head of the household and so long as women were not properly educated: 'The bourgeoisie has torn away from the family its sentimental veil, and has reduced the family relation to a mere money relation.'[214] Marx believed that women were financially dependent upon men due to their childcare responsibilities and argued that state childcare provision and a drive to get women out to work was necessary to achieve equality. He and his fellow communists were contemptuous of marriage:

> 'The bourgeois clap-trap about the family and education, about the hallowed co-relation of parents and child, becomes all the more disgusting, the more, by the action of Modern Industry, all the family ties among the proletarians are torn asunder, and their children transformed into simple articles of commerce and instruments of labour ... The bourgeois sees his wife a mere instrument of production ... He has not even a suspicion that the real point aimed at is to do away with the status of women as mere instruments of production ... Our bourgeois, not content with having wives and daughters of their proletarians at their disposal, not to speak of common prostitutes, take the greatest pleasure in seducing each other's wives. Bourgeois marriage is, in reality, a system of wives in common and thus, at the most, what the Communists might possibly be reproached with is that

they desire to introduce, in substitution for a hypocritically concealed, an openly legalised community of women. For the rest, it is self-evident that the abolition of the present system of production must bring with it the abolition of the community of women springing from that system, i.e. of prostitution both public and private.'[215]

In *A Communist Confession of Faith*, a series of questions are answered. Those relating to the family, nationality, and religion are revealing:

'What will be the influence of communist society on the family? It will transform the relations between the sexes into a purely private matter which concerns only the persons involved and into which society has no occasion to intervene. It can do this since it does away with private property and educates children on a communal basis, and in this way removes the two bases of traditional marriage – the dependence rooted in private property, of the women on the man, and of the children on the parents. And here is the answer to the outcry of the highly moral philistines against the "community of women". Community of women is a condition which belongs entirely to bourgeois society and which today finds its complete expression in prostitution. But prostitution is based on private property and falls with it. Thus, communist society, instead of introducing community of women, in fact abolishes it.

What will be the attitude of communism to existing nationalities? The nationalities of the peoples associating themselves in accordance with the principle of community will be compelled to mingle with each other as a result of this association and thereby to dissolve themselves, just as the various estate and class distinctions must disappear through the abolition of their basis, private property.

What will be its attitude to existing religions? All religions so far have been the expression of historical stages of development of individual peoples or groups of peoples. But communism is the stage of historical development which makes all existing religions superfluous and brings about their disappearance.'[216]

As is clearly set out, what is advocated is not restricted to who owns which property, but the whole basis of society is to be destroyed. Marriage, the family, the bringing up of children, the existence of nations – and hence anything dependent upon that existence such as

32

healthcare, pensions, or the rule of law – and even religion is to be forcibly destroyed, irrespective of the wishes of ordinary people who are of course all suffering from false consciousness. Marx wrote: 'philosophers have only interpreted the world, in various ways: the point, however, is to change it.'[217] *The Communist Manifesto* concluded:

> 'In short, the Communists everywhere support every revolutionary movement against the existing social and political order of things ... The Communists disdain to conceal their views and aims. They openly declare that their ends can be attained only by the forcible overthrow of all existing social conditions. Let the ruling classes tremble at a Communistic revolution. The proletarians have nothing to lose but their chains. They have a world to win. **Working Men of All Countries, Unite!**'[218]

As *The Communist Manifesto* states, communists support '*every* revolutionary movement'. The hatred of society is all consuming. Communists will support anyone who hates the West, be they terrorists, hostile foreign powers, social misfits, or even criminals. Provided that someone is hostile towards the West and Western society, then communists will support them in a bond of common hatred. This is the opposite of patriotism.

THE FRANKFURT SCHOOL AND THE INTER-WAR YEARS

Contrary to Marx's prediction, a communist revolution did not first occur in economically advanced European economies; it occurred in a backward one – Russia. The Russian industrial working class was small, and at least 80% of the population were peasants.[219] Russia had experienced little industrialization compared to the Western European countries. The autocratic rule of Tsar Nicholas II had successfully repressed dissent, and the industrial working class was badly organized. However, WWI led to social and industrial unrest, and the military setbacks led to a disintegration of the army. In October 1917, a Bolshevik revolution seized power. The Tsar was executed in 1918.

The revolution was initiated in Petrograd, supported by the garrison which feared it was about to be sent to the front and, likewise, the Bolshevik crew of the cruiser *Aurora*. Bolshevik support was concentrated in Petrograd. The strain of trying to continue the war was sapping the support for and the strength of the government. Trotsky, the chairman of the Petrograd Soviet and the acting leader of the Bolshevik Party due to Lenin being in hiding after being denounced as a German spy, announced that 'this semi-government only awaits the sweep of history's broom'.[220] The government was indeed swept out by a carefully planned coup. However, Russia was plunged into civil war. That war was won by the Bolsheviks, partly due to the inept White Russians and partly due to the ruthlessness of the Bolsheviks, and Trotsky in particular. Trotsky, the War Commissar, who conducted the war from an armoured train, warned: 'if a unit retreats without orders, the first to be shot will be the commissar, the second will be the commanding officer. Courageous soldiers will be rewarded according to their merits and will be given commissions. Cowards, scoundrels and traitors will not escape bullets ... this I pledge before the entire Red Army.'[221]

Again, contrary to what Marx predicted, and what the Bolsheviks pronounced at the time (Trotsky wrote: 'In our generation the revolution began in the East. From Russia it passed over into Hungary to Bavaria and, doubtless, it will march westward through Europe'),[222] the communist revolution did not spread. The Spartacist uprising in Berlin and attempted communist revolution in Germany failed. The Bela Kun communist revolution in Hungary was overthrown in a counter revolution after only a few months. The Soviet-Polish war of 1920 ended the Bolshevik attempt to expand the revolution by conquest when the Russian attack resulted in fiasco and defeat.[223] Far from spreading the communist revolution, the Bolsheviks were having to resort to terror in order to keep control. This was state policy and openly advocated. Trotsky wrote:

> '*Intimidation* is a powerful weapon of policy, both internationally and internally. War, like revolution, is founded upon intimidation. A victorious war, generally speaking, destroys only an insignificant part of the conquered army, intimidating the remainder and breaking their will. The revolution works in the same way: it kills individuals and intimidates thousands ... The State terror of a revolutionary class can be condemned "morally" only by a man who, on principle, rejects [in words] every form of violence whatsoever ... For this, one has to be merely and simply a hypocritical Quaker.'[224]

For Trotsky, as long as there was class society, 'repression remains a necessary means of breaking the will of the opposing side'. Thus the Red Terror was justified in killing landlords, generals, and capitalists who allegedly sought to re-establish capitalism.[225] In March 1921, in one

34

notorious episode, the sailors at the naval base Kronstadt rebelled at a time when there was widespread discontent. The rebels demanded freedom of speech and a free press, free elections to the Soviets, freedom for political prisoners from socialist parties, as well as an equalization of rations of all workers to be accompanied by the freedom of the peasants to farm their own land as they liked. Trotsky, who dismissed democracy as a 'bourgeois fetishism',[226] issued an ultimatum that 'Only those who surrender unconditionally can count on the mercy of the Soviet Republic.' The sailors ignored the ultimatum. The base was attacked and the sailors massacred.[227]

The Red Terror was made worse by the concept of a permanent revolution. Trotsky wrote:

> 'The permanent revolution, in the sense which Marx attached to this concept, means a revolution which makes no compromise with any single form of class rule, which does not stop at the democratic stage, which goes over to socialist measures and to war against reaction from without; that is, a revolution whose every successive stage is rooted in the proceeding one and which can end only in complete liquidation of class society.'[228]

Trotsky had taken his lead from Marx, who had written in 1850 in an address to the central committee of the Communist League:

> 'The democratic petty bourgeois wish to bring the revolution to a conclusion as quickly as possible ... it is our interest and our task to make the revolution permanent, until all more or less possessing classes have been forced out of their position of dominance, until the proletariat has conquered state power, and the association of proletarians, not only in one country but in all dominant countries of the world, has advanced so far that competition among the proletarians of these countries has ceased and that at least the decisive productive forces are concentrated in the hands of the proletarians.'[229]

The next great communist revolution did not occur until after WWII in China, another backward country (the various communist regimes in eastern Europe were installed by Russia, backed up by tanks and troops after WWII, and were not the product of a communist revolution). This was some considerable time after the Russian revolution. This, again, was not a typical proletariat uprising as predicted by Marx, but a civil war waged first in the countryside to win support from the peasants – not the urban proletariat – followed by the capture of cities. Mao declared in 1949 that 'the centre of gravity of our work has been in the villages – gathering strength in the villages, using the villages in order to surround the cities, and then taking the cities. The period for this method of work has now ended. The period of "from the city to the village" and of the city leading the village has now begun. The centre of gravity of the party's work has shifted from the village to the city.'[230] Mao argued:

> 'In reality, the more backward the economy, the easier, and not the more difficult, the transition from capitalism to socialism. The poorer people are, the more they want revolution ... In the East, countries such as Russia and China were originally backward and poor. Now not only are their social systems far more advanced than those of the West, but the rate of development of the productive forces is far more rapid. If you look at the history of the development of the various capitalist countries, it is again the backward which have overtaken the advanced. For example, the United States surpassed Britain at the end of the nineteenth century, and Germany also surpassed Britain in the early twentieth century.'[231]

This is in fact contrary to Marxist theory, which asserted that the more advanced countries would lead the way to communism due to the passing phase of capitalism and its ultimate crisis. Mao relied on 'People's War' to gain power. This consisted of: an adherence to a comprehensive ideology; the idea that the leadership of the Communist Party must control the army and that both should win the support of the masses; there should be a united front; and that an indigenous leadership should organize an armed struggle.[232] (This is all very different from the ideas developed by Gramsci – see below). Mao further advocated that the united front should use other classes to support the proletarian revolution which, once achieved, would then lead to those other classes being liquidated in an ongoing revolution. Lenin described this process as 'the rope [that] supports a hanged man'.[233] For Mao, China's backwardness was an advantage for the communists. In one speech, Mao scoffed to much laughter: 'If China becomes rich, with a standard of living like that in the Western world, it will no longer want revolution. The wealth of the Western world has its defects, and these defects are that they don't want revolution ... Their high standard of living is not so good as our illiteracy.' Mao said in 1964: 'We shouldn't read too many books. We should read Marxist books, but not too many of them either. It will be enough to read a dozen or so. If we read too many we can move toward our opposite, become bookworms, dogmatists, revisionists.'[234]

As with the French Revolution and the Bolsheviks in Russia, the Chinese Communist Party (CCP) maintained power and continued the revolution by the use of terror. Mao admitted that 700,000 had been executed in China in 1950-52.[235] In 1962 Mao declared: 'Those whom the people's democratic dictatorship should repress are landlords, rich peasants, counter-revolutionary elements, bad elements and anti-communist rightists. ... these classes and bad people comprise about 4 or 5 per cent of the population. These are the people we must compel to reform.'[236] In the Kwangtung province alone, at the beginning of the 1960s, there were an estimated one million people in concentration camps, for a variety of reasons including alleged antisocial behaviour. Roving brigades would dispense summary mass reprisals with, in some instances, public rallies being staged to watch the executions.[237] One set of judges used rest periods and lunch breaks from the agricultural work to decide 35 criminal cases.[238]

Mao came to regard the CCP as the source of counter-revolution and said: 'Cadres who have made mistakes can re-establish themselves, provided that they do not persist with their mistakes, but reform them, and are forgiven by the revolutionary masses.'[239] Almost 90% of the Party's work teams were deemed to have made mistakes at the start of the Cultural Revolution, which was described as a trial of the Party by the masses in order to achieve unity with the masses in an ongoing revolution.[240] Mao's view of the lower classes was 'Rousseauist', and identification with them was a 'background assumption.'[241] In his *Twenty Manifestations of Bureaucracy* in 1967, Mao set out his distaste for bureaucracy. For example:

'They [bureaucrats] are conceited, complacent, and they aimlessly discuss politics. They do not grasp their work; they are subjective and one-sided; they are careless; they do not listen to people; they are truculent and arbitrary; they force orders; they do not care about reality; they maintain blind control. This is authoritarian bureaucracy ...

They are ignorant; they are ashamed to ask anything; they exaggerate and they lie; they are very false; that attribute errors to people; they attribute merit to themselves; they swindle the central government; they deceive those above them and fool those below them; they conceal faults and gloss over wrongs. This is dishonest bureaucracy ...

They fight among themselves for power and money; they extend their hands into the Party; they want fame and fortune;

they want positions, and if they do not get it they are not satisfied; they choose to be fat and to be lean; they pay a great deal of attention to wages; they are cosy when it comes to cadres but they care nothing about the masses. This is the bureaucracy that is fighting for power and money ...'

The increase in the number of state cadres was 2,000,000 in 1948, 720,000 in 1949, 3,310,000 in 1952, 5,270,000 in 1955, and 7,920,000 in 1958.[242] To combat increased bureaucracy, Mao launched a series of *hsia fang* campaigns, which had a reduction of bureaucracy as one of their aims.[243] For all his talk of the masses, Mao was basically a dictator.

The fact that the first communist revolution had occurred in a backward country, Russia, and the failure to spread the revolution led to a questioning of Marxist ideology following WWI. In the forefront of this reappraisal was the Frankfurt School and the Italian communist Antonio Gramsci. The Frankfurt School had been created with an endowment from the son of a millionaire, Felix Weil, at Frankfurt University. The original intention had been to call the institute the Institute for Marxism, but this was rejected as it was desired that the institute's true political leanings were best kept obscure. They therefore called it the Institute for Social Research, which became informally known as the Frankfurt School. Nevertheless, Weil wrote: 'I wanted the institute to become known, perhaps famous, due to its contributions to Marxism.'[244] From its very inception, Marxism was the ruling ideology of the institute,[245] which focused not on the material (i.e. economic) issues that were so prominent in Marxist ideology, but on the culture and superstructure of society to which Marxists had paid less attention.[246] George Lukacs, a Hungarian who was expelled from Germany by the Nazis, saw the Frankfurt School as an answer to the question: 'Who shall save us from Western Civilization?'[247] The views of those creating the Frankfurt School were that the culture of Western societies was acting as a block on the communist revolution. The Frankfurt School focused more on Western culture rather than on examining classical Marxism but, nevertheless, worked within a Marxist framework from the outset.[248] They sought to rework Marxism by combining it with Freud (1856-1939).[249] The Frankfurt School believed that a new culture needed to be created to *increase* the alienation of the population. The philosopher Walter Benjamin said: 'Do not build on the good old days, but on the bad new ones.'[250] They developed Critical Theory, which in its early manifestations was derived from Marxism. The objective of Critical Theory was to criticize in such a way as to debunk the objective of the criticism.

Both Lukacs and Gramsci focused more on the superstructure rather than the substructure, as Marx had done.[251] Gramsci was not a member of the Frankfurt School but was a prominent communist in the 1930s. He became leader of the Italian communist party and argued that there needed to be a long march through the institutions – including the government, the judiciary, the military, the educational system, and the media – before there could be a successful revolution. Gramsci also argued that alliances with other Leftist groups were necessary.[252] Lukacs believed that, for a new Marxist culture to be successful, the existing culture had to be destroyed: 'Such a worldwide overturning of values cannot take place without the annihilation of the old values and the creation of new ones by the revolutionaries.'[253] It should not be taken that the theorists of the Frankfurt School were more patient for a revolution than classical Marxists. With typical extremist logic, Max Horkheimer (1895-1973, and director of the Frankfurt School from 1930 to 1953) wrote:

> 'Present talk of inadequate conditions is a cover for tolerance of repression. For the revolutionary, conditions have always appeared right. What appears in retrospect a preliminary state or premature situation was once, for the revolutionary, a last chance to change. A revolutionary is with the desperate people for whom everything is on the line, not with those that have time … Critical theory … rejects the kind of knowledge that one can bank on. It confronts history with that possibility which is always concretely visible within it … [Humanity] is not betrayed by the untimely attempts of the revolutionaries but by the timely attempts of the realists.'[254]

With the Nazis taking power in Germany, the Frankfurt School was invited to move to the USA with an affiliation with Columbia University.[255] The Frankfurt school, being Marxist, was ideologically at odds with the Nazis. They were also mainly Jewish. Once in the USA, the Frankfurt School moved away from developing a Critical Theory of Germany and towards developing a Critical Theory of American society.[256]

Although William Lind highlights the importance of critical theory, his article does not set out its true extent. It is pervasive and an ideology, not simply criticism. Critical theory has been described as an attempt to comprehend society, criticise its contradictions and failings, and to construct alternatives.[257] Its aim is to replace the existing society with another. Rick Roderick writes: 'Critical theory originated as the first entrance of Marxism into the university system in the West.'[258] Martin Jay states: 'Critical Theory was developed partly in response to the failure of traditional Marxism to explain the reluctance of the proletariat to fulfil its historical role.'[259] David Held, himself a Marxist, describes critical theory as a 'school' of Western Marxism that 'became a key element in the formation and self-understanding of the New Left' in the 1960s, with Marcuse's name being given equal prominence with Marx and Mao in the political slogans of the day.[260] Held describes Horkheimer, Adorno (1903-1969), Marcuse (1898-1979), and Habermas (born 1929) as being 'central figures of critical theory'.[261] For Horkheimer and Lukacs, the practical role of the critical theorist is to develop 'a latent class consciousness'.[262]

Horkheimer sees critical theory as a means of understanding the truth by means of immanent criticism which exposes the difference between accepted truth (false consciousness) and reality (the real truth). By means of immanent critique of capitalism, there would be a transformation of 'the concepts that thoroughly dominate the economy into their opposites: fair exchange into a deepening of social injustice; a free economy into the domination of monopolies; productive labour into the strengthening of relations which hinder production; the maintenance of society's life into the impoverishment of the people's.'[263] By this, he means that beliefs are changed into the opposite by 'scientific' analysis. David Held explains:

> 'It [immanent criticism] starts with the conceptual principles and standards of an object, and unfolds their implications and consequences. Then it re-examines and reassesses the object (the object's function, for instance) in light of these implications and consequences. Critique proceeds, so to speak, 'from within' and hopes to avoid, thereby, the charge that its concepts impose irrelevant criteria of evaluation on the object. As a result, a new understanding of the object is generated – a new comprehension of contradictions and possibilities. Thus, the original image of the object is transcended and the object itself is brought partly into flux.'[264]

For Horkheimer, the aim is to condemn the object as failing by its own standards and thus, by alienating public perceptions, make it vulnerable to radical change.[265]

In the early years of the Frankfurt School, the focus was still on the economic system. Lukacs developed Marx's theory in that he argued that the domination of capitalism was not sustained solely by coercion, but by a process in which people falsely viewed a social reality as natural despite it being created by them.[266] Marcuse was influenced by Lukac's *History and Class Consciousness,* which asserted that commodity fetishism, the capitalist labour market, and mass media all contributed to conformist thought and behaviour, which created a resistance to revolution.[267] This priority affected the application of critical theory as a means of explaining the proletariat's failure to embrace a communist revolution and the reason for the continuance of false consciousness. Raymond Marrow and David Brown wrote:

> 'From this perspective the task of critical theory was one of *immanent critique* that merely required pointing to the discrepancy between the basic liberal values of freedom and equality proclaimed by bourgeois society and the objective realities of economic irrationality that could be subjected to human control – that is, "from a blind to a meaningful necessity".[268]

Habermas, subsequently, concentrated on communication and how it was perpetuating capitalism. From the 1960s onwards, under the leadership of Habermas, the Frankfurt School revised critical theory to focus on what was believed to be advanced capitalism.[269] For Habermas, the task was 'to identify and reconstruct universal conditions of possible understanding'[270] and to establish that the basis of knowledge is language itself as it is the means by which reality is transmitted. As language is subjective, then so is knowledge.[271] Raymond Marrow and David Brown wrote: 'critical theory ... is ... nothing more and nothing less than a theory of the necessity of overcoming distorted communication as a part of an endless process of collective learning.' Habermas advocated that social theory must be critical and not only describe social reality but also criticise it and try to change it. The theory therefore has a 'practical intent'.[272] Habermas regarded the critical theorist as being the 'psychoanalyst of the working class',[273] and believed that 'the problem of language has today replaced the problem of consciousness'.[274] For Habermas, it is the transmission of culture and beliefs from one generation to the next and across society that needs to be prevented. False consciousness is deemed to be sustained by communication, and this communication should be targeted and controlled.

In 1962, Habermas wrote his first book, *Structural Transformation of the Public Sphere*, in which he rejected that notion that the public sphere involved a 'reasoning public' trying to achieve a consensus under conditions of open and free discussions of issues. Habermas alleged that the public sphere was actually comprised of the bourgeoisie and that the 'rational formation of the public will' was never actualised. He further alleged that there was a 'depoliticalisation of the public sphere resulting from the commercialisation of the mass media, increased state intervention in the economy, and an increase in the influence of science and technology.[275] This is a common theme in Habermas's writing.

Habermas argued that Marx's theories could no longer be relied upon to achieve revolutionary change for a number of reasons: with advanced capitalism the state and the economy are interlocked; the increase in living standards with advanced capitalism meant that economic grounds were no longer sufficient for revolution; and 'the proletariat as proletariat, has been dissolved' and cannot be relied upon as a revolutionary agent; and in Russia Marxism had become a 'legitimation science'.[276] The response was for immanent critique to become 'total critique' – an attack on the whole of Western society.[277] Habermas saw those who experienced most deprivation and were likely to be the least integrated into society as being the most likely supporters of revolutionary change.[278] Such unintegrated people needed to be radicalised and promoted into positions of power. Critical theory is a means of justifying and promoting this.

Habermas, Marcuse, and the other members of the Frankfurt School remained committed to 'catastrophic total revolution', but their language changed, and milder terms were used in order to disguise their true politics.[279] In part, this was due to the need for funding from American universities and foundations. Hegel and Freud were used as fronts for Marx. Code words were adopted, with 'emancipation' and 'democracy' often being used for revolution and socialism, respectively. Critical theory was used for the Frankfurt School's version of Marxism.[280] Marcuse advocated that the Left needed to soften its language, partly to differentiate itself from the brutal communist dictatorships, and even to criticize those dictatorships in order to accentuate that differentiation, and partly because socialism, let alone outright communism, alienated the American public.[281] The Frankfurt School shifted their stance from praxis (the process for the realization of theory) for a communist revolution towards education for tolerance.[282]

Whatever its flowery language and pretended scientific intellectual basis, critical theory amounted to an attack, by means of destructive criticism passed off as scientific analysis, upon all aspects of Western culture, including Christianity, capitalism, the family, hierarchy, morality, tradition, patriotism and nationalism, and conservatism.[283] It was an attempt to turn existing understandings and common sense into a state of flux and, eventually, to replace those beliefs with a contrived neo-Marxist ideology masquerading as the truth. The ultimate aim was the destruction of Western civilization and a communist revolution.

The first item from the Frankfurt School to be examined is *The Authoritarian Personality*, a published report, which is more than 1,000 pages long and was published in 1950.

THE AUTHORITARIAN PERSONALITY

The purpose of the report *The Authoritarian Personality* (conducted in the USA) was set out by Max Horkheimer and Samuel Flowerman (both members of the Frankfurt School), who wrote:

> 'Our aim is not merely to describe prejudice but to explain it in order to help in its eradication. That is the challenge we would meet. Eradication means re-education, scientifically planned on the basis of understanding scientifically arrived at. And education in a strict sense is by its nature personal and psychological.'[284]

Mission creep entered into proceedings as the report itself states:

> 'Our study grew out of specific investigations into anti-Semitism. As our work advanced, however, the emphasis gradually shifted. We came to regard it as our main task not to analyze anti-Semitism or any other anti-minority prejudice as a sociopsychological phenomenon *per se*, but rather to examine the relation of antiminority prejudice to broader ideological and characterological patterns. Thus anti-Semitism gradually all but disappeared as a topic of our questionnaire and in our interview schedule it was only one among many topics which had to be covered.'[285]

The report openly states that it has not studied those with fascist opinions or belonging to known fascist organizations. The report instead focuses on those it describes as 'potentially fascistic', or those especially 'susceptible to anti-democratic propaganda'.[286] Even though WWII had recently ended with the destruction of fascist regimes and the exposure of their worst excesses, the report states that the potentially fascistic were easily identified (even in the USA) and that these people would 'readily accept fascism' if it became strong and respectable.[287] This is, of course, all highly subjective, and the political prejudices of the report's authors will undoubtedly colour the conduct and conclusions of the report. The idea was to encourage anti-fascist thinking in order to resist a fascist takeover:

'A fascist triumph in America must reckon with the potential existing in the character of the people. Here lies not only the susceptibility to antidemocratic propaganda but the most dependable sources of resistance to it.'[288]

The report states that it has restricted itself regarding the causes of prejudice and that the wider problems of society are ignored:

'Our findings are strictly limited to the psychological aspects of the more general problem of prejudice. Historical factors or economic forces operating in our society to promote or to diminish ethnic prejudice are clearly beyond the scope of our investigation. In pointing toward the importance of the parent-child relationship in the establishment of prejudice or tolerance we have moved one step in the direction of an explanation. We have not, however, gone into the social and economic processes that in turn determine the development of characteristic family patterns.'[289]

The stress placed on 'the importance of the parent-child relationship' should be noted, as should the exclusion of historical or 'social and economic' factors from any consideration, meaning that any problem identified will be attributed totally to the 'strictly limited ... psychological aspects'. The outcome of the research is a recommendation for indoctrination to counter 'the whole structure of the prejudiced outlook' with 'major emphasis' not upon discrimination against any particular minority group but upon 'phenomena as stereotypy, emotional coldness, identification with power, and general destructiveness' against which 'rational arguments' are unlikely to have a lasting effect due to their irrationality. The report asserts that, if hostility against one minority group were curtailed, then 'the hostility will now very probably be directed against some other group'.[290] Regarding the so-called authoritarian personality, someone broadly condemned as being mentally defective, the report concludes that appeals to 'his reason or to his sympathy' are unlikely to succeed although 'appeals to his conventionality or to his submissiveness toward authority might be effective'. The report goes on to say that since 'acceptance of what is like oneself and rejection of what is different is one feature of the prejudiced outlook', then minorities might gain some advantage by 'conforming in outward appearance as best they can with the prevailing ways of the dominant group', but 'aside from the fact that such conformity works against the values of cultural diversity', this is unlikely to be effective, and there is a danger that 'once the minority group member has conformed in this way there is little reason to suppose that he would not adopt the prevailing ingroup attitudes toward those who have not been able to conform'.[291]

The report recommends that psychologists (presumably only those psychologists who agree with the report's assertions) should be more involved in the running of society and in the *control* of families. The report states that attention should be 'focused upon child training', as 'the earlier the influence the more profound it will be'. The report asserts: 'It would not be too difficult ... to propose a program which ... could produce non ethnocentric personalities. All that is really essential is that children be genuinely loved and treated as individual humans.'[292] The report alleges that 'ethnocentric parents' would be likely to 'exhibit in their relations with their children much the same moralistically punitive attitudes that they express toward minority groups', and that parents' need to 'do the "correct" thing' prevents them from conforming to modern theories. More importantly there are those 'parents who with the best will and the best feelings are thwarted by the need to mould the child so that he will find a place in the world as it is. Few parents can be expected to persist for long in educating their children for a society that does not exist, or even in orienting themselves toward goals which they share only with a minority.' What is needed for the 'modification of the potentially fascist structure' was for the 'total organization of society' to be changed. To change or constrain 'the fascist potential' requires 'an increase in people's capacity to see themselves and to be themselves' and this is prevented by 'social control' and by 'a "blindness" that is rooted in their own psychology.' Consequently, psychologists should develop techniques to overcome 'resistance to self-insight and resistance to social facts' among those deemed 'middle' ethnocentrists.[293]

Thus the report is as brazen in its agenda as it is chilling. It targets children, with a Rousseauist outlook as to the effect of society upon them. It aims to usurp the influence of 'ethnocentric parents'. It advocates that the whole of society be changed. It demands 'a voice' for psychologists – i.e. communists. It advocates psychological techniques be adapted and used on 'a mass scale'. And it insists that people suffer from a 'blindness', i.e. false consciousness, and that they are moulded by the economic system. Quite apart from the doctrinaire and totalitarian nature of the report's recommendations, what might be considered more chilling is its methodology. Adorno admitted:

> 'We never regarded the theory simply as a set of hypotheses but as in some sense standing on its own feet, and therefore did not intend to prove or disprove the theory through our findings but

only to derive from it concrete questions for investigation, which must then be judged on their own merit and demonstrate certain prevalent socio-psychological structures.'[294]

One can read many landmark essays, reports, or books and be disappointed. They fail to live up to expectations and the hype of others as to their exulted status. The telling argument, or brilliant revelation, or insight is just not there. Sometimes the argument is thin, and the work fails to convince, perhaps compounded by the passage of time and a better understanding of the topic involved. *The Authoritarian Personality* goes beyond all these considerations. The book is turgid. More importantly, it is embarrassing. It is bigoted, and the bald assertions contained within it are unsupportable by the so-called research laboriously set out. Were it not for the seriousness with which it is taken, it would be easy to dismiss it as being primitive Looney-Left. The report does not dwell on the middle scorers of the various questionnaires and extrapolates generalities of the entire population by comparing the views and answers of either the low or high quarters of small unrepresentative samples. It is the extreme groups that are openly focused on.[295] Analysis of the report's research is therefore necessary. Even from a basic statistical standpoint, the report is substandard and biased:

> 'The findings rest on an admittedly unrepresentative sample, from which large generalizations are incautiously drawn. What is true of highly educated people, or of extreme ethnocentric or non-ethnocentric individuals, or of active participants in civic affairs, is not necessarily true of the majority of the population. Weaknesses in the authors' handling of the quantitative data invariably work in favour of the assumptions, and the procedures are often inadmissible. Thus, the hypothesized "stereotypy" of ethnocentric individuals is deemed supported by the questionnaire answers, although both high and low scorers were forced, by nature of the scales, to subscribe or not to subscribe to arbitrary, generalized statements. A positive correlation between authoritarianism and political conservatism is claimed, although the contents of the two scales which produce the correlation are clearly overlapping and therefore inflate the value.'[296]

The report admits that 'the present samples are heavily weighted with younger people, the bulk of them falling between the ages of twenty and thirty-five'.[297] The report further admits that it had difficulty in getting people, especially from conservative organizations, to fill in the questionnaires and participate in the research. The report comments: 'Among people of this type there appeared to be a conviction that it was best to let sleeping dogs lie, that the best approach to the "race problem" was not to "stir up anything."'[298] Quite how this dismissive view was formed of conservative opinion is unexplained, and there is an obvious danger that the comment written is as much evidence of the authors' own prejudices as of any conservative opinion. Given the report's contents, a more likely explanation is that many conservatives saw the hatred for what it was and resisted the temptation to lend it any credence, having no wish to be set up and having better things to do. In any event, the report's authors passed off the research as being more of a public opinion survey in order to try and gain cooperation. Payments were offered for the subjects' time as an inducement for participation as well as anonymity for interviewees if requested.[299]

The report conducted research with both questionnaires and interviews to rank the fascist, or anti-fascist, opinions of the subjects. The report used a series of scales to rank respondents: A-S Scale – anti-Semitism; E Scale – ethnocentrism; PEC Scale – political and economic conservatism; F Scale – fascism (NB there is no C Scale for communism. Liberal democracy can be threatened by totalitarianism from both extremes. State socialism is authoritarian, conservatism not so, despite *Authoritarian Personality*. The absence of a C Scale demonstrates the bias of the report's authors). High scores were deemed to indicate prejudice and low scores against prejudice.[300] The report states: 'The distinction between "ideological" and "personal" is artificial – though often useful – is indicated by the fact that in the subject's spontaneous discussion of ideology some references to personal matters such as family and childhood repeatedly crop up';[301] and 'One of the most clearly antidemocratic forms of social ideology is prejudice'.[302] The report defines anti-democratic and introduces the concept of being pseudodemocratic:

> 'An idea may be considered openly antidemocratic when it refers to active hatred or to violence which has the direct aim of wiping out a minority group or of putting it in a permanently subordinate position. A pseudodemocratic idea, on the other hand, is one in which hostility toward a group is somewhat tempered and disguised by means of a compromise with democratic ideals. Pseudodemocratic statements about Jews are often introduced by qualifying phrases which deny hostility or which attempt to demonstrate the democratic attitude of the

47

speaker, e.g. "It's not that I'm prejudiced, but ..."; "Jews have their rights, but ...".[1303]

Using this definition of being pseudodemocratic, then almost all criticism can be deemed to be prejudiced, as a disavowal of prejudice is tantamount to prejudice. The report comments that 'This pseudodemocratic façade is probably relatively untouched by most of the current literature attacking prejudice as "race hatred", "un-American", "un-Christian intolerance", and the like'.[304] Therefore: 'It is necessary ... to understand its external sources in American culture and tradition as well as the inner sources which make certain individuals particularly receptive to these cultural pressures.'[305] The report states:

> 'It is probably an error to regard the pseudodemocratic compromise as a mere surface disguise used deliberately and skilfully by prejudiced people to camouflage their actual conscious antidemocracy. The person whose approach to social problems is pseudodemocratic is actually different *now* from one whose approach is now openly antidemocratic. For various reasons – perhaps because he has internalized democratic values, perhaps out of conformity to present social standards – the pseudodemocrat does not now accept ideas of overt violence and active suppression ... Undoubtedly very many people who are now pseudodemocratic are potentially antidemocratic, that is, are capable in a social crisis of supporting or committing acts of violence against minority groups.'[306]

The logic is that it is those who hold supposed pseudodemocratic opinions who are to be targeted as these are the people more likely to support fascist movements in certain circumstances. Therefore, in the fight against fascism, conservatives are deemed to be the enemy, and by driving out conservative viewpoints from society, fascism is to be opposed. For those who wish to engineer a communist revolution, as those in the Frankfurt School do, this viewpoint has obvious attractions, particularly as communism is deemed to be the only real opposition to fascism. Trotsky himself argued that the 'defence of democracy' was not an effective way to fight fascism, which could only be defeated by hardline Bolshevik policies.[307] The report continues:

> 'Most of the items on the A-S scale have been formulated as pseudodemocratically as possible. This consideration was, in fact, one of the main reasons for the use of negative items only.

48

The following rules have been followed in general: Each item should be made appealing and "easy to fall for" by avoiding or soft-peddling or morally justifying ideas of violence and obvious antidemocracy. Much use is made of qualifying phrases such as "One trouble with Jewish ..."; "There are a few exceptions, but ..."; "It would be to the best interests of all if ...", in order to avoid a categorical, aggressive condemnation. Items are worded so that the person can add at the end: "but I am not anti-Semitic". Seeming tentativeness is introduced by qualifications such as "it seems that", "probably", "in most cases". Finally, an attempt has been made to give each statement a familiar ring, to formulate it as it has been heard many times in everyday discussions ... Pseudodemocratic subjects are likely to make scores on this scale as high, or nearly as high, as those of the antidemocratic ones. It will be the task of later techniques, both questionnaire-style and clinical, to provide further information concerning the distinctions between these two groups of subjects.[308]

Once again, the report merges those deemed to be pseudodemocratic with those who are anti-democratic: 'Many individuals who are not now willing actively to support anti-Semitic programs have nevertheless a negative imagery and an underlying hostility that constitute a definite potentiality for such action.'[309] This assertion is based on the interpretation that the results show that the high scorers 'seem to indicate only weak resistance to these ideas'.[310] The criticism is that people are being condemned not because they hold fascist opinions but because they do not hold the opposite opinions.

The report prefers to use the term 'ethnocentrism' rather than the term 'prejudice', which it states can have several meanings. Ethnocentrism originally was used to have 'the general meaning of provincialism or cultural narrowness; it meant a tendency in the individual to be "ethnically centred," to be rigid in his acceptance of the culturally "alike" and in his rejection of the "unlike".'[311] The report continues: 'Ethnocentrism refers to group relations generally; it has to do not only with numerous groups toward which the individual has hostile opinions and attitudes but, equally importantly, with groups toward which he is positively disposed.'[312] The report states:

'The term "ethnocentrism" shifts the emphasis from "race" to "ethnic group". The everyday use of the term "race" has been criticized from many sides and on many grounds. It was originally suggested as one type of broad classification of human beings on the basis of skin colour. Other anthropometric measures such as head shape and blood type were also suggested. Each of these organic bases of classification divides human beings (also known as the human "race") into groups which are mixed with respect to the other organic characteristics. Thus, the Negroes, a "race" according to the skin colour criterion, are mixed with respect to head shape and blood type.'

The report continues to refer to the debate between the influence of hereditary forces and environmental forces. The report then points out the wide use and misuse of the term race:

'Furthermore, the term "race" is often applied to groups which are not races at all in the technical sense. Sometimes this term is applied to nations, e.g. "the German race" or even "the American race". Sometimes it is misused in connection with American ethnic minorities, such as Italians or Greeks. There is no adequate term, other than "ethnic", by which to describe cultures (that is, systems of social ways, institutions, traditions, language, and so forth) which are not nations, that is, which do not form politico-geographical entities.'[313]

The report prefers the term "ethnic" as a means of focusing on non-hereditary factors rather than 'racial hereditary'. There is a distinction drawn between ingroups, to which an individual identifies himself, and outgroups, 'with which he does not have a sense of belonging and which are regarded as antithetical to the ingroups'.[314] The individual is alleged to have positive feelings towards ingroups and hostile feelings towards outgroups, which he believes should be subordinate to ingroups. The report continues: 'Anti-Semitism is best regarded, it would seem, as one aspect of this broader frame of mind; and it is the total ethnocentric ideology, rather than prejudice against any single group, which requires explanation.'[315]

The report acknowledges that the samples were not representative, alleging that the high scorers were under-represented due to the reluctance of many to cooperate and fill in the forms. Others would cooperate up to a point. The report alleges that 'This difficulty might have been expected on the basis of the ethnocentrists' tendency toward self-deception and concern with prying, which was expressed indirectly in the responses on the A-S and E scales.'[316] That such reluctance to cooperate might be due to the political dogma of the report's authors, readily apparent in the questionnaires, is not considered in the report at all.

The report's favoured example, Larry, is described as having an extremely low score, and 'in the interview he makes every effort to place himself squarely on the side of democratic internationalism and social equality for minorities'.[317] The report attacks what it terms as pseudopatriotism:

> 'A primary characteristic of ethnocentric ideology is the generality of outgroup rejection. It is as if the ethnocentric individual feels threatened by most of the groups to which he does not have a sense of belonging; if he cannot identify, he must oppose; if a group is not "acceptable", it is "alien". The ingroup-outgroup distinction thus becomes the basis for most of his social thinking, and people are categorized primarily according to the groups to which they belong ... Most other nations, especially the industrially backward, the socialistic, and those most different from the "Anglo-Saxon", tend to be considered outgroups ... It would appear that an individual who regards a few of these groups as outgroups will tend to reject most of them. An ethnocentric individual may have a particular dislike for one group, but he is likely nonetheless to have ethnocentric opinions and attitudes regarding many other groups.
>
> Another general characteristic of ethnocentric ideology is the *shifting* of the outgroup among various levels of social organization. Once the social context for discussion has been set, ethnocentrists are likely to find an outgroup-ingroup distinction. Thus, in a context of international relations ethnocentrism takes the form of pseudopatriotism; "we" are the best people and the best country in the world, and we should either keep out of world affairs altogether (isolationism) or we should participate – but without losing our full sovereignty, power, and economic advantage (imperialism). And in either case we should have the biggest army and navy in the world, and atom bomb monopoly.'[318]

Thus what might be described as national pride and a desire to enhance the success and power of the country, patriotism, or nationalism becomes a simplistic pseudopatriotism – a form of ethnocentrism. This makes it easy to target and denigrate the concept of national pride, and particularly nationalism (especially given the ingroup-outgroup focus), and makes opposition to immigration, the EU, or international organizations ethnocentric or prejudiced as the opposition is supportive of the national interest and disapproving of outside entities. Having carried out their research, the report advances the following assertion:

> 'Ethnocentrism is based on a pervasive and rigid ingroup-outgroup distinction; it involves stereotyped negative imagery and hostile attitudes regarding outgroups, stereotyped positive imagery and submissive attitudes regarding ingroups, and a hierarchical, authoritarian view of group interaction in which ingroups are rightly dominant, outgroups subordinate.'[319]

The report further draws in capitalism as well as denigrating wider society:

> 'That political and economic forces play a vital role in the development of ethnocentrism, in both its institutional and individual psychological forms, is no longer questioned by social scientists or even by most laymen. In modern industrial societies ethnocentric ideology has been utilized by a great variety of sociopolitical movements which can be broadly characterized as fascist, prefascist, reactionary, imperialistic, chauvinistic.'[320]

The report therefore moves into more mainstream opinions as a target and not fascism:

> 'The focus of the present study was, therefore, on liberalism and conservatism, the currently prevalent left- and right-wing political ideologies – with an eye, to be sure, on their potential polarization to the more extreme left and right. There is considerable evidence suggesting a psychological affinity between conservatism and ethnocentrism, liberalism and anti-ethnocentrism.'[321]

The report defines liberal thus: 'To be "liberal" ... one must be able actively to criticize existing authority. The criticisms may take various forms, ranging from mild reforms (e.g. extension of government controls over business) to complete overthrow of the *status quo*.'[322] A 'complete overthrow of the *status quo*' is not liberal, but communism. It is the view of the average Leninist. The report is sneaking in communist ideology in a liberal Trojan Horse. By comparison, conservatism is condemned as being ethnocentric. In the attack upon conservatism, many aspects of society are targeted, including Christianity and even charity:

> 'Our religious tradition is one of charity and tolerance; if one cannot excuse the poor, one can at least soften their plight – with Christmas parties, Thanksgiving bazaars, orphanages, and the like. Industrialists like Carnegie and Rockefeller are examples of this combination of weekday toughness and Sunday charity, which Item 8 was intended to measure: "Every adult should find time or money for some worthy service organization (charity, medical aid, etc.) as the best way of aiding his fellow man."
> From the "liberal" point of view charity is mainly a soothing of conscience and a means of maintaining an unjust state of affairs. The causes of poverty are seen, not in the innate stupidity of the poor, but in the politico-economic organization which, by virtue of its concentration of economic power, creates poverty as a symptom. And the answer is seen, not in ineffectual though often well-intentioned charity, but in the elimination of poverty through modification of its societal causes.
> It would appear, then, that liberals tend to view social problems as symptoms of the underlying social structure, while conservatives view them as results of individual incompetence or immorality.'[1323]

And:

> 'The attitude toward charity was also explored in this connection as a possible manifestation of atonement which, in turn, is known to be a reaction to aggression. From a social point of view, charity often has the function of keeping the underprivileged in their place, kindness acting in effect as a humiliating factor.'[1324]

Many genuine liberals might be surprised to be told that they regard society as the cause of all poverty, being a 'symptom' of the 'politico-economic organization' of the economy, or that they are opposed to charity, preferring instead to modify 'societal causes' – i.e. support a communist revolution. The report even goes so far as to assign religious belief as being ethnocentric and atheism as being less ethnocentric: 'It appears that those who reject religion have less ethnocentrism than those who seem to accept it.'[1325] The report's authors define poverty as something that is caused by society and do not embrace the concept of civilization and the process of economic and social advancement, i.e. the idea that poverty might be reduced by the process of civilization. The report defines conservatism thus:

> 'Conservatism is taken to mean traditional economic laissez-faire individualism, according to which our economic life is conceived in terms of the free (unregulated) competition of individual entrepreneurs. Business, accorded such great prestige by conservative values, is regarded as deserving great social power in relation to labour and government. Unions are regarded as threatening, power-seeking, interfering with the traditional functions of management, and promoting radical changes. Unions are likely to be accepted only when their actual power is less than that of business: this means virtual elimination of the right to strike, of a voice in determining company policy, and of political functions – in short, of the possibility of changing to any significant degree the existing balance of politico-economic power. A liberal view point regarding unions is expressed in Item 68: "Labour unions should become stronger by being politically active and by publishing labour newspapers to be read by the general public".
>
> Conservative ideology has traditionally urged that the economic functions of government be minimized. Fear of government power (like union power) is emphasized, and great concern is expressed for the freedom of the individual, particularly the individual businessman.'[326]

The report's authors betray themselves with this last comment. Traditionally, it is liberalism that favours small government and a restriction of government power. Liberals tend to favour the freedom of the individual, and this is not confined to conservatism. Obviously, communists favour powerful government. True conservatism would involve patriotism, a pride in tradition, a desire to protect what is best in society and bequeath it to the next generation. Conservatism does not just appeal to any particular class but is concerned with uniting the whole nation. It is communism that is focused on fostering division and hatred in society. Conservatism is not just about economics, and the report's definition of conservatism betrays the authors' communism. Hostility towards right-wing opinions extends to feelings of patriotism and nationhood.[327] For the Left of the 1930s, especially communists, fascism was the final resort of conservatism in response to the inevitable crisis of capitalism.[328] The report links ethnocentrism with authority and tradition (i.e. conservatism):

54

'There are also theoretical reasons for expecting a relationship between liberalism and anti-ethnocentrism. Both tend to involve a critical attitude toward prevailing authorities and traditions. The identification with the masses (workers, "the common man", "the weak and downtrodden") so often a central theme in left-wing political ideology, finds expression also in opposition to ethnocentrism and outgroup suppression.'[329]

The report identifies what it calls the pseudoconservative:

'The ethnocentric conservative is the *pseudoconservative*, for he betrays in his ethnocentrism a tendency antithetical to democratic values and tradition ... His political-economic views are based on the same underlying trends – submission to authority, unconscious handling of hostility toward authority by means of displacement and projection onto outgroups, and so on – as his ethnocentrism. It is indeed paradoxical that the greatest psychological potential for antidemocratic change should come from those who claim to represent democratic tradition. For the pseudoconservatives are the pseudodemocrats, and their needs dispose them to the use of force and oppression in order to protect a mythical "Americanism" which bears no resemblance to what is most vital in American history.'[330]

In reference to those pseudoconservatives deemed to be highly ethnocentric, the report states:

'This is not merely a "modern conservatism". It is, rather a totally new direction: away from individualism and equality of opportunity, and toward a rigidly stratified society in which there is a minimum of economic mobility and in which the "right" groups are in power, the outgroups subordinate. Perhaps the term "reactionary" fits this ideology best. Ultimately it is fascism. While certainly not a *necessary* sequel to laissez-faire conservatism, it can be regarded as a possible (and not uncommon) distortion of conservatism – a distortion which retains certain surface similarities but which changes the basic structure into the antithesis of the original.'[331]

That the report was biased is scarcely concealed. Research that did not produce the desired outcome was dropped; questions were altered or ignored. This is openly stated. For example:

55

'"The modern church with its many rules and hypocracies, does not appeal to the deeply religious person; it appeals mainly to the childish, the insecure, and the uncritical." The hypothesis here was that disagreement with the item would indicate uncritical acceptance of the church and, hence, ethnocentrism, and that agreement with the item would indicate either an antireligious attitude or a genuinely religious but more intellectual point of view from which the church might be criticized − something which we should expect to go with low scores on the scales for measuring prejudice.'[332]

However, the results were described as 'disappointing', and the report concluded that the question was 'too complex and awkward, and hence, frequently misunderstood'. The question was therefore dropped.[333] It is entertaining to read the logic behind the question and the rationale for its intended inclusion. The report links religion with prejudice:

'Subjects who profess to some religious affiliation express more prejudice than those who do not; but mean A-S or E scores for all the large denominations are close to the theoretical neutral point ... Frequency of church attendance is also not particularly revealing; however, the finding that those who never attend obtain lower E scores than those who do attend is added evidence that people who reject organized religion are less prejudiced than those who accept it.'[334]

The report even goes so far as to state that 'agreement between the subject and his or her mother in the matter of religion tends to be associated with ethnocentrism, disagreement with its opposite. These results suggest that acceptance of religion mainly as an expression of submission to a clear pattern of parental authority is a condition favourable to ethnocentrism.'[335] The purported correlation between religious belief (i.e. Christianity) and ethnocentrism (i.e. racism) does not prove causation, and the purported correlation is only achieved by the manipulation of the results, the exclusion of results that are not what was desired, and the interpretation imposed by the communist authors of the report.

Paternal authority is deemed to be an aspect of ethnocentrism: 'In general, it appeared that gross, objective factors − denomination and frequency of church attendance − were less significant for prejudice than were certain psychological trends reflected in the way the subject accepted or rejected religion and in the content of his religious ideology.

These trends (were) conventionalism, authoritarian submission, and so forth.'[336] Families are a repeated target: 'Very characteristic of high-scoring subjects is an initial statement of great admiration for parents, followed by some criticism which is not, however, recognized as such by the subject.'[337] The report further states: 'The difference in the type of discipline found in the families of our high-scoring as compared with those of our low-scoring subjects, in conjunction with the difference in the family structure and the personality of the parents (stern vs. relaxed) may be considered part of the foundation for an authoritarian vs. democratic approach to interpersonal relationships.'[338]

The report opines that high-scoring men might be expected to consider themselves to be more masculine. However, the report defines them as being more pseudo-masculine, being more inclined to 'boastfulness about such traits as determination, energy, industry, independence, decisiveness, and will power'.[339] Likewise, the report identifies pseudo-femininity as being an overly exaggerated sense of femininity combined with an aggressive attitude towards men.[340] The report is dismissive of women and their traditional roles:

> 'The opportunism found in high-scoring women, together with their underlying hostility towards men ... made us expect that they would tend to see their fathers mainly as sources of provision ... Six of the high- and only one of the low-scoring women stress the provider quality in their fathers. It is this quality that high-scoring women seem to value primarily in men and which, rather than affection, is often the source of their dependency on men. There is indeed little evidence of a genuine positive relation of prejudiced women toward their fathers.'[341]

The attack on the traditional family is persistent, and the family is deemed to be the earliest adverse influence giving rise to prejudice:

> 'Conformity to externalized values in the extremely prejudiced can be observed in a variety of spheres of life. One of the earliest expressions of this conventionality is to be found, probably, in the high scorer's attitude toward his parents. It is one of stereotypical admiration, with little ability to express criticism or resentment. There are many indications that there actually is often considerable underlying hostility toward the parents which – though not always expressed – prevents the development of a truly affectionate relationship.'[342]

What constitutes 'underlying hostility' or 'a truly affectionate relationship', for example, is not explained, and the report simply relies upon the bald assertions of its authors. The repeated use of the term 'probably' betrays that the supposed findings are simply invented allegations.

By contrast: 'The unprejudiced man, especially, seems oriented toward his mother and tends to retain a love-dependent nurturance-succorance attitude toward women in general which is not easily satisfied';[343] and 'The descriptions of the parents given by the low scorers have an aspect of spontaneity: they depict real people with all their inherent assets and shortcomings.'[344]

Intelligence is deemed to be another aspect: 'There is a very low but dependable negative relationship between intelligence and ethnocentrism: the most ethnocentric subjects are, on the average, less intelligent than the least ethnocentric, while the middle scorers on E are intermediate in IQ.'[345] Being impressed by authority, as well as being less intelligent, gives rise to the idea that the prejudiced can be manipulated and educated by using authority:

> 'Efforts to modify the "prejudiced" pattern may have to make use of authorities – though by no means necessarily of authoritarian authorities – in order to reach the individual in question. This follows from the fact that it is authority more than anything else that structures or prestructures the world of the prejudiced individual. Where public opinion takes over the function of authority and provides the necessary limitations – and thus certainties – in many walks of daily life, as is the case in this country, there will be some room for the tolerance of national or racial ambiguities.
>
> It must be emphasized, however, that the potentially beneficial aspects of conformity are more than counterbalanced by the inherent seeds of stereotypy and pre-judgement. These latter trends are apt to increase in a culture which has become too complex to be fully mastered by the individual.'[346]

Supposedly concerned with anti-Semitism, the report meanders along as the mission creep grows, but it does deal with anti-Semitism by linking it to Nazism:

> 'The term "problem" is taken over from the sphere of science and is used to give the impression of searching, responsible deliberation. By referring to a problem, one implicitly claims personal aloofness from the matter in question – a kind of

detachment and higher objectivity. This, of course, is an excellent rationalization for prejudice. It serves to give the impression that one's attitudes are not motivated subjectively but have resulted from hard thinking and mature experience. The subject who makes use of this device maintains a discursive attitude in the interview; he qualifies, quasi-empirically, what he has to say, and is ready to admit exceptions. Yet these qualifications and exceptions only scratch the surface. As soon as the existence of a "Jewish problem" is admitted, anti-Semitism has won its first surreptitious victory.[1347]

The report periodically lobs in some Freudian rationale to try to give credence to its allegations. For example, it cites one subject who commented about Jewish 'drive and ambition to get there'; the comments are designated as 'mainly envy', and the subject is accused of having 'furtive signs' of 'hostility against "the Jew"' that, allegedly, stems from the subject's repressed resentment towards his father: 'This father-ideal is difficult for him to rebel against even by way of displaced resentment against the symbol of "the Jew", because under moralistic pressure from his mother he is deceived into thinking that his submission to this ideal is itself an assertion of independence from his father's values.'[1348] The reader is supposed to be impressed with this. As may well be the case, there are those who cannot keep their mouths shut:

> 'The extreme anti-Semite simply cannot stop. By a logic of his own ... he reaches after having started from relatively mild accusation, the wildest conclusions, tantamount in the last analysis to the pronouncement of death sentences against those whom he literally "cannot stand". This mechanism was encountered in the "screened" interviews of the Labour Study where subjects frequently "talked themselves into anti-Semitism".[1349]

Genocide is seen as the ultimate evolved state of anti-Semitism: 'Our analysis has led us to the extreme consequence of anti-Semitism, the overt wish for the extermination of the Jews. The extremist's Superego has been transformed into an extrapunitive agency of unbridled aggression.'[1350] The Freudian quip does not convince and is nothing more than a throwaway line. The report continues to allege that 'if our basic hypothesis' is correct, then class plays a role in anti-Semitism:

'To the true proletarian, the Jew is primarily bourgeois. The workingman is likely to perceive the Jew, above all, as an agent of the economic sphere of the middle-man, as the executor of capitalist tendencies. The Jew is he who "presents the bill" ... To the anti-Semitic members of the middle classes, the imagery of the Jew seems to have a somewhat different structure. The middle classes themselves experience to a certain degree the same threats to the economic basis of their existence which hang over the heads of the Jews. They are themselves on the defensive and struggle desperately for the maintenance of their status. Hence, they accentuate just the opposite of what workingmen are likely to complain about, namely, that the Jews are not real bourgeois, that they do not really "belong"'.[351]

It should be noted that, as the report slips in, this is all a 'basic hypothesis' and nothing more. There is no evidence, and the report does not claim any. The allegation has simply been invented.

It is not only the anti-Semitists who talk themselves into a more extremist position; the report's authors show themselves to be fully capable of the same impulse:

'It has often been said that anti-Semitism works as the spearhead of anti-democratic forces. The phrase sounds a bit hackneyed and apologetic: the minority most immediately threatened seems to make an all-too-eager attempt to enlist the support of the majority by claiming that it is the latter's interest and not their own which really finds itself in jeopardy today. Looking back, however, at the material surveyed ... it has to be recognized that a link between anti-Semitism and antidemocratic feeling exists. True, those who wish to exterminate the Jews do not, as is sometimes claimed, wish to exterminate afterwards the Irish or the Protestants. But the limitation of human rights which is consumated in their idea of a special treatment of the Jews, not only logically implies the ultimate abolition of the democratic form of government and, hence, of the legal protection of the individual, but it is frequently associated quite consciously, by high-scoring interviewees, with overt antidemocratic ideas.'[352]

In support of the above, Adorno cites one note which states: 'Respondent believes that the "laws of democracy should favour white, Gentile people", yet he "would not openly persecute Jews in the way the Hitler program treated them".' Adorno comments: 'The reservation of

60

the second sentence is disavowed by the momentum of the convictions expressed in the first one.'[353] In fact, the convictions of the first sentence do not disavow the second sentence. It is Adorno's own bigotry that is demonstrated. One would need to delve into why the respondent believed that the laws should favour certain people before passing judgement.

The report draws in capitalism and also draws upon Marx's idea that capitalism needs to replicate itself in order to survive and sustain itself, as well as the Marxist idea that people suffer from false consciousness. Capitalism, it is alleged, is 'on the defence' and 'has to maintain itself somewhat precariously' and 'block critical insights' that are 'viewed as potentially dangerous', all of which makes 'for a one-sided presentation of the facts, for manipulated information, and for certain shifts of emphasis which tend to check the universal enlightenment otherwise furthered by the technological development of communications'. This '*status quo*, struggling for its perpetuation, is reflected by the attitudes and opinions of all those who, for reasons of vested interests or psychological conditions, identify themselves with the existing setup'. Consequently, people are alleged to 'unconsciously' be 'ready to accept superficial or distorted information as long as it confirms the world in which they want to go on living'. 'Psychological repressions' may therefore be more responsible for a supposedly low level of 'political intelligence' and even 'stupidity' as people 'find it difficult to think and even to learn because they are afraid they might think the wrong thoughts or learn the wrong things', which is 'probably often due to the father's refusal to tell the child more than he is supposedly capable of understanding', and this 'is continuously reinforced by [the] educational system'. This 'absence of political training' is at odds with the 'abundance of political news' which 'fictitiously presupposes such training'. This stupidity is allegedly compounded by psychological factors. Politics is allegedly treated as a part of 'the framework of "entertainment"' such as 'sport or the movies', and people are therefore 'conditioned' and are indifferent towards politics. This tendency is 'most often to be observed, perhaps, among young women namely, skipping the political sections of newspapers, where information is available, and turning immediately to gossip columns, crime stories, the woman's page, and so forth, may be an extreme expression of something more general'.[354] Comments such as this betray the contempt held for women who hold traditional values. (That ordinary people are too stupid and disinterested in politics is a viewpoint that will arise below with other members of the Frankfurt School.) The report goes on to express some startling views of women:

'The patient had a great deal of unconscious hostility towards her husband, as well as towards her mother, her favourite brother, and men in general, who were represented as aggressive and sexually brutal. This unconscious imagery of men as "attackers" was expressed consciously in her thinking about certain outgroups such as Negroes and Mexicans. The dreams also suggest a conflict over sexual and oral-aggressive impulses towards men. The contexts in which the orality and aggression appeared (smashing snakes, biting into chicken drumsticks, etc.) suggest infantile wishes to bite, destroy and incorporate a penis … [This subject] could not admit any aggression towards her husband or family, inhibiting most expressions of anger and irritation behind a façade of submissive compliance and somewhat forced cheerfulness. In therapy it was revealed that her shaking and fainting spells always followed incidents in which a man provoked her anger by acting in a deprecating and implicitly aggressive and demanding manner, while she retained a calm and good-humoured attitude.'[355]

The report cites: '[The subject] resented [her father's] treatment of her husband of whom he did not approve, but she was unable to admit this resentment.'[356] Elsewhere, both men and women deemed to be ethnocentric attract Freudian comments:

'The high scorers have rigid, constricted personalities, as shown by their stereotyped, conventional thinking and acting and their violent and categorical rejection of everything reminding them of their own repressed impulses … It is as if they can experience only the one conventionally correct attitude or emotion in any given situation. Everything else is suppressed or denied, or if another impulse breaks through it is experienced as something which is completely incompatible with the conception of the self, and which suddenly overwhelms the ego. In part, this high degree of ego-alienness probably derives from the fact that the impulses emerging from repression are so primitive and, especially in the women, so very hostile.'[357]

The report states: 'the high scorers … are dominated by castration anxiety and more often show anal character traits such as hostile rejectiveness, retentiveness, and anal reaction formations' which was 'particularly strong in the women'. High scoring men also had 'strong but repressed passive-dependent desires … the high-scoring men's passivity and dependency probably is mainly a reaction to their extreme castration anxiety. The high-scoring men often seek protection from this anxiety in a motherly woman, but without having a very differentiated relationship to this woman as a person.[1358]

The report opines that low scorers are confident that 'public figures are good, friendly fathers who take care of one, or of the "underdog", and that this view is the product of a 'positive transference' of the relationship the low scorers had with their parents. Conversely, high scorers seek strength in public figures and this is derived from 'a stern father to whom one "looks up".[1359] The Marxist concept of alienation also creeps in:

> 'The alienation between the political sphere and the life experience of the individual, which the latter often tries to master by psychologically determined intellectual makeshifts such as stereotypy and personalization, sometimes results in a gap between what the subject professes to think about politics and economy and what he really thinks. His "official" ideology conforms to what he supposes he *has* to think; his real ideas are an expression of his more immediate personal needs as well as of his psychological urges. The "official" ideology pertains to the objectified, alienated sphere of the political, the "real opinion" to the subjects' own sphere of the political, the "real opinion" to the subjects' own sphere, and the contradiction between the two expresses their irreconcilability.'[1360]

To try and justify this the report refers to one subject who 'is middle on E and F but low on PEC'. In her case, the deeper determinants are doubtless potentially fascist as evidenced particularly by her strong racial prejudice against both Negroes and Jews. However, the woman admires Russia. She is very different politically from her husband, and the report states: 'One is tempted to hypothesize that she wants him to get mad at her when she speaks in favour of Russia. In her case, the broad-mindedness and rationality of surface opinion seems to be conditioned by strong underlying, repressed irrationalities.'[1361] Another example is described as being 'consciously liberal and definitely nonprejudiced' but, nevertheless, has a 'mildly antistrike attitude' and is condemned for being antistrike for using a 'getting together formula' to solve a dispute as a means of avoiding strike action. The report concludes that 'this man's "political instincts" – if this term is allowed – are against his official progressiveness'.[1362] Another example expresses support for socialism but says that he will not vote for socialists if they were ever likely to win, preferring them to act as an opposition brake on the government. The report concludes that 'This subject wants to be endowed with the prestige of a left-wing intellectual while at the same time, as an empirical being, he is manifestly afraid of a concrete materialization of ideas to which he subscribes in the abstract.'[1363]

The report attaches importance to the unions and is hostile to any adverse criticism of union activity: 'The element of partial truth in the critique of labour is among the most dangerous fascist potentials in this country ... No analysis of the fascist potential is valid which does not give account of the agglomerate of rational critique and irrational hatred in the people's attitude toward labour.'[1364] The report regrets that 'today's labour movement, instead of aiming at a better society, is satisfied with securing certain advantages and privileges within the present setup. This is just the opposite of the typical high scorer's complaint that unions have become too political.'[1365] The report condemns those who believe that unions should confine themselves to industrial relations issues:

> 'One particular aspect of critical feelings toward labour should be stressed. It is the idea that unions should not engage in politics. Since this has nothing to do with those economic experiences with labour at which the complaints of many people aim, it is a matter of plain ideology, derived very probably from some belief that according to American tradition unions offer a means of "bargaining", of obtaining higher shares, and should not meddle in other issues. The anger labour wage disputes and strikes is displaced and becomes rationalized by hasty identification of organized labour and communism. Since unions in this country are incomparably less political and class-conscious than anywhere else, this objection is of an entirely different order from those previously discussed: it is truly an expression of reactionism. However, in this area the reactionary ideology is so strongly backed by preconceived notions that it infiltrates easily into the opinion of people of whom it could hardly be expected.'[1366]

The report again becomes unhinged when attacking those who are critical of unions and lobs in some Freudian phrases to try to lend credence to the report's stance [note the term 'it is our general assumption']:

> 'As to the high scorers, the key theme of their antilabour ideology is that of the "racket" ... Viewed from a purely psychological angle the idea of "labour racketeering" seems to be of a nature similar to the stereotype of Jewish clannishness. It dates back to the lack of an adequately internalized

identification with paternal authority during the Oedipus situation. It is our general assumption that the typical high scorers, above all, fear the father and try to side with him in order to participate in his power. The "racketeers" are those who by demanding too much (though the subject wants as much himself) run the risk of arousing the father's anger – and hence the subject's castration anxiety. This anxiety, reflecting the subject's own guilt feelings, is relieved by projection. Thinking in terms of in- and outgroup, the high scorer who wants to "outgroup" the others is continuously prone to call them the ingroup.[367]

An objection to high taxation is also deemed to be a pre-fascist trait:

'The man who bangs his fist on the table and complains about heavy taxation is a "natural candidate" for totalitarian movements. Not only are taxes associated with a supposedly spendthrift democratic government giving away millions to idlers and bureaucrats, but it is the very point where people felt, to put it in the words of one of our subjects, that this world does not really belong to the people.'[368]

The report is contemptuous of those who express negative opinions towards Russia, such opinions being condemned as irrational and idiotic, which shows the 'vast psychological resources fascist propaganda can rely on' in denouncing communism. Those holding these critical views of Russia were supposedly displacing 'hostility against the defeated enemy upon the foe to be'.[369] If respondents regarded communism as the 'foe to be', then they were fully correct. Communism was the looming enemy and was responsible for far many more deaths in the 20th century than fascism. The report goes even further and, with a caveat, dismisses even the idea that other countries may choose communism:

'The interviews of other subjects show an unmistakably condescending overtone of this same argument, such as *M107*, a medical student who scores high on E but middle on F and PEC: "We can cooperate with Russia; if they want communism they have to have it."
    This type of liberal approach, of which, incidentally, the Hitler regime profited during the Chamberlain era of noninterference, is not as broad-minded as it may appear. It often hides the conviction that there is no objective truth in politics, that every country, as every individual, may behave as it likes and that the

only thing that counts is success. It is precisely this pragmatization of politics which ultimately defines fascist philosophy.

Obviously, the relationship between anticommunism and fascist potential as measured by our scales should not be oversimplified. In some of our earlier studies the correlation between anti-Semitism and anticommunism was very high, but there is reason to believe that it would not be so high today.'[370]

The members of the Frankfurt School were supportive of the communist revolution in Russia and could be disingenuous in being so. Horkheimer wrote in 1930:

'Those who have an eye to the senseless injustice of the imperialistic world which cannot be explained by technical powerlessness, will regard events in Russia as the continued, painful attempt to overcome ... terrible social injustice, or he will at least ask with a beating heart, if this attempt is still continuing. If appearances speak against it, he clings to the hope in the way in which a cancer victim does to the questionable news that a cure for cancer has in all likelihood been found.'[371]

In 1946, Horkheimer wrote: 'At present the only country where there does not seem to be any kind of anti-Semitism is Russia. This has a very obvious reason. Not only has Russia passed laws against anti-Semitism, but it really enforces them; and the penalties are very severe.'[372] It should not be surprising that the theorists of the Frankfurt School were unfazed by the genocide in Russia, not only due to the shared communist beliefs, but also due to their own tendencies. Lukacs, according to eyewitness accounts, when drawing up lists for the firing squad during meetings of the Hungarian Soviet in 1919, used to quote the Grand Inquisitor (from the Spanish Inquisition): 'And we who, for their happiness, have taken their sins upon ourselves, we stand before you and say, "Judge us if you can and if you dare".'[373]

The report alleges: 'The *Authoritarian* type is governed by the superego and has continuously to contend with strong and highly ambivalent id tendencies. He is driven by fear of being weak.'[374] The usage of Freudian terms does not convince, even when those terms are produced at length and linked directly to political issues:

'[The "Authoritarian" Syndrome] comes closest to the over-all picture of the high scorer as it stands out throughout our study. It follows the "classic" psychoanalytic pattern involving a sadomasochistic resolution of the Oedipus complex, and it has been pointed out by Erich Fromm ... According to Max Horkheimer's theory in the collective work of which he wrote the sociopsychological part, external social repression is concomitant with the internal repression of impulses. In order to achieve "internalization" of social control which never gives as much to the individual as it takes, the latter's attitude towards authority and much to the individual as it takes, the latter's attitude towards authority and its psychological agency, the superego, assumes an irrational aspect. The subject achieves his own social adjustment only by taking pleasure in obedience and subordination. This brings into play the sadomasochistic impulse structure both as a condition and as a result of social adjustment. In our form of society, sadistic as well as masochistic tendencies actually find gratification. The pattern for the translation of such gratifications into character traits is a specific resolution of the Oedipus complex which defines the formation of the syndrome here in question. Love for the mother, in its primary form, comes under a severe taboo. The resulting hatred against the father is transformed by reaction-formation into love. This transformation leads to a particular kind of superego. The transformation of hatred into love, the most difficult task an individual has to perform in his early development, never succeeds completely. In the psychodynamics of the "authoritarian character", part of the preceding aggressiveness is absorbed and turned into masochism, while another part is left over as sadism, which seeks an outlet in those with whom the subject does not identify himself: ultimately the outgroup. The Jew frequently becomes a substitute for the hated father, often assuming on a fantasy level, the very same qualities against which the subject revolted in the father, such as being practical, cold, domineering, and even a sexual rival. Ambivalence is all-pervasive, being evidenced mainly by the simultaneity of blind belief in authority and readiness to attack those who are deemed weak and who are socially acceptable as "victims". Stereotypy, in this syndrome, is not only a means of social identification, but has a truly "economic" function in the subjects' own psychology: it helps to canalize his libidinous energy according to the demands of his overstrict superego. Thus stereotypy itself tends to become heavily libidinized and plays a large role in the subject's inner household. He develops deep "compulsive" character traits, partly by retrogression to the anal-sadistic phase of development. Sociologically, this syndrome used to be, in Europe, highly characteristic of the lower middle-class. In this country, we may expect it among people whose actual status differs from that to which they aspire. This is in marked contrast to the social contentment and lack of conflict that is more characteristic of the "Conventional" syndrome, with which the "Authoritarian" one shares the conformist aspect.'[375]

And:

'A basically hierarchical, authoritarian, exploitive parent-child relationship is apt to carry over into a power-orientated, exploitively dependent attitude toward one's sex partner and one's God and may well culminate in a political philosophy and social outlook which has no room for anything but a desperate clinging to what appears to be strong and disdainful rejection of whatever is relegated to the bottom. The inherent dramatization likewise extends from the parent-child dichotomy to the dichotomous conception of sex roles and of moral values, as well as to a dichotomous handling of social relations as manifested especially in the formation of stereotypes and of ingroup-outgroup cleavages. Conventionality, rigidity, repressive denial, and the ensuing breakthrough of one's weakness, fear and dependency are but other aspects of the same fundamental personality pattern, and they can be observed in personal life as well as in attitudes toward religion and social issues.'[376]

This incorporation of Freud into Marxism is deemed an act of genius! Words fail. If this is an accurate representation of Freud, then it requires serious effort not to conclude that he was a charlatan who tried to draw attention to his quack theories by using dirty talk; and the self-appointed psychologists of the Frankfurt School are even worse in that they churn out such filth without a shred of evidence and in preference to practical argument. Dirty talk from self-appointed psychologists does not constitute expert evidence, nor factual evidence, and is not a replacement for intellectual analysis. One of the subjects used to support the ridiculous and unsubstantiated assertions is Mack:

'The general picture of Mack's surface attitudes towards his father is one of submission and admiration. And this despite the subject's claim to stubbornness and independence. One might say that his only recourse in the face of what he conceived to be the father's irresistible power was to submit – and then to gain a

68

sense of adequacy by participating psychologically in the father's power. This, in the last analysis, is the homosexual solution to the Oedipus problem. It is not surprising, therefore, to find in Mack's T.A.T. productions clear indications of his fear of homosexual attack. (This is made manifest, primarily, in his treatment of the "hypnotist" picture.)

Even without this piece of direct evidence we would be led to hypothesize repressed homosexuality in order to explain some of the outstanding features of Mack's personality development. The material is replete with manifestations of authoritarian submission. As clear a manifestation as any, perhaps, is the conception of God "as strictly a man, one who would treat us as a father would his son". There would seem to be no doubt that Mack has longed for his father's love – as we should expect in a boy who lost his mother when he was 6 years old. He has tried to replace the imagery of a bad, dangerous father with imagery of a good father who would spend "*all* of his time with us". But Mack is not able to admit this need. Even while *acting* in a submissive and deferential manner he seems to cling to the belief that he is very manly and self-sufficient. The reason for this self-deception, we can well believe, is that, for this subject, to submit to a man and so to gain his love has definite sexual implications. It may be connected with very primitive imagery of passivity and emasculation. One might say that Mack's homosexuality, repressed in childhood in a setting of sadomasochistic relations with the father, has remained on an infantile level; insufficiently sublimated, it cannot find gratification in friendly, equalitarian relations with men but, instead, it determines that most such relations have to be on a dominance-submission dimension ... it is Mack's repressed homosexuality, very probably, that is mainly responsible for his compelling fear of weakness. If weakness means emasculation, if it means being at the mercy of an irresistibly strong man, then it is not difficult to see why this subject should exert every effort to make himself appear impregnable.[377]

There is no evidence that Mack was homosexual, or even a repressed homosexual. The use of the terms 'hypothesize repressed homosexuality', 'we can well believe' and 'very probably', for example, are telling. The allegations are invented. Nor is there any logic or evidence that homosexuality renders someone more prone to general prejudice, ethnocentrism, or Nazism. Nevertheless, the report asserts:

'As far as our material goes the only outlets for the expression of aggression that Mack has is through his ethnocentrism, that is, through authoritarian aggression against various kinds of outgroups. ... We must understand, however, that in cynicism the destructiveness is directed against the self as well as against the world. It is not only that the subject's own aggressiveness is projected onto other people, who are then accused of being acquisitive and warlike, but contempt for other people seems to be closely related to contempt for himself. In Mack's case – and this probably holds generally for authoritarian personalities – the self-contempt derives from his sense of weakness and this, as we have seen, is the aftermath of his surrender to his father. This surrender cannot be wholly excused, and as long as he cannot permit himself to feel aggressive toward those who are actually strong, there will be a nagging reminder that he, in reality, is weak. He tries to free himself from this thought by projecting the contemptibleness onto mankind, and this there is some basis for saying that he hates other because he hates himself.'[1378]

Once again, the above paragraph consists of nothing more than bald assertions. There is no evidence to support the allegations, which are simply invented. The get out is the parameters of the report, quoted above, in which it is stated: 'Our findings are strictly limited to the psychological aspects of the more general problem of prejudice. Historical factors or economic forces operating in our society to promote or to diminish ethnic prejudice are clearly beyond the scope of our investigation.' What the report's authors are doing, as evidenced above, is to invent 'psychological aspects' of alleged prejudice to fill the void left by the absence of any consideration of historical, economic or other factors. Furthermore, the 'psychological aspects' are limited to Freud and dirty talk. Homosexuality is also cited in another case to justify the respondent's hostility to 'negro men':

'Ronald has a history of severe chronic bed-wetting until the age of 12, for which he has no explanation to offer beyond an externalization of the symptom onto "my kidneys". He has no idea why his enuresis suddenly stopped at the age of 12. That bed-wetting may have represented in part a passive mode of sexual gratification is suggested by his homosexual conflicts. Earlier mention has been made of his righteous condemnation of "sexual perversion" including, explicitly, fellatio. He denies that he has ever "felt any desire of any kind" for homosexual

70

relations, yet subsequently admits to having several times had such relations with a fellow inmate. He implicitly denies any "real" homosexuality in this (blaming it exclusively on prison sex deprivation), and says that he had no special reaction to the experiences except to lose respect for the *other* man. Ronald's paranoid "toughness" toward Negro men might perhaps be a defence against homosexual excitement aroused by them. Ronald's promiscuous heterosexuality, including several, impersonalized, unusual marriage ceremonies, may also be understood as an attempt to deny homosexual impulses.'[379]

Those deemed to be unprejudiced are, apparently, free from all of the above problems:

> 'The contrasting sexual orientations of the prejudiced and unprejudiced interviewees suggest certain crucial personality differences. The unprejudiced men seem to seek, above all, love – which they also have some capacity to give. Despite frustration and conflict their approach to life is influenced by basic respect for themselves and other people. This makes for democratic identification with other people, and for an inclination to identify with underdogs. The prejudiced men, on the other hand, seem to feel basically rejected and to have almost given up hope of experiencing genuine love. They speak as if they dislike and fear themselves as well as others. Their main energies seem to be devoted to defending themselves against any sense of weakness, chiefly by striving for external status and power and "proofs" of masculinity. The result is a power-orientated character structure driven to attack outgroups as symbols of their own suppressed characteristics.'[380]

It should not be forgotten, while reading this, that the report is written by communists, and at a time when the full gore of communist revolution was in full flow with the Stalin purges in Russia, the suppression across Eastern Europe, and the various communist revolutions and wars in China and the Far East.

The report goes to significant lengths to dismiss high scorers as being mentally defective:

> 'All of the material so far presented supports what was stated earlier: that the high scorers anxiously avoid letting themselves think and feel freely, especially about psychological matters. For such inner freedom might lead them to "see" things they are

71

afraid of in themselves. So they externalize their feared impulses, weakness, and conflicts with other people, onto outside situations and events and onto scapegoats. To the extent that these men let themselves feel their real feelings and impulses at all, they tend to keep them undifferentiated and to experience them as alien, as coming from outside their conscious self. Above all, what seems to be the emotional origin of their deepest conflicts – namely childhood and relations with parent figures – tends to be split off by them and regarded as discontinuous with their adult personality.[381]

This is all invention. There is no evidence presented to support the allegations. How could someone measure whether another person is 'letting themselves think and feel freely'? This is nonsense.

One subject is supposedly having a 'complete displacement of hate for the father's harsh discipline, onto the stepmother'.[382] The diagnoses of other high-scorers are just as revealing:

'[One subject's] case reveals in rather pure form the dynamics of a power-ridden type of inverted Oedipus complex: fear-driven homosexual submission to a hated father, and underlying identification with the mother's role as subordinate ... Yet the fearful dependence of a little child apparently forced [the subject] to repress the hate such treatment must have excited: for in the same breath in which he reveals her self-centred cruelty, he idealizes her and is unable to criticize her for these things ... Questioned about her weakness or faults, [the subject] declares: "In my memory, she just doesn't have any faults". His mother's intimidation alone might be thought to have discouraged [the subject's] heterosexual development. But fear of a stern father appears to have combined with this to "stampede" [the subject] into complete homosexual submission to the father and adoption of the mother's manipulative techniques.[383]

'[One high scorer subject's] murder of his hostile, despised mistress was the climax of a flight into sexual promiscuity which has been interpreted as an unconscious attempt to quiet fears of nonmasculinity that his wife's frigidity may have intensified'.[384]

'[One high scorer subject's] sexual assaults on children, with his accompanying paranoid delusions of being "framed by the people in politics", seem to be attempts to "prove" masculinity and suppress homosexual panic. [Another high scorer subject's] statutory rape of a young girl and molesting of his own small children probably have similar meanings. His drunken cheque-writing spree with a despised prostitute seems to have been an attempt to bolster his masculinity by means of heterosexual promiscuity and "big-shot financier" behaviour'.[385]

Other citations include someone involved in gang robberies and drunken brawls and another who committed robbery with a cap-pistol. The report alleges that the high scorers are all trying to prove their masculinity and attempting to deny their nonmasculinity, whereas the low scorers' crimes are motivated by a 'longing to be loved by and to love a mother figure who will both "mother" them and let them "father" her'.[386] The report concludes:

> 'Low scorers offer considerably more promise of rehabilitation than do high scorers. This follows from the apparent greater capacity of the former to establish genuine relationships with other people; just as their criminal behaviour seems to have followed upon frustration of the need of the need for love, or upon some crisis in their love relationships, so would the establishment of new relationships offer the basis for changed behaviour. In the high scorers, on the other hand, relationships based primarily upon love would seem to be very difficult of achievement; rather, we should expect new relationships in their case to conform with the old pattern of dominance-submission, something which, though it might induce conforming behaviour for the moment, would in the end only strengthen those personality structures which are basic to their criminality – and to their fascist potential.'[387]

SUMMARY

The report's methodology is flawed and reflects the political bigotry, the communism, of the authors. Data is put forward and is then explained in the terms of the authors' own theories. There are no safeguards on the interpretations extrapolated, and they are simply bald allegations. Subjects were selected from extreme groups, the groups were small, and statements of experiences were taken as fact when they might have been merely perceptions, faded memories, or self-serving stories (this particularly applies to the prison inmates).

The Frankfurt School's use of Freud has been cited by many as being an act of genius on their part. On reading *The Authoritarian Personality*, the use of Freudian psychobabble is infantile, ham-fisted, unconvincing, and embarrassing to read. Whether the passage of time and the growth of psychology has lessened the impact of Freudian terminology, one cannot say, other than that it fails to convince in the 21st century. The self-appointed psychologists at the Frankfurt School would not be held in such high esteem were such a report to be produced today, and would probably be held in ridicule. But the report was influential at the time, in 1950, and the targeting of conservatism for attack and linking it with fascism, as a version of pre-fascism, is an affected attitude advanced by the politically correct to this day. Tony Blair's speech in 1999 at a Labour Party conference denigrating the forces of conservatism should be viewed as pure political correctness. This speech went beyond the usual knockabout stuff and sought to denigrate Conservatism as something evil:

> 'We renew British strength and confidence for the 21^{s} century; and how, as a Party reborn, we make it a century of progressive politics after one dominated by Conservatives. New Britain where the extraordinary talent of the British people is liberated from the forces of conservatism that so long have held them back, to create a model 21st century nation, based not on privilege, class or background, but on the equal worth of all ... And New Labour, confident at having modernised itself, now the new progressive force in British politics which can modernise the nation, sweep away those forces of conservatism to set the people free ... Today's Tory party – the party of fox hunting, Pinochet and hereditary peers: the uneatable, the unspeakable and the unelectable ... Under John Major, it was weak, weak, weak. Under William Hague, it's weird, weird, weird. Far right, far out.'

The idea that Hague was 'Far right' is as absurd as is the line that somehow people are held back by Conservatism. Blair, like Adorno, was trying to convince people that Conservatism is a stage of fascism.

The contempt for the views and interests of ordinary people is a common theme in Frankfurt School thinking, and communist thinking in general. Ordinary people are to be managed, manipulated, and controlled. They are afflicted by false consciousness, and their views and actions are invalid. They need to be politically educated, and their failure to support a communist revolution is a factor in their lack of political education and understanding.

The Authoritarian Personality is important as it was treated as being so by the Left, and it marks the targeting of conservatism in the supposed fight against fascism – when in fact the real aim is to weaken society in preparation for a communist revolution. It is also important as it openly sets out the case for the state to take over control of the family as a means of 'education' for children. The state's increasing interference in the family, whether it be to force women out to work, with children being brought up by state employees, or whether it be political indoctrination of children, is not only do-gooding and the Nanny State; at its core, there lurks hard-line communist ideology. The British government has introduced a so-called Cinderella Law, imposing jail terms on parents or carers deemed to have imposed 'emotional cruelty' on children. Child abuse now includes 'maltreatment' which harms a child's 'physical, intellectual, emotional, social or behavioural development'. This new law gives rise to opportunity for yet another attempt to demonize ordinary people, to foment hatred, and to allow the state to indoctrinate children in neo-Marxist ideology.

This is not idle speculation. A relatively recent development is in the growth of child-snatching judges, who preside behind closed doors and use court orders to prevent discussion of their decisions. Family members have even been secretly imprisoned for breaching such orders. A recent case (reported in November 2015) involved a mother whose child was taken from her and given to a couple of two homosexual men. One of the men was the biological father and claimed that there had been a surrogacy agreement with the mother. The mother denied this, and there was nothing in writing. The mother had initially been subject to a gagging order to prevent her speaking of what had happened. The judge responsible was Justice Alison Russell, who is unmarried, has never been a mother, and is an ardent feminist who wanted to be referred to as 'Ms Justice'. The two biological parents fell out over the raising of the child, but matters settled down after the court ordered that the father should have the child for two nights and one day each week. Then a social worker listed the matter for 'a change of residence' hearing, at which time custody was given to the homosexual couple. The judge ruled that the mother had wanted to raise the child herself and accused her of being manipulative, of trying to discredit the homosexual couple 'in a homophobic and offensive manner' using 'stereotypical images and descriptions of gay men', and of insinuating 'that gay men in same-sex relationships behave in a sexually disinhibited manner'. The mother denied being homophobic. The judge said that 'attachment which will develop in an infant who sleeps with her mother, spends all day being carried by her mother and is breast-fed on demand raises questions about the long-term effect on the child'.

The judge accepted that the child would be distressed by being 'moved' from the mother, but was young enough to 'settle quickly' with the male couple.

Another example of the danger posed by the Cinderella law is that of the UKIP foster parents in Rotherham, who, in 2012, had a foster child removed from their care due to their membership of the anti-EU UKIP. After the case made news headlines, the council's strategic director of children and young people's services, Joyce Thacker, stated to the BBC that her decision to remove the child from the couple was influenced by UKIP immigration policy, which she alleged advocated the end of the 'active promotion of multiculturalism'. Social workers had told the couple that UKIP had racist policies and that their membership of the party constituted a 'safeguarding issue for the children'. As will be seen below, Rotherham council has been far more tolerant of Asian paedophile gangs.

Communists have long seen the family as a target. Marx dismissed the 'hallowed co-relation of parent and child' as being 'bourgeois clap-trap'.[388] For the Frankfurt School, the bourgeois family helped prepare the conditions for fascism. A project 'Authority and the Family' was conducted to support this view.[389] Marcuse wrote that the family transmitted social norms that 'stands in service of the defence of the bourgeoisie against the growing threat from its own ranks and from the socialist tendencies'.[390] Horkheimer described the family as the 'germ cell of bourgeois culture',[391] while Fromm regarded the family as the agent of society.[392] Marcuse theorized that a liberal individual could be socialized within the family unit to accept fascist authority.[393] Communists are intrinsically hostile to the family and its role in transmitting the values of society to the next generation. For *The Authoritarian Personality* to therefore seek to demonize the family and demand control of it is predictable.

The report was proved correct in its assertion that it would be possible to control and manipulate Conservatives by using the law – certainly so far as Britain is concerned. The Tories are very diligent in implementing the law, even those laws which are hostile to Conservatism and British interests (e.g. the Human Rights Act, or the Equality Act that was dubbed 'socialism in one clause'). Time and again, Tory politicians can be found pontificating about Britain's 'international obligations'. Mindlessly implementing laws based on abstract theories and political correctness renders genuine morality and patriotism redundant.

Next to be examined is Marcuse's essay 'Repressive Tolerance', which, thankfully, is far shorter and less turgid – yet more venomous.

REPRESSIVE TOLERANCE

I n the 1960s the anti-Vietnam War movement gave rise to increased radicalism in America. This radicalism presented an opportunity for the Frankfurt School to indoctrinate students and radicals with neo-Marxist thought. One of the most influential members of the Frankfurt School in this was Herbert Marcuse, who had previously worked for the OSS (Office of Strategic Services, formed during WWII and a predecessor of the CIA) after fleeing Germany. Marcuse wrote a number of articles and books which helped develop Critical Theory and was proclaimed 'father of the New Left' in the 1960s.[394] Some of the Frankfurt School had returned to Germany after the war, but Marcuse remained in the USA.

One of the most influential essays written by Marcuse was 'Repressive Tolerance',[395] which he wrote in 1965, in which the hallmarks of political correctness are evident and in which the logic of the intolerance of political correctness is set out. Martin Jay describes 'Repressive Tolerance' as being 'one of Marcuse's most controversial and influential essays'.[396] In the opening paragraph Marcuse states:

> 'This essay examines the idea of tolerance in our advanced industrial society. The conclusion reached is that the realization of the objective of tolerance would call for intolerance toward prevailing policies, attitudes, opinions, and extension of tolerance to policies, attitudes, and opinions which are outlawed or suppressed. In other words, today tolerance appears again as what it was in its origins, at the beginning of the modern period – a partisan goal, a subversive liberating notion and practice. Conversely, what is proclaimed and practised as tolerance today, is in many of its most effective manifestations serving the cause of oppression.'[397]

Marcuse complains at the 'systematic moronization' of society and states:

> 'Generally, the function and value of tolerance depend on the equality prevalent in the society in which tolerance is practised. Tolerance itself stands subject to overriding criteria: its range and its limits cannot be defined in terms of the respective society. In other words' tolerance is an end in itself only when it is truly universal, practised by the rulers as well as by the ruled,

by the lords as well as by the peasants, by the sheriffs as well as by their victims. And such universal tolerance is possible only when no real or alleged enemy requires in the national interest the education and training of people in military violence and destruction. As long as these conditions do not prevail, the conditions of tolerance are 'loaded': they are determined and defined by the institutionalized inequality (which is certainly compatible with constitutional equality), i.e., by the class structure of society. In such a society, tolerance is *de facto* limited on the dual ground of legalized violence or suppression (police, armed forces, guards of all sorts) and of the privileged position held by the predominant interests and their 'connections'.

These background limitations of tolerance are normally prior to the explicit and judicial limitations as defined by the courts, custom, governments, etc. (for example, 'clear and present danger', threat to national security, heresy). Within the framework of such a social structure, tolerance can be safely practised and proclaimed. It is of two kinds: (i) the passive toleration of entrenched and established attitudes and ideas even if their damaging effect on man and nature is evident, and (2) the active, official tolerance granted to the Right as well as to the Left, to movements of aggression as well as to movements of peace, to the party of hate as well as to that of humanity. I call this non-partisan tolerance 'abstract' or 'pure' inasmuch as it refrains from taking sides – but in doing so it actually protects the already established machinery of discrimination.[1398]

Having established the horrors of tolerance, Marcuse asserts:

'Society cannot be indiscriminate where the pacification of existence, where freedom and happiness themselves are at, stake: here, certain things cannot be said, certain ideas cannot be expressed, certain policies cannot be proposed, certain behaviour cannot be permitted without making tolerance an instrument for the continuation of servitude.'[1399]

In response to this, Marcuse questions the rationale of tolerance: 'Universal toleration becomes questionable when its rationale no longer prevails, when tolerance is administered to manipulated and indoctrinated individuals who parrot, as their own, the opinion of their masters, for whom heteronomy has become autonomy.'[1400] (This last comment is consistent with another of Marcuse's utterances: 'If the worker and his boss enjoy the same television program and visit the same resort places, if the typist is as attractively made up as the daughter of her employer, if the Negro owns a Cadillac, if they all read the same newspaper, then this assimilation indicates not the disappearance of classes, but the extent to which the needs and satisfactions that serve the preservation of the Establishment are shared by the underlying population.'[401] For Marcuse, a lack of class or race hatred is the hegemony of bourgeois ideology. Marcuse does not believe that tolerance is desirable when it is exercised by a society dominated by false consciousness:

> 'Free and equal discussion can fulfil the function attributed to it only if it is rational expression and development of independent thinking, free from indoctrination, manipulation, extraneous authority. The notion of pluralism and countervailing powers is no substitute for this requirement.'[402]

Marcuse then condemns majority opinion:

> 'Those minorities which strive for a change of the whole itself will, under optimal conditions which rarely prevail, will be left free to deliberate and discuss, to speak and to assemble – and will be left harmless and helpless in the face of the overwhelming majority, which militates against qualitative social change. This majority is firmly grounded in the increasing satisfaction of needs, and technological and mental co-ordination, which testify to the general helplessness of radical groups in a well-functioning social system.
>
>   Within the affluent democracy, the affluent discussion prevails, and within the established framework, it is tolerant to a large extent. All points of view can be heard: the Communist and the Fascist, the Left and the Right, the white and the Negro, the crusaders for armament and for disarmament. Moreover, in endlessly dragging debates over the media, the stupid opinion is treated with the same respect as the intelligent one, the misinformed may talk as long as the informed, and propaganda rides along with education, truth with falsehood. This pure toleration of sense and nonsense is justified by the democratic argument that nobody, neither group nor individual, is in possession of the truth and capable of defining what is right and wrong, good and bad. Therefore, all contesting opinions must be submitted to 'the people' for its deliberation and choice. But I have already suggested that the democratic argument implies a

necessary condition, namely, that the people must be capable of deliberating and choosing on the basis of knowledge, that they must have access to authentic information, and that, on this basis, their evaluation must be the result of autonomous thought.

In the contemporary period, the democratic argument for abstract tolerance tends to be invalidated by the invalidation of the democratic process itself. The liberating force of democracy was the chance it gave to effective dissent, on the individual as well as social scale, its openness to qualitatively different forms of government, of culture, education, work – of the human existence in general. The toleration of free discussion and the equal right of opposites was to define and clarify the different forms of dissent: their direction, content, prospect. But with the concentration of economic and political power and the integration of opposites in a society which uses technology as an instrument of domination, effective dissent is blocked where it could freely emerge; in the formation of opinion, in information and communication, in speech and assembly. Under the rule of monopolistic media – themselves the mere instruments of economic and political power – a mentality is created for which right and wrong, true and false are predefined wherever they affect the vital interests of the society. This is, prior to all expression and communication, a matter of semantics: the blocking of effective dissent, of the recognition of that which is not of the Establishment which begins in the language that is publicized and administered. The meaning of words is rigidly stabilized. Rational persuasion, persuasion to the opposite is all but precluded. The avenues of entrance are closed to the meaning of words and ideas other than the established one – established by the publicity of the powers that be, and verified in their practices. Other words can be spoken and heard, other ideas can be expressed, but, at the massive scale of the conservative majority (outside such enclaves as the intelligentsia), they are immediately "evaluated" (i.e. automatically understood) in terms of the public language – a language which determines "a priori" the direction in which the thought process moves. Thus the process of reflection ends where it started: in the given conditions and relations. Self-validating, the argument of the discussion repels the contradiction because the antithesis is redefined in terms of the thesis. For example, thesis: we work for peace; antithesis: we prepare for war (or even: we wage war); unification of opposites; preparing for war is working for peace. Peace is redefined as necessarily, in the prevailing situation, including preparation for war (or even war) and in this Orwellian form, the meaning of the word 'peace' is stabilized. Thus, the basic vocabulary of the Orwellian language operates as a priori categories of understanding: preforming all content. These conditions invalidate the logic of tolerance which involves the rational development of meaning and precludes the closing of meaning. Consequently, persuasion through discussion and the equal presentation of opposites (even where it is really, equal) easily lose their liberating force as factors of understanding and learning; they are far more likely to strengthen the established thesis and to repel the alternatives.'[403]

Marcuse then attacks objectivity:

'In a democracy with totalitarian organization, objectivity may fulfil a very different function, namely, to foster a mental attitude which tends to obliterate the difference between true and false, information and indoctrination, right and wrong … when a magazine prints side by side a negative and a positive report on the FBI, it fulfils honestly the requirements of objectivity: however, the chances are that the positive wins because the image of the institution is deeply engraved in the mind of the people. Or, if a newscaster reports the torture and murder of civil rights workers in the same unemotional tone he uses to describe the stockmarket or the weather, or with the same great emotion with which he says his commercials, then such objectivity is spurious – more, it offends against humanity and truth by being calm where one should be enraged, by refraining from accusation where accusation is in the facts themselves. The tolerance expressed in such impartiality serves to minimize or even absolve prevailing intolerance and suppression. If objectivity has anything to do with truth, and if truth is more than a matter of logic and science, then this kind of objectivity is false, and this kind of tolerance inhuman. And if it is necessary to break the established universe of meaning (and the practice enclosed in this universe) in order to enable man to find out what is true and false, this deceptive impartiality would have to be abandoned. The people exposed to this impartiality are no *tabulae rasae*, they are indoctrinated by the conditions under which they live and think and which they do not transcend. To enable them to become autonomous, to find by themselves what is true and what is false for man in the existing society, they would have to be freed from the prevailing indoctrination (which is no longer recognized as indoctrination). But this means that the trend would have to be reversed: they would have to get information slanted in the opposite direction. For the facts are never given immediately and never accessible immediately; they are established, 'mediated' by those who made them; the truth, 'the whole truth' surpasses these facts and requires the rupture with their appearance. This rupture – prerequisite and token of all freedom of thought and of speech – cannot be accomplished within the established framework of abstract tolerance and spurious objectivity because these are precisely the factors which precondition the mind against the rupture.'[404]

Consequently, Marcuse advocates intolerance: 'The restoration of freedom of thought may necessitate new and rigid restrictions on teachings and practices in the educational institutions which, by their very methods and concepts, serve to enclose the wind within the established universe of discourse and behaviour – thereby precluding a priori a rational evaluation of the alternatives.'[405] After complaining about the 'tyranny of public opinion and its makers', Marcuse advocates: 'Liberating tolerance, then, would mean intolerance against movements from the Right and toleration of movements from the Left.'[406] Marcuse proceeds:

'The false consciousness has become the general consciousness – from the government down to its last objects. The small and powerless minorities which struggle against the false consciousness and its beneficiaries must be helped: their continued existence is more important than the preservation of abused rights and liberties which grant constitutional powers to those who oppress these minorities. It should be evident by now that the exercise of civil rights by those who don't have them presupposes the withdrawal of civil rights from those who prevent their exercise, and that liberation of the Damned of the Earth presupposes suppression not only of their old but also of their new masters.'[407]

In the various communist revolutions in the 20th century, this 'suppression' took the form of genocide. In a postscript written in 1968, Marcuse expands upon his attack on tolerance: 'Under the conditions prevailing in this country, tolerance does not, and cannot, fulfil the civilizing function attributed to it by the liberal protagonists of democracy, namely, protection of dissent.'[408] Once again he is hostile to majority opinion in democracies:

> '... where the majority does not result from the development of independent thought and opinion but rather from the monopolistic or oligopolistic administration of public opinion, without terror and (normally) without censorship. In such cases, the majority is self-perpetuating while perpetuating the vested interests which made it a majority. In its very structure this majority is "closed", petrified; it repels a priori any change other than changes within the system. But this means that the majority is no longer justified in claiming the democratic title of the best guardian of the common interest. And such a majority is all but the opposite of Rousseau's "general will": it is composed, not of individuals who, in their political functions, have made effective "abstraction" from their private interests, but, on the contrary, of individuals who have effectively identified their private interests with their political functions. And the representatives of this majority, in ascertaining and executing its will, ascertain and execute the will of the vested interests, which have formed the majority. The ideology of democracy hides its lack of substance.'[409]

In his postscript Marcuse reiterates his belief that the Right should be denied equal treatment with the Left and again attacks Western democracy:

> 'The alternative to the established semi-democratic process is not a dictatorship or elite, no matter how intellectual and intelligent, but the struggle for a real democracy. Part of this struggle is the fight against an ideology of tolerance which, in reality, favours and fortifies the conservation of the status quo of inequality and discrimination. For this struggle, I proposed the practice of discriminating tolerance. To be sure, this practice already presupposes the radical goal which it seeks to achieve. I committed this *petitio principii* in order to combat the pernicious ideology that tolerance is already institutionalized in this society. The tolerance which is the life element, the token of a free society, will never be the gift of the powers that be, it can, under the prevailing conditions of tyranny by the majority, only be won in the sustained effort of radical minorities, willing to break this tyranny and to work for the emergence of a free and

83

sovereign majority – minorities intolerant, militantly intolerant and disobedient to the rules of behaviour which tolerate destruction and suppression.'[410]

The essay is illuminative as it explains the rationale for the demonization, if not criminalization, of the Right. It demonstrates the logic for the enforcement of the neo-Marxist views of political correctness. The definition of political correctness used in this book is that it is 'the mechanism for the enforcement of neo-Marxist ideology'. 'Repressive Tolerance' concerns itself with the justification of the enforcement of political correctness. The essay was written by a leading, if not the leading, member of the Frankfurt School in the 1960s, someone who was very much a part of the development of the New Left.

SUMMARY

Marcuse is open from the outset that he is advocating intolerance: 'the objective of tolerance would call for intolerance toward prevailing policies, attitudes, opinions, and the extension of tolerance to policies, attitudes, and opinions what are outlawed or suppressed'. Marcuse condemns the tolerance of the 'systematic moronization' of the public. He believes that the tolerance of views from the Right leads to a perpetuation of the existing society, which he condemns for its supposed oppression and lack of freedom and that the tolerance allows discrimination and inequality. Overthrowing the prevailing cultural hegemony requires intolerance of existing views and the promotion of the Left and the views of minorities. Majority public opinion is invalid as it is prejudiced, derived, and influenced by the dominant forces of society and the process of moronization, and the people are suffering from false consciousness. The public are incapable of making an informed opinion because they are not informed. To this end, the banning of right-wing views and promotion of left-wing views is necessary to inform the public. Western society is so bad that those who seek to destroy it should be actively promoted even if they are in a minority, and the majority support for existing society should be ignored. The majority, who are responsible for the oppression of minorities, should have their civil rights withdrawn.

Normally, one might expect the government to protect the interests and views of the majority; Marcuse, however, seeks to destroy them. He

84

partly justifies this by his sneer at the 'systematic moronization' of society, thus rendering the views held by the majority of ordinary people as not worthy of respect. His language (e.g. his references to 'class structure', 'institutionalized inequality', and 'legalized violence or suppression') is that of a communist.

His remark comparing tolerance to the Right as well as to the Left, along with 'to movements of aggression as well as to movements of peace, to the party of hate as well as to that of humanity' equates the Right with being aggressive and hateful, as opposed to the peaceful humanity of the Left. This absolutist stance, typical for communists, ignores the fact that communism was responsible for the deaths of more than 100million in the 20th century. The Right actually fought against Nazism and the aggression of Japan. The communists actually backed Russia, which had made a pact with Hitler; it was the German invasion of Russia that forced the communists into open opposition to Hitler in WWII. It is Marcuse who displays hatred, not the Right.

His dismissal of tolerance being 'an instrument for the continuation of servitude' is hysterical and typical rhetoric for a communist. He has not proved why there is a state of servitude or that tolerance is responsible for it. For him, tolerance cannot apply when there is a lack of independent thinking free of indoctrination, manipulation, and extraneous authority. He neither establishes that people are incapable of rational opinion or that such opinion is a result of indoctrination etc. He merely baldly states this. By comparison, however, minorities, who are deemed to be free from false consciousness, are deemed to be oppressed and alienated. Marcuse regards the black population as being a likely source for rebellion.[411] That is to say, he aims to supplement class war politics with race war politics.

There is nothing contentious in highlighting the commitment to race war politics. Marcuse, as well as other members of the Frankfurt School, sets this out in simple language. As David Horowitz, an outspoken member of the New Left and co-editor of *Ramparts* before coming out as a conservative in a 'Lefties for Reagan' article, explained:

> 'Marxism is a bankrupt creed. It was bankrupt by the 1950s. People understood it didn't work. There was no working class that was going to make revolution. People were happy with capitalism, basically because it spread more money to more people than any other system in history. So they tried to find other sources of revolutionary energy.'[412]

Marcuse asserts that because the people do not have the ability to evaluate and choose between competing arguments, then democracy is redundant. The people are unable to decide for themselves which view is sense and which nonsense, which is right and which wrong. For Marcuse, democracy is flawed and not real democracy; the failure of dissent to overthrow the majority opinion and society is symptomatic of the failure of democracy.

However, democracy is not about challenging the views of the majority but a means by which ordinary views are accorded an outlet and an influence on who is in government. Whether the government is responsive to those views is a different matter. Perhaps minority dissent should be blocked. In fact, there is no reason why minority views of dissent should dominate. For Marcuse, tolerance is an ideology which preserves the status quo of inequality and discrimination. Therefore, tolerance should discriminate against the tyranny of the majority and support radical minorities, who are themselves 'militantly intolerant' of current society.

The focus on language is another hallmark of political correctness. For Marcuse, public language is a mechanism for the interpretation of the message and thus a reason for false consciousness ('false consciousness has become the general consciousness'). Even objectivity is condemned for 'being calm' and not 'enraged'. Such calm objectivity is allegedly false.

Consequently, 'liberating tolerance' means 'intolerance against movements from the Right and tolerance of movements from the Left'. It should be noted that the institutional hostility towards conservative opinion in Britain, for example in the BBC, is not just some innate instinct, subconsciously acted upon. Behind that lurks a communist belief system which seeks to deliberately suppress not only right-wing views *but also the majority views of ordinary people*. Minority views are to be lauded ('minorities which struggle against the false consciousness and its beneficiaries must be helped'). The civil rights of the majority should be denied. The majority should be suppressed. In England, this means that the English must be suppressed, with their views ignored, if not demonized or even criminalized.

That Marcuse is committed to a communist revolution, with all the bloodshed that that entails, should not be doubted. He is openly hostile to Western democracy and its people. For him, the aim, which 'may require undemocratic means', is to create a 'subversive majority' which he claims is currently 'blocked by organized repression and indoctrination'. He believes this would necessitate 'withdrawal of toleration of speech and assembly from groups and movements which promote aggressive policies, armament, chauvinism, discrimination on grounds of race and religion, or which oppose the extension of public services, social security, medical care, etc.'[413] The proposed censorship of those who might even dare to suggest that welfare spending cannot be increased displays an extreme absolutism. This intolerance is to include 'rigid restrictions on teachings and practices in the educational institutions'.[414] It is a total rejection of Western civilization and is the advocacy of violence and revolution:

> 'Even in the advanced centres of civilization, violence actually prevails: it is practised by the police, in the prisons and mental institutions, in the fight against racial minorities; it is carried, by the defenders of metropolitan freedom, into the backward countries. This violence indeed breeds violence. But to refrain from violence in the face of vastly superior violence is one thing, to renounce a priori violence against violence, on ethical or psychological grounds (because it may antagonize sympathizers) is another. Non-violence is normally not only preached to but exacted from the weak ... In terms of historical function, there is a difference between revolutionary and reactionary violence, between violence practised by the oppressed and by the oppressors. In terms of ethics, both forms of violence are inhuman and evil — but since when is history made in accordance with ethical standards? To start applying them at the point where the oppressed rebel against the oppressors, the have-nots against the haves is serving the cause of actual violence by weakening the protest against it.'[415]

Marcuse cannot be accused of getting carried away in the heat of the moment and making comments that he later regretted or was dissuaded from in reflection by an adverse or critical reaction. His postscript, written three years later, is unyielding. If anything, he is even more virulent in his attack on the majority, which he accuses of being 'self-perpetuating while perpetuating the vested interests which made it a majority' and 'the ideology of democracy hides its lack of substance'. Instead, Marcuse advocates support for 'radical minorities' who are 'intolerant, militantly intolerant and disobedient to the rules of behaviour which tolerate destruction and suppression'.

The essay is consistent with other writings of Marcuse. The Frankfurt School accepted the classical Marxist theory that Fascism was the product of capitalism.[416] They attributed the causes as being the inevitable crisis of capitalism, authoritarian personalities and the bourgeois family, ideology and culture that support the capitalist society, and obscure alienation and domination.[417] Marcuse dismissed all liberal capitalist societies as containing the seeds of fascism: 'the turn from liberalist to the total-authoritarian state occurs within the framework of a single social order'.[418] For Marcuse, liberalism 'was the social and economic theory of European industrial capitalism in the period when the actual economic bearer of capitalism was the individual capitalist, the private entrepreneur'.[419] Liberalism's support of capitalism facilitated fascism.[420] Marcuse wrote in *Reason and Revolution* in 1960: 'The defeat of Fascism and National Socialism has not arrested the trend towards totalitarianism. Freedom is on the retreat – in the realm of thought as well as in that of society.'[421] Marcuse believed that 'Marxism is the theory of proletarian revolution and the revolutionary critique of bourgeois society.'[422] Marcuse regarded the capitalist system as causing alienation, exploitation, and oppression, and he believed that total revolution was the only solution, which meant a 'catastrophic upheaval' to completely overthrow the entirety of existing society.[423] (As has been shown above in the *Communist Confession of Faith*, a communist revolution means the destruction of marriage, the family, nationhood, and religion, with the bringing up of children taken over by the state.) There is a shift in reasoning away from the initially Marxist theory of revolution. Originally, the idea was that the proletariat would become so alienated that they would rise up against the crumbling capitalist system. Now, as the Frankfurt School theorists freely admit, the proletariat is not complaining or in a revolutionary frame of mind due to alienation. Marcuse wrote: 'Contemporary society seems to be capable of containing social change ... This containment of social change is perhaps the most singular achievement of advanced industrial society ... The integration of opposites ... is the result as well as the prerequisite of this achievement.'[424] Marcuse asserted that society was 'unfree' and 'irrational' but that the proletariat, as Marx argued, would only rise up in revolution '*if* and *when* the proletariat has become conscious of itself and of the conditions and processes which make up society. This consciousness is prerequisite ....' Therefore, the revolution will not happen until the proletariat has been radicalised and freed from false consciousness. Minority groups are to be encouraged in their alienation. Class war politics is to be reinforced by race war politics.

For Marcuse, the integration into society of supposedly alienated groups acts as a stabilizing force and thereby neutralizes the revolutionary elements which, according to Marxism, should be committed to society's overthrow. The proletariat are being integrated into the capitalist system with class collaboration hiding the true nature of class domination.[425] Marcuse wrote: 'The distinguishing feature of advanced industrial society is its effective suffocation of those needs which demand liberation – liberation also from that which is tolerable and rewarding and comfortable – while it sustains and absolves the destructive power and repressive function of the affluent society.'[1426] He alleged that 'Domination – in the guise of affluence and liberty – extends to all spheres of private and public existence, integrates all authentic opposition, absorbs all alternatives.' His essay 'On Hedonism' states: 'It appears that individuals raised to be integrated into the antagonistic labour process cannot be judges of their own happiness. They have been prevented from knowing their true interest. Thus, it is possible for them to designate their condition as happy and, without external compulsion, embrace the system that oppresses them.'[1427]

Marcuse argued: 'In the last analysis, the question of what are true and false needs must be answered by the individuals themselves, but only in the last analysis; that is, if and when they are free to give their own answer. As long as they are kept incapable of being autonomous, as long as they are indoctrinated and manipulated (down to their very instincts), their answer to this question cannot be taken as their own.'[1428] With this logic, the views of the people can be totally ignored as being invalid. Only the views of communists are valid due to the supposed communist superior intellect and understanding of society. Marcuse wrote:

> 'The basic idea is: how can slaves who do not even know they are slaves free themselves? How can they liberate themselves by their own power, by their own faculties? How can they spontaneously accomplish liberation? They must be taught and must be led to be free, and this the more so the more the society in which they live uses all available means in order to shape and preform their consciousness and to make it immune against possible alternatives. This idea of an educational, preparatory dictatorship has today become an integral element of revolution and of the justification of the revolutionary oppression.'[1429]

Marcuse believed that what was needed was 'the development of an effectively organized radical Left, assuming the vast task of *political education*, dispelling the false and mutilated consciousness of the people so that they themselves experience their condition, and its abolition, as vital need, and apprehend the ways and means of their liberation.'[1430] Marcuse supported the 'long march through the institutions' (like Gramsci) and the strategy of 'working against the established institutions while working in them'.[1431] One advantage of this, of course, is that the wealth of Western society is being used to fund those whose aim it is to destroy Western society.

As Western society continued to enjoy the support of the people, Marcuse's commitment to revolution remained undimmed, and he sought revolution wherever he could see the opportunity. In *An Essay in Liberation* (pages 80-82), written in 1969, Marcuse supported both the Cuban revolution and the Viet Cong as influences furthering revolution in the West.[432] While supportive of Third World revolutionaries, Marcuse criticized both the Soviet Union and European communist parties for not being sufficiently revolutionary.[433] In *Counterrevolution and Revolt*, Marcuse wrote: 'the Western world has reached a new stage of development: now, the defence of the capitalist system requires the organization of counterrevolution at home and abroad'.[434] Marcuse cited the deaths of black militants such as Malcolm X and Martin Luther King, Nixon's conservative appointments to the Supreme Court, as well as civil unrest generally; abroad, he cited the war in Indochina, Nigeria, and the Congo, as well as US interference in Latin America.[435] All of this was to try and suppress 'world-historical revolution'. Marcuse wrote: 'Defeat in Vietnam may well be the signal for other wars of liberation closer to home – and perhaps even for rebellion at home.'[436]

By the 1970s Marcuse no longer regarded the working class as being the same instrument for a revolution as Marx had envisioned, the alienated proletariat, but instead hoped that other groups deemed not to be fully integrated into society – students, intellectuals, the unemployed, racial minorities etc. – would now become the 'catalysts' for revolution.[437] Marcuse sought to supplement class war politics with race war politics and regarded the black population as being the 'most natural' force of rebellion.[438] The New Left were to be the vanguard.

Who is Marcuse to judge all this? What divine wisdom does he have that he, unlike the majority of the rest of society, can see the truth and how society should be? But these questions presume that Marcuse is sincere in his beliefs, that he genuinely believes the face value of what he says. The alternative is that he seeks to spread dissent, hatred, and conflict for the sake of it. This is not merely an idle thought, but is entirely consistent with Marcuse's work.

When David Cameron, a supposed Conservative, claims that he is in favour of political correctness, then we should bear in mind exactly what he and others like him are supporting, even if they are too vain to understand it.

Marcuse's advocacy for intolerance of the Right and of public opinion – i.e. an intolerance of politically incorrect views – lies at the heart of political correctness. His zeal for the radical views of minorities has been taken up by the politically correct and is promoted to this day. The whole concept is subversive and destructive. It is intended to be so. This is set out in the essay in simple language. It is not the case that political correctness has the unfortunate effect of causing harm while trying to do good. The *intention* is to do harm to society. Marcuse and his adherents are communists. They *believe* in the revolution and in the destruction of the West. There has been a failure by those on the Right to grasp this very simple historical fact, and it is one of the reasons for the success of political correctness to this day. It has advanced not by winning public opinion, but by infiltrating the public sector, grabbing the levers of power, and bludgeoning public opinion into adherence to the neo-Marxist creed.

Next to be examined will be an essay by Jurgen Habermas, who had all the influence and prestige that being leader of the Frankfurt School might bring and who is, in 2016, still very much alive and kicking. The essay, 'Citizenship and National Identity: Some Reflections on the Future of Europe', is less venomous and more subtle; nevertheless, the hard line remains.

CITIZENSHIP AND NATIONAL IDENTITY

Written in 1995, Jurgen Habermas's 'Citizenship and National Identity: Some Reflections on the Future of Europe' (Citizenship and National Identity) was predicated on the assertion that that current history was in a state of flux, and that there were three issues that were impacting upon citizenship and national identity: (1) the future of the nation state; (2) the EU; (3) immigration.[439]

Habermas focused on the recent reunification of Germany, which he believed had two interpretations. Either it could be seen as a restoration of the unity of the German nation as a 'pre-political unity of a community with a shared common historical destiny', or it could be seen as a restoration of 'a constitutional state in a territory where civil rights had been suspended in one form or another since 1933', and not a restoration of national unity in a pre-political sense. Habermas favoured the second viewpoint, and he believed that 'loosening the semantic connections between national citizenship and national identity takes into account that the classic form of the nation state is at present disintegrating'.[440]

For Habermas, the evolution of the nation state arose out of unstable European empires and facilitated democracy and capitalism. But more importantly, 'the nation state laid the foundations for cultural and ethnic homogeneity ... although this was achieved at the cost of excluding ethnic minorities'. He believed that the French Revolution was responsible for the 'twins' of the nation state and democracy, although culturally, 'both have been growing in the shadow of nationalism'. For Habermas, nationalism is 'to a certain extent a construct ... susceptible to manipulative misuse by political elites'.[441] He points out that *Natio* for the Romans was the Goddess of Birth and Origin. Unlike *civitas*, *natio* refers to 'peoples and tribes' and was used by the Romans to refer to those who were savage, barbaric, or pagan. Habermas acknowledges, therefore, that, in the classical sense, 'nations are communities of people of the same descent, who are integrated geographically, in the form of settlements or neighbourhoods, and culturally by their common language, customs, and traditions, but who are not yet politically integrated in the form of state organization'.[442] Habermas asserts that the French Revolution changed this:

> 'Since the middle of the eighteenth century, the differences in meaning between "Nation" and "Staatsvolk", that is, "nation" and "politically organized people", have gradually been disappearing. With the French Revolution, the nation even became the source of state sovereignty ... Each nation is now supposed to be granted the right to political self-determination ... in the nineteenth century, the conservative representatives of the German Historical School equated the principle of nationality with the "principle of revolution".'[443]

Habermas alleges that the term 'nation' thus changed from being a reference to a pre-political group of people into a 'political identity of the citizen within a democratic polity'.[444] The nation thus becomes a nation of citizens who do not derive their 'identity from some common ethnic and cultural properties, but rather from the praxis of citizens who actively exercise their civil rights', and 'at this juncture, the republican strand of "citizenship" completely parts company with the idea of belonging to a pre-political community integrated on the basis of descent, a shared tradition and a common language'.[445] In this way, 'hereditary nationality' gave way to a nationality of choice that can be acquired, and 'nationalism and republicanism combine in the willingness to fight and, if necessary, die for one's country'.[446] Habermas asserts that 'republican freedom can cut its umbilical links to the womb of the national consciousness which had originally given birth to it. Only briefly did the democratic nation state forge a close link between "ethnos" and "demos". Citizenship was never conceptually tied to national identity.'[447] This 'concept of citizenship' was developed by Rousseau, and the idea of a political community 'has taken on concrete legal shape in a variety of constitutions, in fact, in all political systems of Western Europe and the United States'.[448]

Habermas dismisses the concepts of *jus soli* and *jus sanguinis* (respectively, that a person's nationality is determined by where he was born or by the nationality of his parents) as functioning 'merely as administrative criteria for attributing to citizens an assumed, implicit concurrence, to which the right to emigrate or to renounce one's citizenship corresponds'.[449] Habermas continues:

> 'Examples of multicultural societies like Switzerland and the United States demonstrate that a political culture in the seedbed of which constitutional principles are rooted by no means has to be based on all citizens sharing the same language or the same ethnic and cultural origins. Rather, the political culture must serve as the common denominator for a constitutional

patriotism which simultaneously sharpens an awareness of the multiplicity and integrity of the different forms of life which coexist in a multicultural society. In a future Federal Republic of European States, the same legal principles would also have to be interpreted from the vantage point of different national traditions and histories. One's own national tradition will, in each case, have to be appropriated in such a manner that it is related to and relativeized by the vantage points of the other national cultures. It must be connected with the overlapping consensus of a common, supranationally shared political culture of the European Community. Particularist anchoring of *this sort* would in no way impair the universalist meaning of popular sovereignty and human rights.'[450]

The term 'constitutional patriotism' is important as it is an ideology with a specific set of beliefs that Habermas has been pushing for some time (this will be examined below). Habermas states: 'although liberal theories often deny the fact, the relation between capitalism and democracy is fraught with tension', there is no 'linear connection between the emergence of democratic regimes and capitalist modernization',[451] and 'to date, genuine civil rights do not reach beyond national borders'.[452] Regarding the EU, Habermas acknowledges that the 'elites of bureaucrats' have become detached from the nation states and 'form a bureaucracy that is aloof from democratic processes'.[453] However, Habermas states:

'The single market will set in motion even more extensive horizontal mobility and multiply the contacts between members of different nationalities. Immigration from Eastern Europe and the poverty-stricken regions of the Third World will intensify the multicultural diversity of these societies. This will give rise to social tensions. However, if those tensions are processed productively, they will enhance political mobilization in general, and might particularly encourage the new, endogenous type of new social movements – I am thinking of the peace, ecological and women's movements. These tendencies would strengthen the relevance public issues have for the lifeworld. The increasing pressure of these problems is, furthermore, to be expected – problems for which coordinated solutions are available only at a European level. Given these conditions, communication networks of European-wide public spheres may emerge, networks that may form a favourable context both for new parliamentary bodies of regions that are now in the process of merging and for a European Parliament furnished with greater competence ... By and large, the national public spheres are culturally isolated from one another. They are anchored in contexts in which political issues only gain relevance against the background of national histories and national experiences. In the future, however, differentiation could occur in a European culture between a common *political* culture and the branching *national* traditions of art and literature, historiography, philosophy, and so forth. The cultural elites and the mass media would have an important role to play in this regard. Unlike the American variant, a European constitutional patriotism would have to grow out of different interpretations of the same universalist rights and constitutional principles which are marked by the context of different national histories.'[454]

While acknowledging that increased immigration will cause tensions, Habermas nevertheless argues that this is beneficial 'if processed productively' and that the EU has the central role to play in this. His advocacy for the development of increased EU networks is a means of bypassing national authority. He even goes so far as to suggest that the EU should have a monopoly of the political culture and that 'the cultural elites and the mass media' would be important in creating this. This elitist view is further expressed with regard to how the indigenous populations might react to the increased mass immigration:

'Europe must make a great effort to quickly improve conditions in the poorer areas of middle and eastern Europe or it will be flooded by asylum-seekers and immigrants. The experts are debating the capacity of the economic system to absorb these people, but the readiness to politically integrate the asylum-seekers depends more upon how citizens *perceive* the social and economic problems posed by immigration. Throughout Europe, right-wing xenophobic reaction against the "estrangement" caused by foreigners has increased. The relatively deprived classes, whether they feel endangered by social decline or have already slipped into segmented marginal groups, identify quite openly with the ideologized supremacy of their own collectivity and reject everything foreign. This is the underside of a chauvinism of prosperity which is increasing everywhere. Thus, the asylum problem as well brings to light the latent tension between citizenship and national identity.'[455]

Although Habermas is keen to undermine the existing national cultures of the European nations, he takes a different stance regarding immigrants and openly advocates mass immigration:

> 'It must not be expected that the new citizens will readily engage in the political culture of their new home, without necessarily giving up the cultural life specific to their country of origin. The *political acculturation* demanded of them does not include the entirety of their socialization. With immigration, new forms of life are imported which expand and multiply the perspective of all, and on the basis of which a common political constitution is always interpreted ... The European states should agree upon a liberal immigration policy. They should not draw their wagons around themselves and their chauvinism of prosperity, hoping to ignore the pressures of those hoping to immigrate or seek asylum. The democratic right of self-determination includes, of course, the right to preserve one's own *political* culture, which includes the concrete context of citizen's rights, though it does not include the self-assertion of a privileged *cultural* life form. Only within the constitutional framework of a democratic legal system can different ways of life coexist equally. These must, however, overlap within a common political culture, which again implies an impulse to open these ways of life to others.
>
> Only democratic citizenship can prepare the way for a condition of world citizenship which does not close itself off within particularistic biases, and which accepts a worldwide form of political communication. The Vietnam War, the revolutionary changes in eastern and middle Europe, as well as the war in the Persian Gulf are the first *world political* events in a strict sense. Through the electronic mass media, these events were made instantaneous and ubiquitous. In the context of the French Revolution, Kant speculated on the role of the participating public. He identified a world public sphere, which today will become a political reality for the first time with the new relations of global communication. Even the superpowers must recognize worldwide protests. The obsolescence of the state of nature between bellicose states has begun, implying that states have lost some sovereignty. The arrival of world citizenship is no longer merely a phantom, though we are still far from achieving it. State citizenship and world citizenship form a continuum that already shows itself, at least, in outline form.'[1456]

The term 'chauvinism of prosperity' is a useful way of denigrating concerns for the economic consequences of mass immigration. The indigenous should be concerned as to the fall in living standards that such a policy must entail (see *The Ponzi Class,* chapter 12, especially from page 300 onwards). Mass immigration is on such a scale that, in England, the English are forecast to become a minority within the 21st century; this is a repopulation policy involving the repopulation of England with non-English people.

Habermas is open that the host nations might be allowed to retain their political culture, such as human rights and democracy, but not their national culture, such as Christianity. For Habermas, the nation state is something to be subject not just to an EU government but to world citizenship and, inevitably, a world government – all as per communist mid-19th century theory. He believes that abstract theories such as human rights can be enforced at a European, if not international, level, and that the sovereignty of the nation state can be usurped with real power being transferred to supranational organizations. More recently, Habermas bemoaned the creation of the new nation states in Europe:

> 'In many countries, the return of the nation state has caused an introverted mood; the theme of Europe has been devalued, the national agenda has taken priority. In our talk-shows, grandfathers and grandchildren hug each other, swelling with feel-good patriotism. The security of undamaged national roots should make a population that's been pampered by the welfare state "compatible with the future" in the competitive global environment. This rhetoric fits with the current state of global politics which have lost all their inhibitions in social darwinistic terms.'[457]

Habermas described those of his view as 'Europe alarmists', who were concerned at the lack of EU integration. He further bemoaned the 'undermining of acceptable social standards':

> 'The justified criticism of the inconsistencies of neo-liberal orthodoxy cannot hide the fact that the obscene combination of rising share prices and mass layoffs rests on a compelling economic logic. Little can be done about this within the national context alone, because the relationship of politics to the market has gotten out of balance on a global scale. It would take a European Union with a cogent foreign policy to influence the course of the world economy. It could drive global

environmental policy forward while taking first steps towards a global domestic policy. In so doing, it could provide an example to other continents of how nation states can be fused into supra-national powers. Without new global players of this kind, there can be no equilibrium between subjects of an equitable world economic order.'[458]

Habermas advocated cultural pluralism and more integration to be conducted at a European level, believing that 'a common European identity will develop all the quicker, the better the dense fabric of national culture in the respective states can integrate citizens of other ethnic or religious groups'.[459]

Turning to Islam, Habermas advocated that liberal values needed to be adapted to accommodate Muslims:

> 'The transformation of consciousness that will enable these norms to be internalised requires a self-reflexive opening of our national ways of living. Those who denounce this assertion as "the capitulation of the West" are taken in by the silly war cry of liberal hawks. "Islamofascism" is no more a palpable opponent than the war on terrorism is a "war". Here in Europe, the assertion of constitutional norms is such an uncontested premise of cohabitation that the hysterical cry for the protection of our "values" comes across like semantic armament against an unspecified domestic enemy.'

As has been pointed out above, what Habermas is advocating is constitutional patriotism (also known as civic nationalism). Before constitutional patriotism is examined, certain definitions need to be clarified. In 'Citizenship and National Identity', Habermas wrote:

> 'The meaning of the term "nation" thus changed from designating a pre-political entity to something that was supposed to play a constitutive role in defining the political identity of the citizen within a democratic polity. In the final instance, the manner in which national identity determines citizenship can in fact be reversed. Thus, the gist of Ernest Renan's famous saying, "the existence of a nation is ... a daily plebisite", is already directed *against* nationalism ... The nation of citizens does not derive its identity from some common ethnic and cultural properties, but rather from the *praxis* of citizens who actively exercise their civil rights. At this juncture, the republican strand of "citizenship" completely parts company

with the idea of belonging to a pre-political community integrated on the basis of descent, a shared tradition and a common language. Viewed from this end, the initial fusion of republicanism with nationalism only functioned as a catalyst ... Hereditary nationality gave way to an acquired nationalism, that is, to a product of one's own conscious striving.'

Despite Habermas's best efforts, his argument fails to convince as it is wrong. The term 'nation of *citizens*' is important as he is redefining the concept of a nation. To rely upon Rousseau's theory of the General Will, when as a matter of historical fact that attempt to implement the theory led to anarchy, civil war, The Terror, and eventually the Napoleonic wars is not convincing. Rousseau's theory did not find favour beyond France, mercifully. The reason why the term nationality has been loosely used to mean both citizenship and nationhood is that, up until recently, the nation was the founder of the various nation states, and once citizenship was granted/created it applied to the nation only. It is only recently with mass immigration, both from beyond the EU and within the EU, that there is now a difference between the membership of a nation and citizenship.

Although the terms nation and national are used loosely, there are certain differences which need to be clarified. A 'state' is a legal and political entity that has a government; the term might also be used to refer to a piece of territory over which the government rules. Collins English dictionary has the following definition:

> 6. a sovereign political power or community. 7. the territory occupied by such a community. 8. the sphere of power in such a community: *affairs of state*. 9. (often cap.) one of a number of areas or communities having their own governments and forming a federation under a sovereign government, as in the US. 10. (often cap.) the body politic of a particular sovereign power, esp. as contrasted with a rival authority such as the Church.[460]

Collins defines a nation state thus:

> An independent state inhabited by all the people of one nation and one nation only.[461]

A country refers to a territory:

1. A territory distinguished by its people, culture, language, geography, etc. 2. an area of land distinguished by its political autonomy: state. 3. the people of a territory or state: the *whole country rebelled*.[462]

Collins defines a nation thus:

1. an aggregation of people or peoples of one or more cultures, races, etc., organized into a single state: *the Australian nation*. 2. a community of persons not constituting a state but bound by common descent, language, history, etc.: *the French-Canadian nation*.[463]

Collins defines nationality thus:

1. the state or fact of being a citizen of a particular nation. 2. a body of people sharing common descent, history, language, etc.,: a nation. 3. a national group: *30 different nationalities are found in this city*. 4. national character or quality. 5. The state or fact of being a nation: national status.[464]

Collins defines citizen thus:

1. a native registered or naturalized member of a state, nation, or other political community. Compare alien. 2. an inhabitant of a city or town. 3. a native or inhabitant of a place.[465]

Collins defines citizenship thus:

1. the condition or status of a citizen, with its rights and duties. 2. a person's conduct as a citizen: *an award for good citizenship*.[466]

The term 'state', therefore, refers to the constitutional and political entity, although it can also refer to a territory over which a state governs. A nation state refers to a state consisting of only one nation (it will be taken for granted that this is not meant to mean racial purity, as there will always be some non-nationals in any country, but will be taken to mean that the non-nationals are not so numerous as to dilute the attachment of the nation state to its nation). A country refers to territory, although it can also be used in such a way as to refer to the country's people. There is an emphasis on the people, culture, and language, as well as geography, that is lacking in the term state. The term nation can refer to those living in a state (this is not inconsistent with Habermas's theory). It also has a meaning of a community within a state sharing a common culture and having common descent (this definition is the pre-political nation). Nationality can refer to those who are citizens of a nation and also a community sharing a common culture and descent. A citizen is someone who is either an indigenous or naturalized member of a state or nation – the political dimension is emphasized in this. A citizen is not defined by culture. Citizenship is the status of being a citizen.

The Soviet Union was a state comprised of many nations (for example, Estonians, Russians, Ukrainians). Britain is generally treated as a nation state, although it strictly is comprised of several nations. A similar situation could be held to apply to Spain or Belgium, both of which have restless minorities demanding national status. However, the difference between the British nations is more pronounced, especially between England and Scotland. The British nations have separate teams for many sports, for example, although it is Britain itself which competes in the Olympics. The term 'British nation' is common, and Winston Churchill referred to the 'British race'. The British can be considered a nation only so long as the various composite nations are happy to be subsumed into the British. Citizenship is British citizenship; the inhabitants of the UK are all British citizens and have British passports. Immigrants become naturalized British citizens and acquire British passports; they do not become English. The English are a nation sharing a common descent and culture. British is the inclusive citizenship shared by all the inhabitants of Britain, while English is an exclusive nationality. There is no such thing as English citizenship. Englishness is the pre-political nation; Britishness is citizenship. (There are many who would regard British *nationality* to be comprised of the English, Scots, Welsh, and Northern Irish, and this is technically correct).

Collins defines the term populate thus:

> 1. to live in; inhabit. 2. to provide a population for; colonize or people.[467]

To repopulate, therefore, is to people a territory again. The term is an accurate description of the British government policy towards England (ethnic cleansing is more focused on driving out a particular set of inhabitants, and this term is therefore less accurate). The British state's policy (including the Tories) is to repopulate England with non-English peoples who are then given British citizenship. The English are to become a minority in England.

With past immigration over the centuries between 1066 and WWII, the numbers of immigrants were of such numbers that they could be assimilated into the English nation. That is not so now. The scale of immigration to Britain is massive. Prior to WWII, immigration into Britain since 1066 was no more than 250,000 or so; in other words, there was no mass immigration. Currently, there are more immigrants in one year than the total between 1066 and 1950, excluding wartime (see *The Ponzi Class,* pages 300 to 305). Frank Fields, a Labour MP, picked up on the scale and effect of immigration in an article in 2006:

> 'Newcomers to Britain are arriving at such a rate that, over a five-year Parliament, the population increase will be equal to 47 new Parliamentary constituencies. On the other hand, the rate at which a number of our fellow citizens are deciding to go in the opposite direction and make their lives beyond our shores is equivalent to 26 constituencies. The result is a turnover in our population of almost a million each year. This statistic is based on official figures for 2004 – the latest available. But the recent trend shows a sharp escalation. The truth is that this is simply not sustainable.
>
> Over the centuries, Britain has generally been a net exporter of people. There was only one year during the period from 1964 to 1982 when there was a net migration into this country. In 1983, there was a net migration of 17,600 – and the figures have swollen to almost a quarter of a million by 2004. The Government's estimate of future movements of population is so wide of the mark it's pitiful ... Movements of population on this scale are having a massive social impact which will, if not addressed, cause sweeping political changes ... The Government projections for future population growth, which is now driven by immigration, show a net migration policy in England producing the equivalent of a new city the size of Birmingham every five years. Given that new arrivals concentrate in the poorest areas ... the sheer numbers arriving in such a short space of time transform the communities into which they arrive. Within the space of five years, an English working-class community with first-generation, settled immigrants and their children, is transformed out of all recognition. Neighbourhoods in which people have spent the whole of their days are literally being changed before their eyes.'

Frank Fields adds that 'Britain is sleepwalking into becoming a global labour station. If the Prime Minister believes this scenario is right, he has a duty to test it openly with the electorate.' This has not happened, and importantly, the churning effect of English people leaving and immigrants from alien cultures arriving has not been discussed at all.

There has been a 4.6million population rise between 2001 and 2012, of which 3.8million was attributable to immigration once children were included. In the 2011 census, it was revealed that 4.2million people, 7.7% of the population, do not speak English as their first language; in London, the figure is 1.7million people, or 22.1% of the population. Annual immigration to March 2015 reached 330,000. 25.9% of the babies born were to mothers who had been born abroad. In August 2015, ONS figures showed that there were 8.3million immigrants in Britain. MigrationWatch UK reported in June 2014 that the total number of illegal immigrants was estimated to be as high as 2million.

It is accepted that a state can determine its own immigration policy, but it is denied that a nation has the same right. The politically correct are very keen to promote the victim status of ethnic minorities and encourage them to demand that the state formulate policies to suit their interests. Yet such is denied to the majority, even though the English are a minority in the world and in the EU.

The Collins definition of a patriot is:

> A person who vigorously supports his country and its way of life

The Collins definition of patriotism is:

> Devotion to one's own country and concern for its defence

The Collins definition of nationalism is:

> 1. a sentiment based on common cultural characteristics that binds a population and often produces a policy of national independence of separatism. 2. loyalty or devotion to one's country; patriotism. 3. exaggerated, passionate, or fanatical devotion to a national community

To flesh out the definition of patriotism, it can be defined thus:

> Patriotism can be defined as love of one's country, identification with it, and special concern for its well-being and that of compatriots.[468]

The distinction between patriotism and nationalism can be slight, although patriotism is often presented as defensive while nationalism is presented as aggressive. A useful method could be to rely on the origin of the words:

> Both patriotism and nationalism involve love of, identification with, and special concern for a certain entity. In the case of patriotism, that entity is one's *patria*, one's country; in the case of nationalism, that entity is one's *natio*, one's nation (in the ethnic/cultural sense of the term). Thus patriotism and nationalism are understood as the same type of set of beliefs and attitudes, and distinguished in terms of their objects, rather than the strength of those beliefs and attitudes, or as sentiment vs. theory.[469]

There is much in common between the issues and beliefs involving patriotism and nationalism. However, where a country is not ethnically homogenous, or where a nation does not have a country of its own, the issues and beliefs can differ. Patriotism involves a sense of loyalty to one's country. Our country is home for our culture, and it educates us and provides for our welfare as well as protecting our freedoms. But while a patriot is a citizen of a country, not all citizens are patriots. Furthermore:

> Patriotism involves special concern for the *patria* and compatriots, a concern that goes beyond what the laws obligate one to do, beyond what one does as a citizen; that is, beyond what one ought, *in fairness*, to do.[470]

The origins of constitutional patriotism can be attributed to Karl Jaspers, who, immediately after WWII, wrote *The Question of German Guilt*, which drew distinctions between criminal, moral, political, and metaphysical guilt. Jaspers also advanced the idea of 'collective responsibility', which he linked with the idea of German unity, believing that Germany's appalling past could in fact become a source of unity and social cohesion.[471] Jaspers believed that Germany needed to address its past with a new version of cosmopolitanism. Immediately after WWII, many German thinkers were concerned by the failure of the Weimar Republic, where the progressive constitution had failed and the Weimar Republic had struggled as a 'democracy without democrats'. The constitution by itself had been unable to resist the enemies of democracy.

Subsequently, Carl Schmitt advanced the idea that democratic integration should be achieved by the use of plebiscites, democratic symbols, including the flag and national anthem, territory, and also a pride in the political system. This came against the backdrop of the German Constitutional Court as being the main defence of democracy.[472] The constitution, it was believed, would reflect not only legal and institutional framework, but would also embody the values derived from the political culture and traditions. In this way, people would not object to 'government by judges' but would support the political system. Eventually, the Constitutional Court became as respected as the central bank in West Germany. Consequently, in 1979, Dolf Sternberger introduced the concept of constitutional patriotism on the 30th anniversary of the introduction of the Federal Republic. Sternberger argued that, until the end of the 18th century, all patriotism had been a form of constitutional patriotism – i.e. a support for the laws and liberties. Therefore, constitutional patriotism could be regarded as a pre-national patriotism.[473] Sternberger was focused on loyalty to the state. He also advocated a 'militant democracy' which would deal aggressively with those who sought to oppose it. Karl Loewenstein argued that democracies were unable to resist the emotional inspiration of fascism simply by the rule of law; instead democracies needed to fight fire with fire and adopt more authoritarian measures against anti-democratic forces.[474] The effect of constitutional patriotism, therefore, is to try and bind the people to the institutions and develop a feeling of pride in the institutions of the state rather than an attachment to 'kith and kin' as a basis of patriotism.

Constitutional Patriotism re-emerged into the political debate in 1986 as a consequence of the 'historians' dispute' about the comparability of the Nazis and the Holocaust with Stalinism and the Gulags. Jurgen Habermas accused conservative historians of trying to revert to a more conventional sense of patriotism and normalize German identity. Habermas advocated constitutional patriotism. Habermas believed that universal ideals needed to be implemented by a nation state and in a 'post traditional society' where patriotism would be subject to critical reflection and revision.[475] National traditions and historical beliefs would, therefore, not be the basis of identity, but would be criticized, while patriotism would be focused on rights and democratic processes. Citizenship would not be a passive, inherited nationality. Habermas argued that 'the overcoming of fascism forms the particular historical perspective from which a post-national identity centred around the universalist principles of the rule of law and democracy understands itself'; 'conventional morality' such as adherence to the rule of law, abiding by 'common sense', or supporting national traditions had failed to prevent the Third Reich.[476] Habermas argued:

'Tradition means, after all, that we continue something as unproblematic, which others have started and demonstrated. We normally imagine that these "predecessors", if they stood before us face to face, could not completely deceive us, that they could not play the role of deus malignus. I for one think that this basis of trust has been destroyed by the gas chambers.'[477]

What was required for West Germany, according to this view, was a 'Holocaust identity' that rejected tradition as well as fascism. This view further rejected the idea of West Germany adopting an identity as an economic miracle or of being anti-totalitarian, which meant anti-communist in the Cold War. 'Holocaust identity' would therefore supplement the universalist norms of constitutional patriotism for Germany, which would become a process of self-interrogation about the past. History and memories would be contested rather than being sources of national pride, and this process would be a means of 'coming to terms with the past'. Patriotism would therefore become a process of rejecting the past and of embracing universal moral values. It would establish collective responsibility for the Holocaust, which was the product of the culture that was passed onto new generations. Habermas argued:

'Our own life is linked to the life context in which Auschwitz was possible not by contingent circumstances but intrinsically. Our form of life is connected with that of our parents and grandparents through a web of familial, local, political, and intellectual traditions that is difficult to disentangle – that is, through a historical milieu that made us what and who we are today. None of us can escape this milieu, because our identities, both as individuals and as Germans, are indissolubly interwoven with it.'[478]

Subsequent generations, too, were therefore obliged to share a collective responsibility for the Holocaust. Constitutional patriotism was therefore particular to each country's national culture as well as a means of promoting universalist moral principles:

'Each national culture develops a distinctive interpretation of those constitutional principles that are equally embodied in other republican constitutions – such as popular sovereignty and human rights – in light of its own national history. A "constitutional patriotism" based on these interpretations can take the place originally occupied by nationalism.[479]

The social bond in a state should be 'juridical, moral and political, rather than cultural, geographical and historical'.[480] Thus, peoples' culture and ethnicity have no role in patriotism, which is based on attachment for universalist ideals rather than attachment to a dominant culture of society. The challenge to constitutional patriotism is whether a set of universalist principles foisted upon a community by law is sufficient to replace the community allegiance based on shared culture, ethnicity, and history, particularly given that that set of universalist principles are implemented by each country in its own cultural and political context. Furthermore, even immigrant countries, such as the USA, and supposedly civic countries, such as France, rely upon a culture derived from an historical majority; the national heroes, the monuments, holidays, and political institutions are products of a particularistic national culture which the civic identification relies upon.[481] Habermas described constitutional patriotism as 'patriotism based upon the interpretation of recognized, universalistic constitutional principles within the context of a particular national history and tradition'.[482] Those who support Habermas tend to fall into two groups: a critical group consisting of those who see constitutional patriotism as a means of destabilizing homogenous, hegemonic national identities and a means of undermining identification and the traditional understanding of national identity, i.e. 'citizens ... must learn to fear, be angry at, and be ashamed of the very institutions and cultures that claim their attachment and allegiance';[483] and a neutralist group of those who see constitutional patriotism as a means of decoupling culture and patriotism, and basing patriotism on a support for universalist values. Recent discussions have focused very much on the de-culturalization and de-ethnicization aspects of constitutional patriotism:

> 'Constitutional patriotism is thus interpreted as valorizing "universalism" over "particularism" ("constitutional patriotism de-ethnicizes citizenship by replacing cultural attachments, which by definition are specific, by allegiance to institutions and symbols which are potentially universalizable"); "values" over "identity" ("sharing universal values of democracy and respect for justice and rights – as opposed to sharing an – identity, in the sense of shared language, associations and culture"); and "procedures" over "substance" ("constitutional patriotism does not entail loyalty to a specific substantial community, but has the sole meaning of being loyal to the democratic procedures of

the constitution"). In addition, constitutional patriotism is brought to bear on two other important developments within liberal thought: the process of disaggregation of democratic citizenship and legal rights (the latter being increasingly grounded in the universalistic basis of personhood), and the search for a "liberal" (that is, non-cultural and universalistic) form of nationalism, of which constitutional patriotism is often presented as the "purest" version.[1484]

The definition of national identity, or citizenship to be exact, and what forges it is thrown into question:

'Many recent writings on nationalism and patriotism have relied on a well-established distinction between "civic" (or universalist, or constitutional) nationalism and "ethnic" (or particularist, or cultural) nationalism, usually to endorse the former and repudiate the latter. Few dichotomies have been more unhelpful than this. Between the so-called "civic" pole of national identity (which emphasizes shared liberal democratic values) and the "ethnic" pole of national identity (which stresses racial and cultural membership), there is a whole range of intermediate positions which, on reflection, describe the nature of citizens, attachment to their national polity more accurately. National identity is a complex, multi-layered phenomenon, which eludes any simplistic "either/or" approach. For our purposes here, we can identify at least four layers of identity in a national community. The first is that of ethnic, "primordial" links based on birth and kinship. The second is that of the broad culture, language, ways of life and social customs characteristic of a particular community. The third is that of the political culture, embodied in political institutions, practices, symbols, ideological and rhetorical traditions, and so forth. The fourth level is that of abstract, universalist political ideals and procedures, usually expressed in the form of general principles outlined in the constitution. Seen in this way it is obvious that levels two and three of the "pyramid" of identity may provide a better account of what, in practice, binds people together than either levels one or four, upon which ethnic and civic accounts concentrate exclusively. This, of course, is not to suggest that normative theory should endorse popular understandings of national identity, but it provides a more realistic starting point from which to begin to articulate a viable civic patriotism.[1485]

Michael Ignatieff, a liberal, opposes ethnic nationalism as 'ethnic nationalism claims ... that an individual's deepest attachments are inherited not chosen. It is the national community that defines the individual, not the individuals who define the national community', whereas, 'according to the civic nationalist creed, what holds a society together is not common roots but law. By subscribing to a set of democratic procedures and values, individuals can reconcile their right to shape their own lives with their need to belong to a community.' This, of course, is more wishful thinking than analysis. What is being promoted is what someone wants to believe rather than what someone actually believes is fact. Ignatieff himself has conceded the pull of ethnicity and the power of historical roots.

With constitutional patriotism, national identity is a matter of choice based on support for the institutions and laws which uphold universalist values. It is not based upon what people are, unlike the more traditional sense of national identity where history and a pre-political identity are more important.[486] The primary concern for nationalism is the protection and maintenance of a distinctive nation. However, the dichotomy that one is either a civic or an ethnic patriot is simplistic for the reasons set out by Cecile Laborde and takes no account of the concept of a Staatsvolk, who create the state, its institutions, and culture. The only way that civic patriotism can replace traditional patriotism is by a forced sterilization of the national culture from the state's institutions. No explanation is given as to why the Staatsvolk would agree to this, nor why they should owe any allegiance to a set of abstract universalist theories instead of their own culture. A criticism arises that both civic and constitutional patriotism are statist and that there is a problem with legitimacy and the ability to command support from the people. It therefore becomes imperative for the people to identify their interests with the state; otherwise the concept fails:

> 'For a liberal state to be secure, the citizens must understand the national interest as something other than the interest of the state. Only the first can evoke in them the sacrificial spirit upon which the second depends.'[487]

The strength of loyalty to constitutional patriotism is likely to be weak. There are those who help the poor and needy in other countries. For philanthropy based on patriotism, the act is exclusive and selective. It is motivated by a desire to do the best for one's own countrymen. It is not neutral, but instinctive and pre-political. Yet constitutional patriotism rejects the pre-political ties that nation states have traditionally appealed to and prefers an appeal to universalist values such as democracy and human rights.[488] It seeks to decouple the national political culture from the majority culture of the Staatsvolk.[489] For Habermas, citizenship can be divorced from nationality:

> '... the modern understanding of ... republican freedom can ... cut its umbilical links to the womb of national consciousness of freedom that originally gave it birth. The nation state sustained a close connection between "demos" and "ethos" only briefly ... Citizenship was never conceptually tied to national identity.'[490]

The EU has been seen to be the future in a post-national world. It was created, in part, as a rejection of nationalism.[491] For civic and constitutional patriots, it affords a sense of identity devoid of national cultures. Instead, a sense of European identity needs to be forged, based on a commitment to democracy and human rights. This leaves the nation states to rely upon the preservation of the 'cultural integrity of national identities'.[492] The EU therefore offers a new opportunity for both the civic and constitutional patriots. As with Germany and its post-WWII repudiation of Nazism, the EU has been seen as a mechanism for condemning European history:

> 'In Europe, notwithstanding national differences in history, in language, in customs, Habermas suggests, people can decide, collectively and deliberatively, to construct a new identity built from their (selectively appropriated) European experiences and European traditions. Together with French philosopher, Jacques Derrida, Habermas has suggested several candidates: several traditions that might be appropriated and that might inform a new transnational European identity. These include a tradition of keeping religion separate from the public sphere, a tradition of relying upon the state to correct market failures, and a tradition of engaging in collective action with a view to promoting social justice. As in the German national case, Habermas envisions this new European political identity, as, in part, the product of critical engagement with what is illiberal and what is anti-democratic in Europe's past. For instance, he suggests that by reflecting critically on the experience of empire and by deliberating together about this deplorable aspect of their shared past, Europeans might construct a political identity that includes an explicit repudiation of Eurocentrism.'[493]

In this way, ordinary people are to be taught, if not forced, to reject the values and beliefs of their nations, to reject their own national culture, and instead to embrace a hatred of their countries and their history. This is a corruption and the opposite of genuine patriotism. Habermas is substituting patriotism with hatred.

The problem, however, is whether the EU can establish popular support and democratic legitimacy with the peoples of Europe. Presently, it is widely accepted that the EU has a democratic deficit. By acquiring competences over matters as diverse as food safety, tourism, law and order, and immigration, in addition to economic redistributive activities (e.g. grants to new member states to try and raise their living standards up to an EU level), the EU has acquired many of the attributes of a nation state.[494] This is despite the lack of democratic legitimacy; the EU does not have a demos in the same sense as a nation state, and there is therefore no legitimacy for a minority to accept the majority decision. Furthermore, due to the diffusion of power in EU governance between the Commission, the EU parliament, the Commissioners (now including a president), and the national governments there is no political party or choice of rival policy agendas that a public can vote out of office.[495] This has led to calls for an EU citizenship to be developed as per constitutional patriotism based on civic rights and obligations.[496] This is the approach favoured by Habermas, who advocates that the creation of new political institutions by a European constitution would have an 'inducing effect' as regards the creation of a democratic community.[497]

This strategy is a continuation of the 'Monnet method' of integration, which envisioned a series of crises that could only be solved by further powers being acquired at supranational level and, hence, the power of the EU growing to create 'a Europe united by bureaucracy'.[498] Monnet believed that the 'supranational agency' would steadily extend its authority so as to inevitably undermine the sovereignty of the nation states, and the supranational agency would actively promote this transfer of power.[499] The first step was the Schuman Plan and the creation of the European Coal and Steel Community, and Schuman himself stated that his plan created 'common bases for economic development as a first step in the federation of Europe'.[500]

Thus far, EU integration has resulted in an increase in power for EU bureaucrats and a decrease in power of the democratically elected national governments. The power of the European parliament, having no executive powers, is too weak to confer democratic legitimacy on EU governance. Furthermore, the EU is too remote from voters for them to effectively hold it to account. For many, this is not a problem as the EU *should not* even attempt to be democratic.[501] For these same people, 'it is a good thing that regulatory policy-makers are isolated from democratic majorities', and 'the EU may be more "representative" precisely because it is, in a narrow sense, less "democratic"'.[502]

From a civic nationalism perspective, the people are seen 'as a group of individuals rationally united within shared structures of citizenship, structures that can be fostered – and indeed created by – an elite, although this may require overcoming the reservations of less rational individuals'.[503] But this statist approach ignores the interests of the indigenous nations of Europe. Civic patriotism does affect the status of the Staatsvolk:

> 'Civic patriotism takes as its starting point this fact of the non-neutrality of the public sphere. It recognizes that most liberal-democratic political cultures reflect the norms, history, habits and prejudices of majority groups ... only those democratic institutions will be legitimate which can effectively secure the loyalty of all citizens (including members of cultural minorities). On the other hand, in contrast to nationalists, civic patriots believe that the value of national identity primarily lies in its contribution to sustaining feelings of solidarity between all citizens. So the conflation of 'national' identity with the historic majority's culture cannot be justified on civic patriotic grounds. Rather, expressions of banal nationalism in the public sphere which are found to be offensive or alienating to certain groups in society will have to be challenged. In this respect, civic patriotism takes the existing imbrication of politics and culture seriously and urges a considerable "thinning out" of national cultures.'[504]

This, as has been argued in the name of multiculturalism, will allow the ethnic minorities a veto on the existence of and content of the public culture, which itself is a reflection of the culture of the Staatsvolk. In this way, multiculturalism is entirely compatible with and complementary to constitutional patriotism:

> 'Multiculturalism's approach to socialization and incorporation is clearly different from that of nationalism ... it to some extent at least deprives the receiving community of automatic resort to a given set of norms and traditions. Traditions – this is how we do things here – do not only have to be communicated to the newcomers (with the assumption that they be adopted and emulated) but have to be explained and justified; hence are open to deliberative challenge and change.'[505]

Multiculturalism is the twin of constitutional patriotism (or civic nationalism). Multiculturalism advocates mass immigration and the

113

imposition of foreign cultures onto the host population; constitutional patriotism advocates the disavowal by the state of any loyalty to the host nation, the Staatsvolk, and the forced removal of any trace of national culture, the culture of the host nation, from state institutions. Any disagreement with either of these aggressive ideologies is demonized as racist. The impact of the twin attack on the institutions of the host nation is lethal, as is now evidenced across Europe with the breakdown of social cohesion, terrorism, and economic ruin. Collins defines culture thus:

> 1. the total of the inherited ideas, beliefs, values, and knowledge, which constitute the shared bases of social action. 2. the total range of activities and ideas of a group of people with shared traditions, which are transmitted and reinforced by members of a group: the *Mayan* culture. 3. a particular civilization at a particular time. 4. the artistic and social pursuits, expression, and tastes valued by a society or class, as in the arts, manners, dress, etc. 5. the enlightenment or refinement resulting from these pursuits.[506]

The first three definitions are the ones associated with culture's understood meaning in the debate about multiculturalism and will be taken to be the meaning for the purposes of this book, although the fourth and fifth definitions are not totally irrelevant. The key aspects of culture are threefold: it is inherited; it consists of 'ideas of a group of people with shared traditions, which are transmitted and reinforced by members of a group' – that is to say that it binds the group together, distinguishing the group; and it is self-perpetuating in that it is 'transmitted and reinforced' by members of a group. This is a big issue for the neo-Marxists and, as they see it, is the manner in which false consciousness is maintained. The attachment of a people to their culture is a major obstacle to the much hoped for communist revolution. Political correctness aims to break that attachment and, if possible, to destroy the concept of a national culture.

In his essay 'Cultural Diversity and Liberal Democracy', Bhikhu Parekh (born in 1935 in Gujarat, and awarded a life peerage in 2000), a leading British multiculturalist, states that most modern states are culturally diverse, and he raises the question as how to establish common citizenship in such states. Parekh identifies a number of different types of cultural peoples, each of which he believes requires different treatment. His essay concentrates on those he describes as 'ethnic, cultural and religious minorities' within society. This is the group most relevant to the debate in Britain.

114

Parekh asserts that these groups wish to preserve their identity and then examines how this might be achieved in a liberal society. He categorizes three possible alternatives – assimilationist liberalism, cultural laissez-faire, and cultural pluralism – and then examines the merits of each. Parekh favours the latter.

Parekh's rationale will be compared below with that of the liberal Brian Barry. There are four major flaws in Parekh's argument: he accuses liberalism of separating government from society when, in fact, it is he; he favours minorities but neglects the rights of majority nations; he ignores that minority cultures exist worldwide, and so they cannot be destroyed by liberal society; and his goal of a 'community of communities' and 'multicultural post-nation' is against the interests of the English or indigenous British. From a multiculturalist viewpoint, multiculturalism being a political process, Parekh advocates a coherent programme to achieve his goal. Regarding Britain, since most immigrants settle in England, it is the English within Britain who are most affected. There is a large overlap in multiculturalist ideology as set out by Parekh with constitutional patriotism as set out by Habermas. Parekh defines the purpose of his essay as to analyse the problems of territorially dispersed 'ethnic, cultural and religious minorities' seeking to preserve their distinct ways of life.[507] This includes immigrants. Parekh states:

> 'These groups wish to participate as equal citizens in the collective life of the community, but they also wish to preserve their way of life and demand recognition of their cultural identities. This raises the question as to how a liberal state should respond to their demands.'[508]

This description makes two assumptions: first, that the minority groups wish to retain their distinctive ways of life; second, that the onus is on liberal society to respond to minority demands. The first potential response which Parekh analyses is assimilationist liberalism. He says this model 'presupposes and is a custodian of a way of life centred on such values as personal autonomy, freedom of choice and independent thought'.[509] Parekh further states:

> '[Minorities] threaten the integrity of the liberal way of life. Being self-contained communities' they also prevent their members from fully integrating into the wider society. Furthermore, their demand for the recognition of their differences is incompatible with their demand for equality.'[510]

115

According to Parekh, an assimilationist is therefore in favour of a culture-blind or colour-blind equality and opposed to special treatment for minorities, and will refuse to recognize cultural diversity in favour of integration. However, Parekh rejects assimilation for four reasons. First, he asserts that liberalism recognizes individuals and not their culture, which is disrespectful due to the importance of culture.[511] Second, he asserts that the assimilationist liberal equates equality with uniformity which leads to inequality.[512] He cites the effect of a requirement to wear trousers at work on Muslim women, who are culturally forbidden to expose their bodies in public. Parekh asserts that society needs to be discriminating. Third, Parekh asserts that a diversity of cultures enriches society and that assimilation is therefore detrimental to that enrichment.[513] Fourth, he says that if minorities are confronted with a process of assimilation then they are likely to exploit whatever freedoms liberalism has to offer in order to preserve and promote their own cultures and that this will lead to friction with wider society. Parekh highlights religion in this context:

> 'It is not often appreciated that fundamentalism is often provoked by liberal intolerance, and that once it arises, liberalism feels mortally threatened and unwittingly takes over many of the characteristics of its enemy.'[514]

This assertion blames the majority for the actions of the minority. Parekh dismisses the notion that immigrants, by entering another country, should be prepared to accept the culture of that country, as such is tantamount to treating them as second-class citizens.[515] The Parekh Report (produced by the Commission on the Future of Multi-Ethnic Britain that had been set up by the Runnymede Trust), written at the same time, goes further: (i) it denies that Britain is or has ever been a homogenous unified whole, and so integration is impossible as there is no culture to integrate into; (ii) it dismisses assimilation as immoral as it suppresses difference and renders those who do not share majority norms to second-class citizenship; (iii) it states that assimilation is impossible due to globalization.[516] None of this addresses the interests of the host nation or takes into account the need to maintain national unity. Parekh's hostility to assimilation is in step with Marcuse's own hostility to assimilation.

Parerkh bases his definition of the cultural laissez-faire model on arguments put forward by John Gray.[517] This model would divorce the state from culture and allow individuals to choose which culture they might have. This would extend to the education system too. While Parekh sees some merit in the proposed cultural neutrality of the state, he nevertheless rejects the laissez-faire approach for four reasons. First, culture is pervasive and intrinsic and cannot be chosen as one might choose clothes. Furthermore, Parekh asserts that some cultures cannot properly survive in an individualist culture.[518] Second, if the state is to maintain an individualist culture, then doing so would result in the state promoting that culture and it would be unable to maintain total neutrality.[519] Third, liberalism would have an advantage in the competition of cultures as it is the product of several centuries of history. It is embedded in society, and people are attached to it. By comparison, other cultures would be at a disadvantage not being a part of the development of society. Liberal culture would therefore remain dominant.[520] In other words, Britain would remain British, and England would remain English. Fourth, a state's authority and constitution must be founded on some moral basis. Parekh states that 'Whatever its structure, the state is inescapably grounded in and biased towards a specific way of life.'[521] Furthermore, the laws of the state must reflect cultural bias – be it the legalization or not of slavery, capital punishment, abortion, polygamy, etc. Therefore, Parekh asserts that 'A morally neutral state, making no moral demands on its citizens and equally hospitable to all human choices, is logically impossible. And since every law and policy coerces those not sharing the underlying values, a morally non-coercive state is a fantasy ... no state can be wholly free of a moral bias and of the concomitant coercion.'[522] Parekh sees the concept of state morality as a problem. His view is an attack on the existence of the nation state since he regards state morality as unavoidable and unacceptable.

Parekh then comes to his preferred option, that of cultural pluralism. Parekh describes people as 'cultural beings' who are 'culturally embedded'[523] and states:

> 'Cultural diversity, then, is a collective good ... it cannot be safeguarded by a policy of cultural laissez-faire. Since it is a valuable public good and since it cannot be left to the vagaries of a distorted cultural market, the state needs to play an active part in promoting it ... Respecting and promoting cultural diversity requires action at several levels. It requires that cultural minorities should be protected against conscious or unconscious discrimination.'[524]

Parekh believes that liberals are particularly likely to assume that only their interpretation of morality is correct.[525] Parekh condemns this and also the concept of a division between public and private culture as it weakens cultural diversity.[526] The result of a prevailing public culture, according to Parekh, is that minorities tend to be nervous about their culture and choose to conform to the host society, which is undesirable as cultural diversity is a collective good. Therefore, the state should promote minority cultures, including minority schools.[527] Parekh even advocates minority self-governance:

> 'There is much to be said for the state encouraging self-governance among [minorities] and becoming a community of communities ... there is no obvious reason why [decentralization] should be based only on territorial and occupational and not on communal grounds as well.[528]'

Parekh cites the Jews as a precedent.[529] In examining the limits on cultural autonomy, Parekh sums up the liberal position as consisting of three elements: the autonomy principle, which needs to be sustained and minority cultures that threaten it should be discouraged or banned – Parekh dismisses this as assimilationism; the no-harm principle, which Parekh also sees problems with if it includes matters that conflict with minority cultures; and finally, the concept of fundamental or core values of society, which Parekh rejects, believing the concept should be redefined to what he calls: 'operative public values'. He defines these as being: 'respect for human dignity, equal respect for persons, secure spaces for self-determination, freedom of dissent and expression, and the pursuit of collective interest as the central *raison d'etre* of political power',[530] and all should be obliged to conform. The definition of these values should be open to change, and Parekh asserts that '[society] ought also to bear in mind that the values are a product, of historical consensus and need to win the allegiance of and be revised to meet the legitimate grievances of new groups'.[531] This is almost identical to Habermas's constitutional patriotism, albeit looking at matters from an immigrant point of view, and would give immigrants a veto on the values of society. Parekh proposes that his operative public values should displace the current national culture or fundamental values, that the product of history should be replaced with theory.

The philosopher Edmund Burke MP pointed out that 'Rage and frenzy will pull down more in half an hour, than prudence, deliberation, and foresight can build up in a hundred years. The errors and defects of old establishments are visible and palpable. It calls for little ability to point them out.'[532] Whatever its faults, liberal society is the product of civilization. It allows the cooperation, legal system, and security which JS Mill regarded as being so important.[533] Mill further attached importance to individuality, which he regarded as essential to avoiding civilization's stagnation and decline.[534] Parekh is firmly at odds with Britain's liberal tradition. Although Parekh does not regard his pluralist vision as being liberal, he does believe that it retains what he sees as the best aspects of liberalism[535] and he believes that liberal societies are themselves moving in a pluralist direction.[536] He states that they should 'develop not liberalism but a critical theory of liberal practice[537]' (the manner of the use of the term 'critical theory' should be noted).

Brian Barry opposes Parekh, rejects multiculturalism, and is critical of those other liberals who adopt their own version of multiculturalism. Barry defines his usage of the term 'multiculturalism' as a description of the process, or 'the variety of programmes' of the 'politics of difference'.[538] This definition is to be contrasted with the state of cultural diversity in a society and is also adopted by others,[539] including Parekh himself.[540] It is consistent with the point made by Collingwood when describing civilization as 'the act of civilizing'[541] and a barbarist as someone who wishes to barbarize and destroy civilization.[542]

A multiculturalist, then, is someone who promotes multiculturalism. Multiculturalism is a political process. Barry points out that acceptance of the fact of ethnic or cultural diversity is not an acceptance of the normative process of multiculturalism, and opposition to multiculturalism is not a denial of ethnic or cultural diversity.[543]

Barry accepts that there can be an abuse of hospitality by immigrants and that there is a limit on the amount of difference to which liberalism can tolerate.[544] Barry believes that it is legitimate to try and assimilate all immigrants, subject to the host population being prepared to change too.[545] He also distinguishes between assimilation and acculturation, which he defines as becoming more similar culturally. This puts him at loggerheads with Parekh. He disagrees with Parekh's advocacy of a 'community of communities', disagrees with Parekh's demand that there should be a devolution of power to communities, and instead recommends that devolution should be territorial and cut across communal boundaries.[546] Barry's rationale is that communities should be encouraged to cooperate together, and he highlights the bloody outcome of the Ottoman millet system, which resulted in the mass expulsion of Christians from various countries and the Armenian genocide.[547] This was despite those peoples having lived within the Ottoman Empire for many centuries. Their status as *dhimmis* had been separate from that of the Muslims. Uri Ra'anan, an Austrian/American political scientist, also emphasizes the difficulty of nation-building:

'Historians have been well aware that the Sultans in five centuries were unable to "build" an "Ottoman nation" out of Turks, Arabs, Armenians, Kurds, Greeks etc., the Tsars in several centuries could not "build" a single nation out of Great Russians,

Ukranians, Belorussians, Poles, Finns, Georgians etc., nor could the Habsburg Emperor-Kings, in a similar time span, "build" one nation out of Germans, Hungarians, Czechs, Croats etc.[1548]

More recently, there is Yugoslavia, and since 2014, there are the problems of Ukraine, which consist of the desire by many of the Russians living there to rejoin Russia and Russia's eagerness for them to do so, as with the Crimea. Ra'anan highlights the concept of Staatsvolk, 'which denotes the ethnic group that created the state, is largely identified with it, constitutes the bulk of its elite, and is responsible for the predominant culture'.[549] The English are the Staatsvolk of England. Parekh accepts this.[550] Ra'anan points out the difference between the Western definition of a nation and the Eastern or Southern approach.[551] In the West, the term nation is also used to mean 'state' and also 'citizen'. Some nations are larger than the states they inhabit, and some are smaller. The West relies upon the *jus soli* (territorial) definition of nationality, whereas the Eastern approach relies upon *jus sanguinis* (ethnic, religious identity etc.). Barry, who recognizes that a Staatsvolk consider a state's territory to be their homeland,[552] believes that citizenship should apply on a *jus soli* basis but believes that a citizen should have genuine attachment to his country and condemns the multiculturalists, who he says are only interested in the entitlement to passports.[553]

Barry rejects Parekh's objection to the confinement of non-liberal cultures to the private sphere on the basis that this, in fact, allows those cultures the same rights as everyone else.[554] Barry highlights that it is impossible for a liberal society to give equal respect to both individuals and all cultures when certain cultures do not involve such equal respect themselves (e.g. regarding the treatment of women or homosexuals).[555] Barry also rejects diversity for its own sake as only illiberal cultures are threatened by liberal institutions and they should not be artificially kept alive.[556] Jeremy Waldron, a New Zealand academic, also takes issue with the notion that cultures should be protected lest they wither away as cultures tend to interact and the prospect of erosion of allegiance is a test of a culture's viability and popular support.[557] Barry contends that some cultural norms should not be preserved (e.g. cannibalism).[558]

Nonetheless, Parekh's rationale is flawed. Cultures are not threatened by liberalism. Britain would not kill off Islam, Hinduism, or Buddhism, for example, even if those cultures lost the allegiance of their former members within Britain as those cultures are widespread in many other countries. What Parekh is demanding is that such cultures are promoted *within Britain* – in particular England.

This failure to appreciate the global perspective also affects Parekh's rationale regarding the rights of nations. Will Kymlicka, a liberal multiculturalist, to Parekh's dismay, assigns more rights to indigenous national minorities than to immigrants.[559] Parekh does not contest the right of national minorities to defend themselves and their culture, but is silent regarding national majorities such as the English, who in turn are a very small ethnic minority globally and also in the EU. If applied consistently, globalization would afford the English the right to protect themselves.

Parekh takes exception to individual autonomy[560] and uses it to justify multiculturalism. This places him at odds with Mill. In reality, it is Parekh who seeks to divorce government from the individual as the one community he cannot accept is the nation. The nation created the nation state and its culture.

Parekh acknowledges the conflict that can arise between cultures[561] and even violence.[562] But he is untroubled by the breakdown of former empires and nations. This is not a weakness in his argument as he is dismissive of the nation state as being out of date.[563] Others share this view.[564] However, the fact is that, in the second half of the 20th century, the number of nation states which joined the United Nations quadrupled.[565] Many of these new countries were new states born out of the demise of the old European empires, but they also included the split of Czechoslovakia, those states emerging from the break-up of the Soviet Union, and the bloody break-up of Yugoslavia. This is the age of the nation state. Even in Western Europe, Belgium is struggling to stay as one, and Britain is itself seeing greater self-awareness of its constituent nations. The idea that national identity and loyalty is outdated is factually untrue, is the exact opposite of reality, and the allegation undermines the concept that the evolution of the nation state is to protect the nation from outsiders[566] and defies nationhood.[567]

In the Parekh Report, Parekh goes further. The Runnymede Trust set up the Parekh Commission in 1998, boasting that the commission consisted of '23 distinguished individuals drawn from many community backgrounds ... with a long record of active academic and practical engagement with race-related issues in Britain and elsewhere.' The commission was very much the establishment and took two years deliberating its report. The Labour government not only acted on the report, but subsequently promoted several members of the Parekh commission. Both Parekh himself and Sir Herman Ouseley were awarded peerages. Trevor Phillips, described by *The Times* as the key man behind the setting up of the report, was promoted to chairmanship of the Commission for Racial Equality and then appointed as chairman for the replacement Equality and Human Rights Commission. In promoting the report, Lord Parekh wrote in *The Independent*:

> 'National identity is not given once and for all and cannot be preserved as if it were an antique piece of furniture. The so-called white majority itself consists of groups of people divided along cultural, religious and other lines. This is equally true of the minority. Since Britain does not consist of cohesive majorities and minorities, we should think of it as a looser federation of cultures held together by common bonds of interest and affection and a collective sense of belonging.'

One could easily have written something very similar in the name of constitutional patriotism rather than multiculturalism. In response to the howls of outrage that greeted the report's launch, Gary Younge (a black communist) of *The Guardian* wrote:

> '*The Telegraph's* front page headline yesterday: "Straw wants to rewrite our history" begs two central questions. Who do they mean by "our" and precisely what version of history are they talking about ... The "our" *The Telegraph* refers to is essentially white, English and nationalistic. For huge numbers of Scots, Welsh and Irish, not to mention those of Caribbean, Asian, African and Chinese descent the idea that "the description of British will never do on its own" is not news ...
>
> Unlike the French tricolore or the American stars and stripes, we do not have a national emblem that stands for a set of notional egalitarian principles or a constitution that would give it meaning. The union flag is a conqueror's flag that owes its design to the subjugation of England's neighbours and its reputation to the predatory expeditions which saw Britain steal huge amounts of land, labour and natural resources ... So "Britishness" like the union flag is not neutral.'

The Parekh Report asserts that there are different versions of racism: 'many varieties of racism and exclusion that disfigure modern Britain and that have been woven into the fabric of British history for many centuries'. It is unashamed in its condemnation of British society as racist: 'Britain continues to be disfigured by racism; by phobias about cultural difference; by sustained social, economic, educational and cultural disadvantage; by institutional discrimination; and by a systematic failure of social justice or real respect for difference. These have been fuelled by a fixed conception of national identity and culture.

They are not likely to disappear without a sustained effort of political will. Is it possible to reimagine Britain as a nation – or post nation – in a multicultural way?'. It also condemns the whole of Europe, saying that 'European societies, it is sometimes said, are multi-racist societies ...' and that 'race-based nationalism interacted with a race-based imperialism. In Britain, for example, the Empire was frequently celebrated as the achievement of "an imperial race". The revival of rabid antisemitism, leading to the pogroms against Jews in central and eastern Europe and Hitler's Final Solution, was the product of this pan-European trend'. In fact, Hitler's Final Solution was a product of Nazi ideology and not part of a 'pan-European trend'. Britain bankrupted itself fighting Nazi Germany, and many millions of people died in WWII fighting against Nazism. The allegation is as vile as it is untrue and can only help stir up anti-European hatred.

The report alleges:

> 'Anti-Muslim racism has been a feature of European culture at least since the Crusades, but it has taken different forms at different times. In modern Britain its manifestations include discrimination in recruitment and employment practices; high levels of attacks on mosques and on people wearing Muslim religious dress; widespread negative stereotypes in all sections of the press, including the broadsheets as well as the tabloids; bureaucratic obstruction or inertia in response to Muslim requests for greater cultural sensitivity in education and healthcare; objections and delays in planning permissions to build mosques; and non-recognition of Muslims by the law of the land, since discrimination on grounds of religion or belief is not unlawful. Furthermore, many or most anti-racist organisations and campaigns appear indifferent to the distinctive features of anti-Muslim racism and to distinctive Muslim concerns about cultural sensitivity ...'.

What the report is doing is fostering a sense of victimhood in Muslims while ignoring the fact that the Muslim population of Britain was virtually non-existent until recently. The report portrays any objection to Muslim immigration, and the attendant issues, as racist. The Parekh report is a long attack on Britain, with a multitude of allegations of racism. Three paragraphs (amongst others) which caused outrage state:

> '3.28 Does Britishness as such have a future? Some believe that devolution and globalisation have undermined it irretrievably ...

123

It is entirely plain, however, that the word "British" will never do on its own.

3.29 Where does this leave Asians, African-Caribbeans and Africans? For them Britishness is a reminder of colonisation and empire, and to that extent is not attractive. But the first migrants came with British passports, signifying membership of a single imperial system. For the British-born generations, seeking to assert their claim to belong, the concept of Englishness often seems inappropriate, since to be English, as the term is in practice used, is to be white. Britishness is not ideal, but at least it appears acceptable, particularly when suitably qualified – Black British, Indian British, British Muslim, and so on.

3.30 However, there is one major and so far insuperable barrier. Britishness, as much as Englishness, has systematic, largely unspoken, racial connotations. Whiteness nowhere features as an explicit condition of being British, but it is widely understood that Englishness, and therefore by extension Britishness, is racially coded. "There ain't no black in the Union Jack", it has been said. Race is deeply entwined in political culture and with the idea of nation, and underpinned by a distinctively British kind of reticence – to take race and racism seriously, or even to talk about them at all, is bad form, something not done in polite company. This disavowal, combined with "an iron-jawed disinclination to recognise equal human worth and dignity of people who are not white", has proved a lethal combination. Unless these deep-rooted antagonisms to racial and cultural difference can be defeated in practice, as well as symbolically written out of the national story, the idea of a multicultural post-nation remains an empty promise.'[568]

A post-nation is the ultimate logic of multiculturalism, to which English or British nationhood is an obstacle. Taken to its conclusion, as Parekh advocates, multiculturalism will destroy the British nation state, regardless of how the English might react, being England's Staatsvolk, and despite overwhelming hostility to multiculturalism even in traditional immigrant countries.[569] What entity someone would be a citizen of if Parekh achieves his goal is unexplained – possibly the EU, or a global parliament, or a state bureaucracy completely detached from the nation. This national destruction is entirely in keeping with the communist agenda set out in *The Communist Manifesto* of 1848, and entirely in keeping with the neo-Marxism promoted by the Frankfurt School.

The term 'multicultural post-nation' is appropriate and emphasizes the fact that multiculturalism combined with mass immigration, as is practised in England, when taken to its ultimate conclusion, must result in the destruction of the host nation. The existence of the English nation is incompatible with multiculturalism. Tony Linsell, an English nationalist, sets out his definition of a nation thus:

> 'It is widely recognized that it is difficult to define a nation but that does not mean that nations do not exist. A fairly simple definition, or collection of guidelines, as to what constitutes a nation is that it is a group of people who share all or most of the following: a collective name; a perceived or real common ancestry; a history; a culture; a language; and sometimes a common religion. There is nearly always an association a nation and a specific territory that is regarded as its homeland. A nation has myths, legends, heroes and loyalties. It is a community with a sense of solidarity and common identity; there is a *we* sentiment and a *they* sentiment; *insiders* and *outsiders*. A greater degree of empathy and sympathy exists among insiders than between insiders and outsiders. Indeed, the notion of *insiders* and *outsiders* derives from the concept of a community living closely together within a physical boundary, e.g. an encampment or settlement enclosed by a fence or ditch. A nation's boundary markers are more often cultural and perceptual than physical.
>
> One of the most important things that bind a nation together is the fact or perception of insiders sharing a common history and ancestry. The members of a nation usually have real ancestral links, but even in those instances where the links are weak the illusion of common ancestry is possible because insiders share certain physical characteristics that make it possible for them to believe in a shared ancestry. As is so often the case, perception is more important than fact but pretence has its limits. For example, it would be difficult for a Japanese to pretend to be a Zulu because whatever clothes that person wore or the language they spoke, their appearance would remain so different from that of Zulus that any claim to share a common ancestry would obviously be doubtful.
>
> That we have mental images of Zulus, Swedes and Japanese indicates that the linked factors of common physical characteristics and common ancestry are important considerations in determining membership of national communities. Despite the instinctive links we make, some

ideologues are outraged by the idea that common ancestry has any part in determining nationality, not because it is untrue but because it is ideologically inconvenient.[570]

Linsell and Parekh are in agreement as to what constitutes a nation and of who the English are. Where they differ is that Parekh wishes to repopulate England with non-English peoples and regards any legacy of English culture and nationhood as racist; he firmly rejects the idea that immigrants should assimilate. The process of multiculturalism is aggressive and hostile to the host nation. It is immoral in that, as the nation is deliberately damaged by the multicultural programme, that which is dependent upon the nation is likewise damaged, such as the funding for the welfare state or equipment for the armed services. Linsell's view is that 'Nationalism is the expression of a will to avoid communal extinction.'[571] Therefore, nationalism is the opposite of multiculturalism. Nationalism seeks to preserve the nation and nation state. Multiculturalism seeks to destroy the nation and the nation state. All the three main political parties in England (Labour, Tories, and the Liberal Democrats), are fully and openly committed to multiculturalism.

Parekh strongly criticizes liberal citizenship, rejecting virtually all aspects of liberal society. He demands public recognition for minority cultures, the end of national culture as currently understood, and the end of the nation state, irrespective of public opinion. Such demands come against a backdrop of Trotskyist infiltration of immigrant groups in order to incite racial consciousness and division.[572] In addition to the communists, of whatever sect, there are also their fellow travellers and those whom Lenin described as 'useful idiots'.

Liberal tolerance has created a society defined by individual autonomy, something which is cherished. Barry, unlike many liberals, is prepared to defend liberalism and reject multiculturalism. His reasoning is persuasive. Multiculturalists will favour Parekh, who has produced a coherent programme to implement multiculturalism to the point of seeking to establish a post-nation. This is what is meant by a community of communities. But his rationale is flawed and clouded by his hostility to English or British nationhood.

National culture is deemed to be malleable and subject to a process of universalization.[573] With constitutional patriotism, it is deemed that the adherence to abstract theories about universalist principles and the commitment to constitutional processes will build a constitutional identity or culture. This will be adhered to even by minorities as they will use the constitution and universalist principles to contest majority decisions; the majority are deemed to welcome this as part of their own commitment to the constitution and universalist principles.[574]

Constitutional patriotism is therefore not a means of achieving unity through agreement, but of achieving a unity of the method of disagreement. For England, so far as ethnic minorities are concerned, immigration is necessary in order to create the disagreement to create the need for the type of unity offered by constitutional patriotism. Habermas has referred to modern democratic citizenship as 'an abstract, legally mediated solidarity between strangers'.[575] Constitutional patriotism does not offer a means to achieve a consensus on values, only a consensus on procedures.[576] Each country may have its own procedures and disagreements, creating a constitutional patriotism that is specific to each country but embodying universalist principles. Ideologically, constitutional patriotism is held to bridge the gap between so-called civic nationalism and ethnic nationalism:

> 'Constitutional patriotism dispenses with the distinction between "good civic" and "bad ethnic" nationalism that sociologists have rightly called "conceptually ambiguous, empirically misleading, and normatively problematic." Consequently, we also should not call constitutional patriotism a fancy version of civic nationalism: it is a transformative conception of living-together different from civic nationalism; and it does suggest a different moral psychology than nationalism of any sort, whether ethnic or civic.'[577]

But for democracy to function, it needs an identity. The bonds of attachment offered by constitutional patriotism are weak:

> 'Identity is, thus, a problem for democracy in the sense that democracy cannot work without it, and yet cannot unequivocally embrace it. If the democrat's fantasy is Rousseau's band of happy peasants regulating the affairs of state under an oak tree, her nightmare is the American Japanese internment camp. In recent years, a number of political theorists have attempted to find a safe place for identity in democracy: a place between the fantasy and the nightmare. Not only German philosopher Jurgen Habermas … but also civic nationalists, republican patriots, and others have attempted to resolve democracy's identity problem by searching for forms of civic identification that meet the democratic polity's need for allegiance and solidarity, while at the same time fostering tolerance toward those defined as outside the civic "we".'[578]

127

It is suggested that this new, contrived definition of identity, one that is based on passports and adherence to universalist values, i.e. abstract theories, is inclusive and nice. Unlike a differentiation based upon nationality, where outsiders are excluded due to their different nationality, with constitutional patriotism, likewise with civic patriotism and civic nationalism, differentiation is based upon passports and belief. Either someone is entitled to a passport – i.e. citizenship – or they are not; either they agree with the universalist ideology, or they are condemned as illiberal, if not racist etc. In fact, to differentiate based upon the criteria defined by constitutional patriotism is every bit as exclusive and is, by demonizing non-believers, distinctly illiberal, intolerant, and hateful. On the other hand, there is no reason to hate those who are not of the same nationality.

The Habermasian view of the nation state regards it as consisting of nationalism and republicanism, with nationalism being the pre-political nation and republicanism being the ideal of voluntary citizenship[579] (as per Rousseau's Social Contract). Civic nationalism consists of the republican definition of citizenship and has been cited as being the opposite of nationalism proper. For republicanism to prevail, the national culture of a nation state must be divorced from the Staatsvolk:

> 'For historic reasons, in many countries the majority culture is fused with the general culture that claims to be recognised by all citizens ...' , 'this fusion must be dissolved if it is to be possible for different cultural, ethnic and religious forms of life to coexist and interact on equal terms within the same political community' (Habermas). In as far as this process of decoupling is successful, it breaks the historical link between republicanism and nationalism and shifts the solidary of citizens onto a constitutional patriotism, which re-directs citizen's sense of loyalty and attachment away from pre-political entities such as the nation, ethnos or the family and towards the fundamental principles enshrined in the political culture and the basic law.[580]

In this way, the nation state no longer relies upon shared culture, language, and history as a basis of unity, but instead relies upon a political culture of universalist values. By divorcing the majority culture from the national culture, citizens of different backgrounds can claim citizenship on equal terms. This view is also fully endorsed by multiculturalism. Multicultural societies will, with constitutional patriotism and republican (civic nationalist) ideology, possess a political culture in which all religious and cultural forms of life are treated equally (not necessarily the same). What is not examined is the willingness of the Staatsvolk to see its culture divorced from the national culture; it is merely assumed that they will not forcefully object, even though the nation is being dispossessed of its homeland. Furthermore, as with multiculturalism, although citizens are to be integrated into the political culture, they should not merge into one culture. Assimilation is deemed to be bad. Immigrants should not have to abandon their own culture. However, the political culture must exist and does have an intolerance of those deemed politically incorrect. It positively rejects the political norms of the majority culture and instead imposes a view of its own. For this reason:

> 'Constitutional patriotism is therefore best seen as the expression of a distinctively liberal form of civic nationalism. While such a civic nationalism can undoubtedly mitigate the violence and exclusion associated with other forms of nationalism, it is not as amenable to diversity as supporters such as Habermas assume. These difficulties lend credence to the worries expressed by critics who have questioned attempts to sharply distinguish between civic and ethnic nationalism. Even in a political community "based solely on a shared commitment to political principles", there would be "plenty of room (for) exclusion and suspicion of difference" (B Yack). In the final analysis constitutional patriotism too entails some of the political risks associated with other forms of nationalism.[581]'

SUMMARY

'Citizenship and National Identity' is an attack on the traditional nation state and on the understanding of nationhood. The argument that nationality has changed is untrue, although it is accurate to say that there is an attempt to impose a new definition. There are differences between citizenship and nationality. Citizenship, to put it simply, is the entitlement to passports. Nationality is the pre-political identity of the nation and is inherited. Although the usage of the term nationality has been hitherto loose due to the homogeneity of the various European nation states and the small numbers of non-European immigrants until relatively recently, this does not alter the differences of which people are increasingly aware. Habermas's contrived choice of words will not change this. It takes more than fancy language to create nations, as the failure to create an Ottoman nation over five centuries demonstrated. The Ottoman Empire culminated in the Armenian genocide.

Citizenship can be created easily, simply by issuing passports. The Tories have continued the previous Labour government's policy of issuing British passports on an industrial scale. Even paedophiles, rapists, and other criminals have been given British citizenship (although there has been some rowing back on this, with those criminals uncovered by the press losing their newly awarded citizenship). Yet citizenship, passport identity, is insufficient to hold together a nation. This insufficiency is a subject of dispute between so-called ethnic nationalists and those advocating civic nationalism (or constitutional patriotism) – although the either/or distinction is simplistic.

The nation which comprises the Staatsvolk confers upon the state the culture of the nation, as is reflected by the religion, the holidays, and the history for example. In this way, the civic institutions of the state reflect the culture of the nation. For the civic nationalists and multiculturalists, this is a problem. The civic nationalists respond by trying to drive out the nation's culture and influence from the civic institutions, while the multiculturalists seek to multiculturalize those institutions with immigrant cultures.

Regarding the problem of national unity, there are three positions. First, the ethnic nationalists stress the weakness of civic nationalism/constitutional patriotism and its likely failure to hold the nation together. Second, there is the liberal wing of civic nationalism/constitutional patriotism which disagrees and promotes the idea that citizens can be taught to give allegiance to the state devoid of any national culture. Third, there is the communist wing of civic nationalism/constitutional patriotism, the Habermasian view, that the likely weakening of national loyalty is desirable, should be encouraged, and is a prerequisite for a communist revolution. With the Habermasian view, civic nationalism/constitutional patriotism is a mechanism for promoting the opposite of patriotism – that is, promoting a hatred of the country's history and hence the Staatsvolk. With the Habermasian view, the state is owed allegiance by all citizens; immigrants and other disaffected groups are to be encouraged to challenge existing national culture and tradition. The state owes no loyalty to the nation. Multiculturalists likewise reject the concept of a national culture; Parekh and his supporters even go so far as to advocate a 'multicultural post-nation'.

In this way, civic nationalism/constitutional patriotism is a means of destroying the nation state and replacing the national culture, the culture of the Staatsvolk, with universalist values – i.e. abstract theories such as international human rights laws, with the state implementing these theories in preference to defending the national interest. International and superstatist organizations are to be promoted – in particular the EU. This anti-nation-state stance is at odds with the quadrupling of the number of nation states. The nation state is not defunct. It is the embodiment of civilization.

There should be no doubting the malevolence of what Habermas advocates. This is especially so regarding immigration and the EU. He openly states that immigration will 'give rise to social tensions', which if 'processed productively ... will enhance political mobilization in general, and might particularly encourage the new, endogeneous type of new social movements' such as 'peace, ecological and women's movements', which would in turn create pressures that could be resolved 'only at a European level'. This, in turn, would create a European-level civil society that would diminish the sovereignty of national governments, and 'cultural elites and the mass media would have an important role to play' regarding this, a concept that might appeal to the more vain. In simple language, Habermas openly advocates that immigrants should be used to attack nationhood. This is race war politics. Despite the carefully crafted forms of words and flowery language, what is being advocated is the fomentation of anti-white racial hatred. Race war politics should be used to generate a revolution, the overthrow of Western society and the destruction of the nation state.

Habermas condemns the 'chauvinism of prosperity', which is a term as manipulative as it is dishonest. If a nation seeks to better itself by developing a thriving manufacturing industry and creating a welfare state, then that is nothing to be ashamed of, and the nation is perfectly entitled to protect that which has been created. The Staatsvolk is entitled to protect itself, including the right to protect its culture, traditions, and living standards. The nation is entitled to its own homeland.

Passports and abstract theories about human rights will not create the necessary national unity for a peaceful coexistence that has taken European countries centuries to establish. What is being advocated by Habermas is the opposite of patriotism and is intended to create division and conflict.

CURRENT INFLUENCE

'Political correctness does not legislate tolerance; it only organizes hatred' – Jaques Barzun (1907-2012), French/American writer and historian

'Americans have to be fearful of what they say, of what they write, and of what they think. They have to be afraid of using the wrong word, a word denounced as offensive or insensitive, or racist, sexist, or homophobic.' – William Lind

'Political correctness is the natural continuum from the party line. What we are seeing once again is a self-appointed group of vigilantes imposing their views on others. It is a heritage of communism, but they don't seem to see this.' – Doris Lessing (1919-2013), writer and ex-communist

That political correctness is an aggressive and influential ideology is evidenced by its pervasive presence and dominance. Despite never being openly advocated by a political party, it steadily infiltrated into British society in the late 1980s and 1990s – under Tory governance. William Lind emphasized that universities were seriously affected by politically correct orthodoxy and referred to 'small ivy covered North Koreas' prosecuting any politically incorrect statement that offended feminists, 'homosexual-rights activists', ethnic minorities or 'other sainted "victims" groups'. William Lind focused on the totalitarian aspect of political correctness and the attempt to force people 'to live a lie' by ensuring that 'reality must be forbidden'.

Since William Lind's speech in 2008, the spread of political correctness has continued. In Britain, in October 2015, Professor Frank Furedi, in the Daily Mail wrote of: 'the increasingly totalitarian attitudes on our university campuses: the bullying dressed up as tolerance, the obsession with political correctness and "identity", the pretentious, overblown language, and the eagerness to portray as many as possible as victims'. Furedi continued: 'This new censorship is spreading like a cancer across British universities, imposing ever more heavy-handed restrictions on what can be read or said.'

Furedi pointed out that the drive to make universities 'safe spaces' meant that there was a drive to remove views that some students might deem to be offensive and ban 'a heretical thinker against the new credo'. There was also the introduction of 'trigger warnings' to alert potential readers of books and publications that might be deemed politically incorrect and traumatising.

Furedi said: 'Much of this is, I believe, a childish form of narcissism, with some students, like oversized toddlers, eager to draw attention to themselves by making a drama of something "unacceptable" in their studies. It is a kind of attention-seeking self-indulgence, using a self-diagnosis of vulnerability as a vehicle for parading one's championing of "victimhood" and thereby gaining social status.' To use a different terminology, the motive is one of snobbery.

In the USA, in Harvard, for example, students objected to a law course lecture about rape, claiming that the course was unacceptable, and one student claimed that the word 'violate' was traumatising. At the Ivy League Brown University in the USA, a special room was established for students who felt that they had been 'triggered'. The room contained Play-Doh and videos of puppies to help the traumatised students recover.

Another perspective, which is very similar but which takes a broader analysis, was that voiced by Dr Wayne Mapp who, as MP for Auckland's North Shore constituency in New Zealand, was appointed by the National Party to a ministerial role as 'Political Correctness Eradicator' to stamp out political correctness in public institutions. Speaking in June 2005, Dr Mapp pointed out:

> 'Political correctness has three features. First, political correctness is a set of attitudes and beliefs that are divorced from mainstream values. Second, the politically correct person has a prescriptive view on how people should think and what they are permitted to discuss. Third, and most importantly, political correctness is embedded in public institutions, which have a legislative base, and which have coercive powers. It is this third aspect that gives political correctness its authority. Without this capture of power the views of the politically correct would simply be another view in the marketplace of ideas. A person, an institution or a government is politically correct when they cease to represent the interests of the majority, and become focussed on the cares and concerns of minority sector groups.
>
> The minority capture of public institutions by the politically correct is a basic cause of people losing faith in the institutions of government. There is a profound belief that the current government is not concerned with nurturing the fundamental values and beliefs of our society.'

Dr Mapp stressed the importance of free speech and said that its demise was a key hallmark of the politically correct agenda: 'Under the guise of protecting minorities, we lose one of the most important values in a free society; the right to freely express one's opinion.' This is not disputed, and the rationale for the hostility by the politically correct towards free speech was openly set out in Marcuse's essay 'Repressive Tolerance'. Dr Mapp continued:

> 'The minority, therefore, has come to dominate the majority, which is an inherent feature of political correctness. This is not done with the intention of protecting minority rights, which is a legitimate aspect of any democracy. Instead, the intent is to ensure that minority world views take precedence over the reasonably held views of the majority.
>
> Political correctness is a real challenge for National and other moderate centre-right parties. There is a natural abhorrence of the agenda of the politically correct, it being so rooted in leftist liberalism. Simply railing against political correctness will not do. There needs to be a clear political programme to reverse it; to remove the viewpoints and language of the politically correct from the institutions of government. Unless there is such a programme, the public who are intensely irritated about political correctness, are unlikely to believe anything will materially change, other than the most obvious examples of government silliness. There needs to be a commonsense strategy that deals with the central issue; what to do about those state institutions that foster the ideas of political correctness.
>
> Political correctness is grounded in the capture of state institutions, with official spokespeople, legislative powers and ultimately sanctions for breach. Without these features, the attitudes and beliefs of the politically correct would be just another viewpoint in society, able to be debated and discussed in the same manner as any other set of ideas. Political correctness requires capture of state institutions by a minority so that the public institutions that deal with discrimination have now been taken over by people who are outside mainstream values. Removing the power of the politically correct means removing their institutional and legislative base.'

Political correctness is not a conspiracy, although its conception by the Frankfurt School, in particular, and implementation is highly effective. There are not groups of the politically correct sitting around a table and conspiring to take over the country, although undoubtedly, as is the nature of politics, such groups do exist. More dangerously, it is a belief system. It is an outlook that has become the basis, if not definition, of morality. This false morality is enforced upon society because the politically correct have successfully taken over state institutions and also civil society (as per Gramsci). They have further re-routed public monies towards themselves and their own pet projects. This is where the politically correct have triumphed. They have *not* triumphed in the battle of ideas. There has been no such battle. The politically correct have captured state institutions and used the power thus gained and the monies thus hijacked to impose their views on society irrespective of what anyone else thinks and believes. Dissenters are simply shouted down, risk losing their jobs, and may even face criminal prosecution.

A good example, in Britain, of the consequences of the capture of a public sector organization by the politically correct, a problem identified by Dr Mapp, is the National Lottery Community Fund. This fund was so loony in its handouts of grants that the body had to be abolished and replaced with another, The Big Lottery Fund, which has been more discreet in its political correctness. Even so, it hit the ground running. To take just a few examples from the first few months of 2005, shortly after its creation:

- A mountain rescue team was refused a grant as it did not rescue enough asylum seekers, elderly, disabled, or ethnic minorities. The volunteers had applied for a £200,000 grant to build an emergency response base, but they were told that they did not meet 'the needs of those at greatest disadvantage in society'. They were then told who constituted the disadvantaged in modern Britain. The grant was refused by a regional committee of the outgoing Community Fund, which stated that the application did not fulfil the criteria for he large grants programme, which was meeting the needs of those at most disadvantage. This decision was upheld by the Big Lottery.
- The residents of the villages of Sandiway and Cuddingham in Cheshire were refused funding assistance to help build a new village hall by the Big Lottery Fund on the basis that the village hall would not benefit enough asylum seekers and ethnic minorities.
- The Big Lottery Fund distributed £714,686 to two asylum seeker organisations. This was one third of the money distributed in the latest round of grants. Student Action for Refugees was awarded £428,498, while a Children's Society scheme was given £286,188. Student Action for Refugees

encouraged students to write to MPs and newspapers in a campaign to influence public opinion.

- In January and February 2005, the Big Lottery Fund made the following handouts:
    1. £235,000 to fund lawyers for asylum seekers.
    2. £168,000 to the Kent Refugee Action Network, whose activists traveled to Calais to distribute supplies to asylum seekers who were trying to smuggle themselves into the UK. The grant was to 'provide a range of services to refugees to help them to integrate into a new way of life in the UK'.
    3. £60,000 for Befriending Refugees and Asylum Seekers to pay for 'drop in sessions for asylum seekers and refugees in Bolton'.
    4. £60,000 to the Shpresa Programme in East London to 'enable Albanian-speaking refugees, asylum seekers and migrants to settle fully and participate in society'.
- The Big Lottery Fund turned down a request for funding from the Samaritans, while at the same time handing out £360,000 to a pressure group for 'sex workers'. The Samaritans were criticised for not meeting the needs of 'target groups'. What the UK Network for Sex Work Projects promised to do to meet the needs of 'target groups' is unknown.

Another example of the consequences of the politically correct taking over an organization is the so-called Commission for Racial Equality (CRE), which itself was ultimately merged into the Equalities and Human Rights Commission. One former CRE commissioner, Raj Chandran, who had been one of three Tories on the commission (all of whom were purged under Labour) wrote in April 2001 (before 9/11 with the accompanying anti-British hostility from many Muslims in Britain, and before the London bombings):

'My message is that the CRE has grossly exceeded and distorted its mission, which was defined by the 1976 Race Relations Act as being to fight discrimination and to foster good race relations.

Instead, this generously funded and largely unaccountable body has fostered prejudice and self-pity. It devotes its energies to stigmatising the white majority population and stirring up resentment among Britain's black and Asian minorities. It attempts to perpetuate two myths: the first is that all racism, prejudice and discrimination is a matter of dominant whites mistreating downtrodden members of ethnic minorities.

The second is that the ethnic minorities are a single group bound together by their experience of prejudice and discrimination.

But this is simply not the case. Last week, parts of Bradford burned during riots which – to simplify greatly – were rooted in bitter conflicts not just between Asians and whites but also between Hindus and Muslims, and within the Muslim community. In Oldham, Asian youths were attempting to turn their rundown council estates into no-go ghettos from which whites would be excluded for fear of violence.'

Patriotism and a desire to do the best for ordinary people has been replaced with a hatred of the nation and the country and a willingness to sacrifice the interests and monies of ordinary people, who are dismissed as prejudiced and afflicted by false consciousness, in adherence to abstract theories such as human rights and constitutional patriotism with its commitment to international bureaucracies such as the EU. Whereas, in past centuries, a man might take pride in attending church, marrying and being a devoted husband, providing for his family and helping to bring up his children, and being a brave patriot, today things are very different. In addition, the same applies to women, especially in regard to their roles as being a wife and mother. Today, the constructive ethos of bygone ages has been replaced with the destructiveness of political correctness. Today, morality is based on hatred of country and a willingness to condemn one's fellow countrymen and society as being racist, sexist, homophobic, etc. The adverse economic consequences of politically correct high-mindedness can be far reaching, whether it be the calamity of the euro or the strains put on public services by mass immigration.

Without understating the pervasiveness of political correctness, and not being exhaustive, this book will highlight a dozen different ways that political correctness affects British society. First, whereas in previous centuries Britain and the Royal Navy were directly engaged in asserting the rule of law, abolishing the slave trade, and combating piracy, now they are more 'concerned' for the human rights of pirates and illegal immigrants. In 2008, European navies trying to control piracy off the coast of Somalia would neither arrest nor hand over pirates to the Somali government. The navy commanders did not believe that they

138

could successfully prosecute the pirates if they brought them back to Europe, and there was a real prospect that the pirates would then claim asylum, and they would not give them to the Somali authorities because the pirates might be executed. Nor were they allowed to simply sink the pirates.

The Americans did arrest and transfer Somali pirates to the USA to stand trial. Those convicted received life sentences; those acquitted or convicted of less serious offences were granted asylum.[582]

People smugglers, including IS and Al Qaeda, earn considerable wealth from their criminal operations, no matter the number of deaths they cause. This wealth is gained because illegal immigrants and those calling themselves asylum seekers are prepared to pay to be smuggled into the EU and Britain, in particular, from where they are almost certain not to be deported no matter how spurious their claim for asylum or no matter how heinous any crimes they might commit are. The judiciary and a whole host of lawyers and human rights groups are on hand to ensure that the flow of money to organized crime rackets and terrorists, which is what the people smugglers are, continues undisturbed. In 2015, the Royal Navy has even been engaged in the Mediterranean helping immigrants get safely to the EU. The days of Palmerston are long gone (see *The Ponzi Class,* page 38).

The activities of the judges and lawyers is anti-democratic, and they display scant regard for the interests and views of ordinary people. This is openly stated and is a long-standing viewpoint, as the judge Lord Bingham showed when he described the Human Rights Convention as 'intrinsically counter-majoritarian' and that decisions to uphold the rights of minorities 'should provoke howls of criticism by politicians and the mass media. They generally reflect majority opinion.'[583] Britain has become a lawyers' dictatorship.

In a speech in Melbourne, Australia, Lord Neuberger, the President of the Supreme Court and Britain's most senior judge, said that the Human Rights Act allowed judges to 'interpret statutes in a way which some may say amounts not so much to construction as to demolition and reconstruction. We can give provisions meanings which they could not possibly bear if the normal rules of statutory interpretation applied. Parliament has written us judges something of a blank cheque in this connection ... this new judicial power of quasi-interpretation can be said to involve a subtle but significant adjustment to the balance of power between the legislature and the judiciary ... The [British] approach can be seen as effectively conferring a law-making function on the judiciary.'

Neuberger, in June 2015 in a speech to commemorate the Magna Carta, said: 'The need to offer oneself for re-election sometimes makes it hard to make unpopular, but correct decisions. At times it can be an advantage to have an independent body of people who do not have to worry about short term popularity.' In reference to 'judicial aggrandisement', Neuberger highlighted that the EU law and the Human Rights Act had given the judges a 'quasi-constitutional function'.

Britain's judges have embraced their own interpretation of their newfangled human rights role with eagerness. In reference to his decision to allow a Bangladeshi murderer to move to England, overturning a Home Office decision, Judge Peter King proclaimed: 'There seems to be an expectation that the public interest trumps everything else. It seems to me that is not necessarily the case.' The Bangladeshi was further granted anonymity to protect his identity and his criminal record.

An illegal immigrant from Sri Lanka who had committed 35 criminal offences in Britain while fighting deportation, in November 2014 was awarded £600 compensation after being supposedly unlawfully detained for eight weeks in 2008. He had cost £1million in legal costs in a 22-year fight to remain in Britain.

In 2015, the High Court judge Justice Nicol, ruled as unlawful the government's fast track system to decide those asylum claims deemed to be totally without merit. The Detained Fast Track process had been introduced in 2003 by the Labour government. The judge objected to 'serious procedural disadvantage' to the asylum seekers and their lawyers, who had limited time to prepare their cases. A significant number of claims for compensation were expected following the judgement. The government suspended the scheme and released all the detained asylum seekers.

In July 2014, High Court Judges ruled that to limit entitlement to legal aid to those living in Britain was 'unlawful and discriminatory' and the justification for such was 'little more than reliance on public prejudice'. The ruling rendered illegal proposed government reforms to the legal aid system, such as that to restrict legal aid to those who had lived in Britain for at least one year. The reforms were dismissed as a 'joke' by Lord Justice Moses. (see *The Ponzi Class*, page 324.)

In July 2015, an Afghan Taliban gunman, Serder Mohammed, who was suspected of large-scale involvement in the planting of roadside bombs which had killed British troops, was found by the High Court to have been unlawfully detained. He had been held beyond a 96-hour limit – he was held for 106 days. He was convicted and sentenced to 10 years in prison by the Afghan authorities but released early in unknown circumstances. He lived in Helmand province. He sued Britain, citing Human Rights legislation. It was expected that he could receive up to £1million in damages.

In October 2015, it was announced that the police would investigate claims of more than 100 Afghans, including Taliban, who claimed that they had been mistreated by British troops. The investigation, Operation Northmoor, involved the Royal Military Police, Greater Manchester Police, and the National Crime Agency. The investigation was launched after allegations were presented to the police by the Public Interest Lawyers firm, who are believed to have Pashtun-speaking workers approaching local Afghans and asking them if they consider themselves to have been mistreated and inviting locals to report allegations of mistreatment to them. This is similar to the experience in Iraq, where a 145 strong team from the Iraq Historical Allegations Team toured the country trying to find allegations of mistreatment over a five-year period; no criminal convictions have resulted. Since 2003, £100million has been spent by the Ministry of Defence on investigations and compensation relating to Iraq. Another £150million has been spent defending British soldiers from the allegations. A source told the *Daily Mail*: 'If it is anything like Iraq, in a few years there will be thousands of claims coming through. One of the cases includes a detainee who is complaining because he didn't like the food.'

In January 2016, it was revealed that one British sniper, who had served in Iraq, was under investigation because he shot an insurgent who was about to fire a grenade. Apparently, the sniper should have shouted a warning first! It was further revealed that one soldier was threatened with arrest if he did not answer questions on his doorstep at home, when challenged by two ex-police officers about an incident in Iraq that had occurred 10 years ago.

Judges are not alone in their attempt to hijack the governance of Britain. For example, in July 2014, a group of UN poverty ambassadors sent a 22-page letter to Britain's ambassador to the UN, complaining that, 'According to concerned sources, the package of austerity measures enacted [by the British government] could amount to retrogressive measures prohibited under the International Covenant on Economic, Social and Cultural Rights, ratified in 1974.'

In April 2014, Rashida Manjoo, a South African and a UN special rapporteur on violence against women, condemned Britain as being sexist, saying: 'What is clear from these indications of portrayals of women and girls is that there is a boys' club sexist culture that exists and it does lead to perceptions about women and girls in this country. I haven't seen that so pervasively in other countries. I'm sure it exists but it wasn't so much and so pervasive.' Manjoo cited alleged harassment on the Tube and cuts to benefits and demanded that there be compulsory lessons for schoolgirls on 'bullying, harassment and sexual violence'.

In July 2015 in a report to the UN, Britain's four Children's Commissioners (for England, Scotland, Wales, and Northern Ireland) claimed that Tory economic policy and benefit reforms were pushing millions of families into poverty. They claimed that 3.7million children (27% of the total) were in poverty. The commissioners also complained about zero-hours contracts, food banks, and possible changes to the Human Rights Act.

These attempts to hijack the governance of Britain are entirely consistent with constitutional patriotism. As per Gramsci's plan to seize control of civil society, it was disclosed in August 2014 that 11 of Gordon Brown's 25 special advisers took posts in charities. Brown changed the law to allow charities to join political campaigns, and the Tories accused them of opposing government policies. The charities included NSPCC and Citizens Advice.

There is an ongoing campaign to render democratically elected government subordinate to judges and a host of international and supranational institutions and to force democratically elected government to adhere to political correctness and abstract theories, rather than to represent ordinary electors. The pity is that the elected politicians have been so keen to aid and abet this process.

Second, another example of the harm done by abstract theories about human rights is the penchant for human rights wars. It has been estimated that the cost of the most recent wars, primarily Iraq and Afghanistan, was between $3trillion and $4trillion. The cost to Britain of the war in Afghanistan was around £40billion and 453 soldiers killed. Over 250,000 people have died in such wars over the last 15 years. This is, as Robert Cooper, an adviser to Tony Blair urged for, 'a new kind of imperialism, one acceptable to a world of human rights and cosmopolitan values ... which like all imperialism aims to bring order and organization but which rests today on the voluntary principle'.[584] Despite the penchant for human rights wars, the human rights theories and the legal profession's opportunism crippled the ability to fight such wars or defend the country. This was demonstrated by the lawyers, with judicial permission, bringing claims against Britain and its troops for alleged human rights breaches.

Wars have not necessarily been fought in defence of the national interest but have been increasingly motivated by a determination to impose human rights theories on imperfect countries. Prime examples are, in general, those countries affected by the so-called Arab Spring and, in particular, Syria. While it might be welcome to see people who have been oppressed by a tyrant gain their liberty, that liberty cannot exist without law and order.

David Cameron and the Tories might have been keen to intervene in Libya to topple Gaddaffi, an understandable aim, but were not prepared to intervene either to prevent Libya from becoming a failed state nor to prevent various gangs of people smugglers, including IS, from sending thousands of immigrants across the Mediterranean. They were not prepared to defend the national interest.

A commitment to military action in the name of human rights very nearly embroiled Britain in the Syrian civil war in 2013 and was only thwarted by a defeat in a vote in Parliament. This defeat likewise influenced the USA to keep out. The Syrian President, Assad, allegedly used chemical weapons against rebels. Cameron wanted to attack Syria with some cruise missiles in response, presumably in the belief that blowing up some Syrians would assuage Assad's lack of human rights credentials. It certainly would not have had much effect on the civil war, and eventually, after pressure and the threat of military reprisals, Assad agreed to destroy his chemical weapons arsenal. Subsequently, IS has been reportedly using chemical weapons.

The Tory policy on Syria was firmly that of the constitutional patriot. Abstract theories determined policy. There was no realpolitik but a willingness to escalate the conflict in the name of human rights. Assad, understandably, looked at the outcome of the Arab Spring in nearby countries, with the bloodshed and killing of the former dictators, and was faced with the barbarity of IS against whom he was defending. It should come as no surprise that he was prepared to fight to the last with every weapon to hand when defeat would probably spell the murder of himself, his family, friends, and supporters and would plunge Syria into barbarism in the event of an IS victory. Winston Churchill was prepared to use chemical weapons to destroy the German troops on the beaches if needs be, rather than allow the Nazis to conquer Britain. Assad was surely faced with at least an equally bad situation.

But this was not the perspective of the high-minded British government, the maxim of a dictator being 'our son-of-a-bitch'. (In 1939 President Franklin Roosevelt is alleged to have said: 'Somoza may be a son of a bitch, but he's our son of a bitch.'). The Tories backed the puny moderate Syrian rebels, some of whom had defected to IS with the weapons they had been supplied with and about whom the Pentagon had to reveal a truly embarrassing fact. The Tory/Liberal Democrat coalition Foreign Minister, William Hague, believed that by arming the moderate Syrian rebels the West could put Assad under military pressure and so force him to negotiate if not force him out. At the time, Assad was perceived to be winning. In the Spring of 2015, the USA had launched a $500million programme to train 5,400 Syrian fighters a year for the next three years. In September 2015, the general in charge admitted that the outcome thus far was that there were only three or four US trained rebels still in combat and only another 120 in training (this is not a typing error)! Even if these do not defect to IS, they are too few to overthrow Assad or to counter IS.

Nevertheless, so high-minded was Tory policy that both George Osborne and Cameron, in full knowledge of the failure of the USA training programme, announced that neither Assad nor IS were to their liking and demanded action to rid Syria of them all. So determined was Cameron to involve Britain in Syria that he convinced himself and the majority of the House of Commons that there was a 70,000 strong Free Syrian Army ready to take on IS and that, therefore, there was a ground force to supplement British air strikes. This was tripe, and these 'bogus battalions' were not much more than a rag-tag bunch of Islamist and local militias too busy fighting among themselves and fighting Assad to march against IS.

One puzzle that afflicts Britain alone is the defectiveness of the Tories. They style themselves as the Conservative and Unionist Party, but they have abandoned any pretence of being Conservative. Cameron's speech to the 2015 conference was a good example of this (see below). One might have thought that the Tories, Britain having lost its empire, would have retrenched to represent and defend British interests. Given that nearly all their support lies in England, they might be expected to defend English interests within Britain. But they do not. Despite specific commitments to introduce English Votes for English Laws, a poor substitute for an English Parliament, they have not honoured even those feeble commitments. Instead, they have merely fiddled about with the parliamentary standing orders. Despite Scottish and Welsh parliaments, MPs from those countries still vote on English affairs. The Tories are unable to represent English interests. They see nothing wrong with the English being denigrated in England and being victims of a politically correct witch-hunt.

Apart from the wet Liberal politics of the Tories, part of the reason lies in Britain's imperial past. Presiding over the empire and placating the natives has been absorbed into the psyche of the British ruling class. That class might have mislaid the empire, reduced the Royal Navy to a token force, squandered North Sea oil, and ruined the economy of the world's first industrial nation, but they remain firmly convinced that they should be big players on the world stage. Disavowing any loyalty to Britain, England in particular, and concentrating on getting their feet under the conference tables of a variety of international institutions, they are more than willing to sacrifice British interests in furtherance of their own worldly status. It should be noted that Cameron was keen to bomb Syria in 2013 in response to Assad's alleged use of chemical weapons and keen again in 2015 to bomb following the terrorist attacks in Paris. He did not, however, urge a military response to the murder of more than 30 British nationals in Tunisia. Somewhere along the way, Britain's imperial role damaged the Tories, rendered them unable to govern properly, and made them highly susceptible to political correctness.

Third, the outcome of this posturing was that the civil war rumbled on, the casualties escalated, IS continued to advance, and Assad struggled to cling on. Meanwhile, in response to the UN withdrawing help for refugees in nearby camps (even turning refugees away), and in response to the German Chancellor Angela Merkel's offer to accept any Syrian who reached Germany, a flood of immigrants, only a minority of whom were actually Syrians, poured across Europe, lining the pockets of people smugglers along the way.

The EU immigration crisis of the summer of 2015 needs to be viewed against the backdrop of political correctness. It should be noted that the EU bureaucracy has been found wanting in recent years. Since the treaty changes leading to a reorganization of the EU relating to the President and the High Representative of the Union for Foreign Affairs and Security Policy, bureaucrats now make political decisions, and the nation states are even more subservient to a supranational organization. One outcome has been that the EU launched into three very serious blunders: it meddled in the Ukraine, where a coup was closely followed by a civil war and the annexation of the Crimea by Russia; it ploughed on with its new single currency, the one size fits all euro, laying waste the southern EU countries in the process; and it bungled the response to the 2015 immigrant invasion – which is what it is.

The EU bureaucrats' initial act as the numbers surged of immigrants setting sail for Europe from what was formerly Libya, a failed state, was to agree with UN bureaucrats that those found in the Mediterranean in their barely seaworthy vessels would be brought to Europe rather than be sent back to Africa. Seeing that the Royal Navy (as well as other navies) was now engaged in people smuggling, needless to say, the numbers getting out into the Mediterranean multiplied. Meanwhile, the flow across land to Greece also increased.

The EU's reaction needs to be contrasted with that of Australia, which has experienced similar problems. The former Australian prime minister, Tony Abbott, made a speech at the Second Annual Margaret Thatcher Lecture in London in October 2015, and he explained Australia's policy towards people smuggling and illegal immigration. He pointed out that 'stopping the flow of illegal immigrant boats' was important 'because a country that can't control its borders starts to lose control of itself'. He said that there was a need to manage 'the nation-changing, culture-shifting population transfers now impacting on Europe' and to win 'the fight in Syria and Iraq ... and [assert] Western civilisation against the challenge of militant Islam'. Tony Abbott continued (italics my own):

'Naturally, the safety and prosperity that exists almost uniquely in Western countries is an irresistible magnet. These blessings are not the accidents of history but the product of values painstakingly discerned and refined, and of practices carefully cultivated and reinforced over hundreds of years.

Implicitly or explicitly, the imperative to "love your neighbour as you love yourself" is at the heart of every Western polity. It expresses itself in laws protecting workers, in strong social security safety nets, and in the readiness to take in refugees. It's what makes us decent and humane countries as well as prosperous ones, but – right now – this wholesome instinct is leading much of Europe into catastrophic error. *All countries that say "anyone who gets here can stay here" are now in peril, given the scale of the population movements that are starting to be seen.* There are tens – perhaps hundreds – of millions of people, living in poverty and danger who might readily seek to enter a Western country if the opportunity is there.

Who could blame them? Yet no country or continent can open its borders to all comers without fundamentally weakening itself. This is the risk that the countries of Europe now run through misguided altruism.

On a somewhat smaller scale, Australia has faced the same predicament and overcome it. The first wave of illegal arrivals to Australia peaked at 4,000 people a year, back in 2001, before the Howard government first stopped the boats: by processing illegal arrivals offshore; by denying them permanent residency; and in a handful of cases, by turning illegal immigrant boats back to Indonesia. The second wave of illegal boat people was running at the rate of 50,000 a year – and rising fast – by July 2013, when the Rudd government belatedly reversed its opposition to offshore processing; and then my government started turning boats around, even using orange lifeboats when people smugglers deliberately scuttled their vessels.

It's now 18 months since a single illegal boat has made it to Australia. The immigration detention centres have-all-but-closed; budget costs peaking at $4billion a year have ended; and – best of all – there are no more deaths at sea. That's why stopping the boats and restoring border security is the only truly compassionate thing to do...

146

In Europe, as with Australia, people claiming asylum – invariably – have crossed not one border but many; and are no longer fleeing in fear but are contracting in hope with people smugglers. However desperate, almost by definition, they are economic migrants because they had already escaped persecution when they decided to move again.

Our moral obligation is to receive people fleeing for their lives. *It's not to provide permanent residency to anyone and everyone who would rather live in a prosperous Western country than their own*. That's why the countries of Europe, while absolutely obliged to support the countries neighbouring the Syrian conflict, are more-than-entitled to control their borders against those who are no longer fleeing a conflict but seeking a better life.

This means turning boats around, for people coming by sea. It means denying entry at the border, for people with no legal right to come; and it means establishing camps for people who currently have nowhere to go. It will require some force; it will require massive logistics and expense; it will gnaw at our conscience – yet it is the only way to prevent a tide of humanity surging through Europe and quite possibly changing it forever.

We are rediscovering the hard way that justice tempered by mercy is an exacting ideal as too much mercy for some necessarily undermines justice for all. The Australian experience proves that the only way to dissuade people seeking to come from afar is not to let them in. Working with other countries and with international agencies is important but the only way to stop people trying to gain entry is firmly and unambiguously to deny it – out of the moral duty to protect one's own people and to stamp out people smuggling.

So it's good that Europe has now deployed naval vessels to intercept people smuggling boats in the Mediterranean – *but as long as they're taking passengers aboard rather than turning boats around and sending them back, it's a facilitator rather than a deterrent*.'

The point is that the existence of European societies is now under threat. Australia has confronted the issue and dealt with it firmly and effectively. Europe is still wallowing in its own political correctness and snobbery. Of course, to use immigrants to overthrow Western society is precisely what the doctrinaire politically correct, the communists, want. But Tony Abbott has explained the need to take on the people smugglers

147

and the benefits of doing so. The immigrant tide is unnecessary and can be stopped – but only if there is the will.

Regarding Syria, Tony Abbott made the important point that it was 'a fight between bad and worse'. The Assad regime might be brutal, but it is preferable to the alternative of 'a caliphate seeking to export its apocalyptic version of Islam right around the world', and that 'everywhere [IS] gains a foothold' there are 'beheadings', 'crucifixions', 'mass executions', 'hurling off high buildings', 'sexual slavery' and 'its perverse allure across the globe'.

The deal between EU and UN bureaucrats that all immigrants found at sea should immediately be brought to Europe was the precise opposite of what was needed. For the Tories to be using the Royal Navy to help people smugglers get immigrants, including IS terrorists, into Europe, and hence into Britain, was positively harmful. Contrary to the Palmerston approach in dealing with pirates in the 19th century, the Tories acted as a 'facilitator' to people smuggling. The EU, yet again, blundered about, leaving a trail of chaos.

'We can do it,' insisted Merkel, saying that Germany was prepared to accept as many as 800,000 immigrants. Germany has a falling population, and there have been concerns as to the economic consequences of this. The lure of Merkel's promises and the fact that UN funding for the refugee camps in Turkey, Lebanon, and Jordan was running out combined to turn a flow into a flood. When that flood of immigrants proved too much, with columns of immigrants trekking through Eastern European countries to reach Germany, Merkel reinstated border controls and demanded that the rest of Europe agree to take more immigrants. As with German reunification and the ERM, Germany acted in its own selfish interests irrespective of the impact on the rest of the EU.

Meanwhile, Hungary fell foul of the EU when it insisted on processing the immigrants properly and then erected border fences with razor wire to stem the flow. Britain refused to join a quota system to distribute the immigrants already in the EU but then announced it would take 20,000 from camps near Syria, despite being warned by the Lebanese minister Elias Bousaab that two in every 100 Syrian immigrants were IS terrorists.

Given the storming of the Channel Tunnel by up to 2,000 immigrants and nightly incursions (with an estimated 70% of Calais immigrants getting into Britain) had finally forced authorities to clamp down on the Calais people smuggling, attention turned to Dunkirk, where the flow of immigrants waiting to be smuggled into Britain proved so numerous that it was reported by one charity worker that even the people smugglers could no longer cope. Once again, the authorities finally reacted, and three British people smugglers were arrested, along with the seizure of

148

three cars, following the use of Kalashnikovs. Also arrested were Vietnamese members of the gang.

In Britain, the Tories had been very busy bragging of their largesse with foreign aid and that they were now giving away 0.7% of national income. (It should be noted that Cameron was so keen on it that he refused Nick Clegg's offer on behalf of the Liberal Democrats in 2012 to delay the introduction of the target.) They had managed to find something to spend the money on, including a variety of politically correct schemes relating to climate change awareness and Wimmin's issues in Africa. This was at a time when the UN was turning Syrian refugees away due to a lack of funds.

Fourth, the media's response to the immigrant invasion was to portray all immigrants, no matter where they were from, as refugees fleeing war and poverty and seeking a new life and that they all deserved sympathy and the right to barge into Europe. Cameron was attacked for using the term 'swarm' in reference to the numbers of immigrants. The Tory reluctance to take quotas of immigrants was met with continuous attack. The media simply assumed that anyone who claimed to be a refugee should be allowed to settle in Europe, and there was barely any analysis as to the best way to help genuine refugees. Those responsible for the news output were not simply news reporters; as per Habermas, they were the 'cultural elite' managing the views of ordinary plebs, the majority of whom were against accepting any more immigrants. As per Marcuse, right-wing or patriotic viewpoints were not tolerated.

A variety of EU and UN officials popped up repeatedly on television to denounce Britain's refusal to agree to take more immigrants and refusal to become a part of an EU quota system. The 'cultural elite' did not see fit to query the UN officials as to their responsibility and their failure to deal with the immigrants.

It is not the case that the left-wing media bias is purely subconscious. In fact, there is a deliberate policy to exclude right-wing views. There is a ruling class monopoly on the definition of morality. This is a phoney definition. It is all very well for the politically correct to pose for photo opportunities, knee deep in the sea, clutching immigrant children just getting off a boat, before jetting back to Britain to demand that Britain take more immigrants, but this does not help genuine refugees. A genuinely compassionate report would explore why the UN was apparently so short of funds that it was turning away refugees and explore the wisdom of why Britain was spending money on Wimmin's issues in Africa from its bloated foreign aid budget while the UN was allegedly so underfunded.

One can compare the morality of these journalists and others, who pose as champions of compassion for those in the Third World from a variety of television studios where they demand that 'we', i.e. the taxpayer, should do more, with 19th century missionaries. Those missionaries, many of them young women, including nuns, ventured into the barely explored Third World to help the native population. They put their own lives at risk and made considerable personal sacrifices. The politically correct sacrifice nothing themselves, are extravagant in their largesse with other people's money and interests, and seek to use the plight of the refugees and immigrants for their own political ends.

The public reaction to the crisis was divided. Some were enthusiastic about accepting more immigrants. However, public opinion was overwhelmingly out of step with the ruling class: 45% considered the figure of 20,000 Syrian immigrants to be too high; 27% supported the decision to allow in 20,000; only 15% wanted more than 20,000. This anti-immigration view was not reflected in the news output of the media, 'the cultural elite'. In fact, Eurostat figures showed that, of the 213,000 immigrants logged as arriving in the EU, only 44,000 were from Syria.

The media were not alone in condemning the Tories, as 84 Church of England bishops signed an open letter to Cameron demanding that he let in at least 50,000 Syrian immigrants. This followed another letter by numerous judges and 300 lawyers a week earlier likewise demanding that the number of Syrian immigrants be increased.

One of the bishops, the Right Reverend David Walker, the Bishop of Manchester, remarked that it would be 'a sad reflection' on society if ordinary people did not welcome more Syrians. Although the Archbishop of Canterbury offered a cottage and the Manchester diocese offered an empty vicarage, the bishop balked at welcoming refugees into his own house, which has six bedrooms and is owned by the church. The bishop explained: 'Refugees need ... a place where they can be with their families, not try to share the breakfast table with a couple whose language they don't understand and whose culture is alien to them.'

In October 2015, a leaked Home Office document put the cost of allowing in Syrian refugees at more than £24,000 per immigrant per year (£8,520 cost to the local councils, £12,700 in benefits and £2,200 for medical expenses). This figure is an underestimate as it does not take into account the impact on ordinary English families, such as on the cost of lower wages or the inability to get social housing. It also doesn't take into account other factors, such as was evidenced by a doctors' report which revealed that 1 in 20 so-called asylum seekers are HIV positive, the infection being particularly bad for those from Zimbabwe, the Democratic Republic of Congo, and Somalia, but also for the obvious inevitable costs of the spread of the infection into the UK population as a whole. Accepting the £24,000 figure, the total figure for 20,000 immigrants is therefore around £480million per year. This should be compared to the poorest in the LDCs who survive on around a dollar a day – around £240 per year. That £24,000 would provide for 100 of the poorest people in the LDCs for a year; the £480million would provide for almost two million people in their own countries.

Also, by comparison, following a tsunami in December 2004, an appeal was made for funds, and it was set out that £5 will provide 100 litres of purified water to a refugee family, £12 will vaccinate a child for life against six killer diseases, £15 will buy a hot meal for 125 people in an emergency feeding centre, £25 buys plastic shelter and food parcels for two families for two weeks, £30 buys enough water purification tablets to give 320 children a litre each, £59 buys tarpaulin shelters for 10 families, £100 buys a tent for one refugee family, or food parcels to feed 60 families for one month, and £250 provides emergency food and shelter for 100 people.

If these bishops, lawyers, and others were sincere in their loudly proclaimed determination to help refugees, then they would be rushing through laws to prevent the people smuggling activities as fast as possible – not aiding and abetting those activities. Any objective analysis clearly shows that shipping people to overcrowded Western countries is the worst possible way to help the poor. What the bishops and lawyers are trying to do, along with a whole host of others, is to show off. They wish to parade their moral superiority (in other words, the motive is snobbery), and, for the communists, to foment a race war in Britain.

Subsequently, in response to IS terrorist attacks in Paris and an IS attack in the USA itself, Donald Trump, who was campaigning to become the Republican presidential candidate, dared to voice the opinion that Muslims should not be allowed to enter the USA until there was a proper grip on the threat of terrorism. This stance instantly provoked howls of outrage from the politically correct from across the West. In Britain, calls were made for Trump to be banned from entry. A petition was set up calling for Trump to be banned from Britain, which attracted 431,000 supporters within days. News reports made much of this petition. However, the media totally ignored another petition which had more supporters which called for all immigration to be stopped until IS was defeated. Once again, the media was manipulating news reporting to peddle their own politically correct propaganda.

In the USA, the attacks on Trump's idea were more rabid. He was accused of being 'un-American'. Even senior Republican Party members weighed in. House speaker Paul Ryan condemned Trump's idea as a violation of the constitution and that it was 'not who we are as a party'. He went on to say: 'This is not conservatism. Some of our best and biggest allies in this struggle and fight against radical Islam terror are

Muslims.' Mitt Romney, the 2012 Republican nominee for president, supported Ryan, his former running mate, and accused Trump of having 'fired before aiming'. Party chairman Preibus said of Trump's idea: 'I don't agree. We need to aggressively take on radical Islamic terrorism but not at the expense of our American values.'

Trump was defiant. Speaking aboard the USS Yorktown, he readily ceded that his proposal was 'probably not politically correct', before announcing, 'But I don't care', to a cheering crowd. He continued: 'We need a total and complete shutdown of Muslims entering the United States while we figure out what the hell is going on. We are out of control.' Hillary Clinton issued an 850-word statement which denounced Trump's idea as 'shameful' and 'dangerous'.

Fifth, while the EU bickered over a proposal to impose a quota system to distribute 120,000 immigrants across the EU, UNICEF's director for the Middle East and North Africa, Peter Salama, said: 'There could be millions and millions more refugees leaving Syria and ultimately (going) to the European Union and beyond.' There are an estimated 8million displaced people in Syria with another 4million refugees in neighbouring countries.

The European Commission President, Jean-Claude Junker, in a state of the union speech announced: 'We are an ageing continent in demographic decline. Migration must change from being a problem to being a well-managed resource. Migration has to be legalised. We have to organize legal ways to Europe. The Commission will come forward with a well-designed legal migration package in early 2016.' No matter the crisis or the hostility of ordinary people, especially in Eastern Europe, to the immigration tidal wave, the unelected and unaccountable bureaucrats of the EU were as defiant as they were determined to increase the scale of the immigration. One EU commissioner, Dimitris Avramopoulos, even went so far as to state: 'The commission is here for five years to do its job and we did it with vision, responsibility and commitment. Because what is driving us is not to be re-elected. That is why for us the political cost means nothing.' This was civic nationalism/constitutional patriotism in practice. Even the subsequent IS terrorist attacks and the number killed did not affect the determination to continue the policy of mass immigration.

Sixth, with immigration running in excess of 500,000 per annum in Britain (net immigration had reached 330,000 by the summer of 2015), the strain on public services was as inevitable as it was predictable (see *The Ponzi Class*, page 306). The country into which they were coming was one where, as set out by both Habermas and Marcuse, they must be encouraged not to assimilate and where a hatred of the English should be encouraged. English history was deemed bad, along with the

British Empire. The 'noble savage' is a victim of colonialism. Immigrants are victims of English racism. Even the Irish are. Multiculturalism is the ideology used to justify what is in effect colonisation. Despite all the grandstanding about human rights, arranged marriages, many if not most of them forced marriages, are tolerated as a means of further immigration, as is child abuse of English children by Asian paedophile gangs (the authorities' policy was to cover it up until public pressure finally exposed the practice – see below). The result is discord and rising extremism among the Muslim community in particular.

The impact of mass immigration, a policy never supported by the majority of the English, on the host English nation is devastating. In addition to the economic consequences there is the certainty that, unless the process is halted, the English will become a minority in England. The English nation will cease to exist and so will the culture of that nation. The politically correct will succeed in their aims. This repopulation policy is fully endorsed by the Tories, who, in the run up to the general election of 2015, announced that they would be seeking a quota of 20% for ethnic minorities on the boards of British companies. Cameron made what he considered to be a noble pledge during the election campaign that he would be setting a series of race quotas for the police, the armed forces, apprenticeships, university students, and jobs, the aim being to impose a quota of 20% for ethnic minorities – despite the fact that they comprise roughly 14% of the total population according to the 2011 census. The Liberal Democrat Vince Cable announced the same target of 20% for company boardroom directors for ethnic minorities in November 2014. The target was adopted in consultation with Trevor Philips and Lenny Henry and was supported by the Institute of Directors. A genuine Conservative would be firmly opposed to such a policy.

Seventh, opposition to both the repopulation policy and political correctness is crushed. Free speech is restricted in Britain – unlike in the USA, where it is vigorously defended. In Britain, what is the British Inquisition even targets children for signs of political incorrectness.

Despite Cameron's promises that those who believed that marriage was between a man and a woman would not be persecuted, that in fact was exactly what happened. For example, a small bakery in Northern Ireland, Ashers, which was open about the devout Christian beliefs of its owners was prosecuted by the so-called Equalities Commission, Northern Ireland. This followed a complaint from a Queerspace activist who had demanded that the bakery make him a cake with the slogan 'Support Gay Marriage'.

A former Church of Scotland minister was sacked as a volunteer chaplain to Strathclyde Police for pointing out on a blog that Cameron had not had an electoral mandate for changing 'God-ordained institution of marriage as between a man and a woman'.

Trafford Housing Trust cut an employee's salary by 40% and issued him with a written warning after he posted on Facebook that gay weddings in churches were an equality too far. A Red Cross volunteer was also sacked when staff saw a photograph of him in a local newspaper and gay press of him holding up a placard which said 'No to Gay Marriage'.

In August 2014, a sociology academic even denounced Gardners' Question Time as racist for using terms such as 'non-native' in reference to plants, saying the radio programme was 'saturated' with racist language.

Worst of all is the manner in which the politically correct targeted children. In 2008-09, there were allegedly 10,436 racist incidents in primary schools in England and Wales, another 19,223 in secondary schools, and 41 in nursery schools. The majority of incidents involved name-calling. In 51 cases, the police became involved. Under the Race Relations (Amendment) Act 2000, teachers were required to name the alleged perpetrator of such incidents, name the alleged victim, and set out the alleged incident and punishment in reports to the Local Educational Authorities. Heads who sent in 'nil' returns were condemned for 'under-reporting'.

The persecution, which is what it is, of even English schoolchildren continued under the Tory/Liberal Democrat coalition and showed the extent of the hatred of English society by the politically correct. Using terms such as 'Chinese boy', 'Somalian', 'gay' or even 'girl' can be sufficient for a child, even a nursery child, to be branded as racist, homophobic, and prejudiced. Ofsted became the government's engine for the persecution.

In June 2014, a small rural primary school in Devon was criticized for being insufficiently 'multicultural'. The school then organized sleepovers for pupils, at parents' expense, with a London school with a high number of non-English children. Another village primary school in Cumbria, with only 13 pupils, was put into special measures by Ofsted, which accused the school of having too many incidents of racist and homophobic bullying, stemming from one incident of children using the term 'gay' in a politically incorrect way. The school is all white. In November 2014, one high-performing primary school was condemned for lacking 'first-hand experience of the diverse make-up of modern British society' by Ofsted, which consequently downgraded the school's performance. A Christian school in Reading was threatened with closure for not inviting imams and other religious leaders to take assemblies. Another school in Market Rasen was criticized because 'The large majority of pupils are White British. Very few are from other ethnic groups, and currently no pupils speak English as an additional language'; the school was told to 'extend pupils' understanding of the cultural diversity of modern British society by creating opportunities for them to have first-hand interaction with their counterparts from different backgrounds'. In January 2015, two schools fell foul of Ofsted. One was put into special measures because a 10-year-old did not give a politically correct answer to a question as to what lesbians 'did'; the other school was told it would be closed because one child gave a politically incorrect answer to a question as to what a Muslim was. An 11-year-old girl was asked if she was a virgin.

The persecution of schoolchildren was not confined to issues of race. The Tory Education Secretary, Nicky Morgan, gave her very full backing to Ofsted in its campaign. One 10-year-old schoolgirl was upset to be held responsible for her school being placed into special measures because she gave a politically incorrect answer to the question 'What is a lesbian?' The girl had replied that she did not want to talk about it. In another example, an 11-year-old girl was asked if she had any gay friends and even whether she had ever felt she was in the wrong body! The questions were aggressive and intimidatory. Nicky Morgan unveiled a £2million programme to tackle alleged homophobic bullying in schools, targeting even the youngest children. Recommendations included encouraging teachers to refer to gay people more in class.

Incredibly, even during the 2015 election campaign, it was revealed that one primary school, with children as young as three years old, required pupils to sign a contract that they must 'Be tolerant of others whatever their race, colour, gender, class, ability, physical challenge, faith, sexual orientation or lifestyle and refrain from using racist or homophobic or transphobic language in school.'

In guidelines from the government in October 2015, children are encouraged to spy on and report fellow children for using supposedly racist or sexist language. For example, the use of the term 'Man Up' is deemed sexist.

It is not the case that ethnic minorities do badly at school due to racism. The victims are poor English children. The extent to which those termed White British children were underperforming in schools was highlighted in a report by the Commons Education Select Committee, which showed that the percentage of poor children (those receiving free school meals) achieving A to C grades in five GCSEs was for girls and boys respectively: White British 37% and 28%; Black Caribbean 48% and 37%; Pakistani 51% and 43%; Black African 56% and 47%; Bangladeshi 63% and 56%; Indian 67% and 57%; and Chinese 80% and 74%. The Committee urged schools to stay open for longer to ensure that children completed their homework.

Research by Lambeth Council and the University of London, in their report 'Raising the Achievement of White Working Class Pupils', reported that white working class children did poorly in school because the curriculums do not 'reflect the culture and lives of white working class children'. The research showed that white working class children were alienated by multiculturalism and were being marginalized and losing their identity. The report recommended that schools should 'give confidence for White British pupils to proudly assert their identity as an ethnic group'.

The politically correct paedophilia was justified as being the promotion of British values. That is bunk. The whole concept of British values will fail because the politically correct are, as they were bound to do, interpreting those values as being political correctness. What has held Britain together is not shared British values, but a sense of national unity, a shared history, and a common British *culture*. With that in mind, the government's disdain for the celebration of the Battle of Waterloo, for example, was divisive and damaging to any *genuine* attempt to promote national unity. Children should be encouraged to take pride in our national victories.

The idea that children should be prevented from accepting the values of their family stems unashamedly from *The Authoritarian Personality*. The determination to bring up children in institutions with mothers forced out to work is pure political correctness. Mothers are perfectly capable of deciding for themselves how to run their lives without the Tories taxing them and then offering them their own money back if they put their children into child care and go out to work. A genuine Conservative would have no truck with such a policy.

Not only is government commitment to political correctness destabilizing the family, it is also, as intended, destabilizing the country. Patriotism pulls people together in a common cause. The pride in national history and culture is important. The attempt to impose civic nationalism/constitutional patriotism onto the country is, as it is intended to, steadily weakening national unity. The evidence can be seen not only in the increased civil strife, but also in the increasing prospect of Britain breaking apart into its constituent countries.

Eighth, while children were bullied and targeted by the politically correct, the scale of immigration into Britain combined with multiculturalism to create what become known as the Trojan Horse plot for school takeovers.

A booklet produced by the Muslim Council of Britain in February 2007 called 'Meeting the Needs of Muslim Pupils in State Schools', supposedly to 'promote greater understanding of the faith, religious and cultural needs' (according to the Foreword) of Muslim children, amounted to a blueprint for the Islamicization of Britain's schools. Demanding changes to the way biology, music, art, sports, and religious education were taught, it even went so far as to call for a ban on 'unIslamic' activities for Muslim children, such as dancing. It further called for the banning of swimming during Ramadan and said that 'girlfriend/boyfriend as well as homosexual relationships' were 'not acceptable practices according to Islamic teachings'. It demanded single sex prayer rooms in schools. It advocated that school balls, discos, and fashion shows should be avoided to not 'inadvertently exclude' Muslims. Raffles were also to be banned. Halal food was to be made available. Sex education, advice about contraception, and diagrams of reproductive organs were condemned as being 'completely inappropriate and encouraging morally unacceptable behaviour'. Mixed gender PE, swimming, and sports were condemned as objectionable, with mixed swimming being 'unacceptable for reasons of modesty and decency to Muslim parents'. The booklet demanded that all British children should be able to study Arabic and that morning assemblies should be segregated between Muslim and Christian pupils.

Critics criticized the 'Taliban-style' decrees and regarded the report as divisive. As the furore unfolded, the MCB quietly withdrew the report from its website. However, the report's author, Tahir Mahmo Alam, a governor of five schools in Birmingham, subsequently became a central figure in the so-called Trojan Horse plot to take over several schools in Birmingham. In details leaked in an anonymous letter, the 'jihad' Operation Trojan Horse involved a five-step strategy: target schools would be identified in predominantly Muslim areas; Muslim parents would be encouraged to join the school's governing board; non-Muslim teachers would be targeted for removal from influential positions; and then the schools' culture, curriculums, and timetables would be quietly subordinated to Muslim beliefs. A primary aim of the plan was to ensure that the process was covert and subversive.

The objective was to spread the subversion to other schools across Britain where British teachers were 'corrupting children with sex education, teaching about homosexuals, making children say Christian prayers and mixed swimming and sports'. Alam dismissed the letter as a hoax and denied that there was any plot. Even so, non-Muslim headteachers in Alam's locality had been forced out in the previous six months, and there was evidence and allegations of attempts to Islamicize local schools. The general secretary of the National Association of Head Teachers said that there had been 'concerted efforts' to infiltrate and take over at least six Birmingham schools and 'alter their character in line with the Islamic faith'. Even Khalid Mahmood, a local Labour MP, admitted that 'There has been a serious bid to take over most of the schools in the east and south of the city,' and the local council suspended the recruitment of new school governors after receiving more than 200 complaints. The government launched enquiries into 25 Birmingham schools.

Allegedly, in some of these schools, GCSE syllabuses had been restricted to adhere to Islamic ideology; teenage boys had been told that rape within marriage is legal; children had been told to try and convert Christian teachers to Islam; there had been classroom segregation; an extremist preacher had been invited to speak; non-Muslims had been described as 'Kuffar'; Christmas events were banned; at one school, assemblies were taken where a teacher would chant: 'We don't believe in Christmas, do we?', 'Do we send Christmas cards? No!' and 'Do we celebrate Christmas? No!'; and children had been given anti-American and anti-Western propaganda. One teacher stated: 'I've no idea whether the Trojan Horse document is real. But the stuff it says is happening certainly is. Everything in that letter is what I experienced at Park View (one of the affected schools). It has been going on for years.'

The investigations and inspections that followed confirmed the problems alleged. In one school, Western women had even been described as 'white prostitutes', and a female member of the inspectors was shunned, with a teacher refusing to shake her hand. One school had even organized a 5-star trip costing £32,000 to Saudi Arabia from which non-Muslims were barred.

Five Birmingham Schools were put into special measures, and others were required to make changes. The school governors accused Ofsted of an 'Islamophobic witch-hunt'. A report by Ofsted alleged in October 2014 that those put into special measures still had problems. The local council admitted that it had been aware of Islamicization but had not acted in order to avoid being accused of racism.

In May 2015, it was reported from the conference of the National Association of Head Teachers that 'fear and intimidation is still prevalent' for those teachers who opposed the Islamic hardliners at the affected schools. One headteacher said that he had received death threats, and some schools had had dead cats and dogs deposited on school premises. The headteachers claimed that those Islamic governors involved had received no sanctions and that matters were once again getting worse. One female headteacher said: 'Trojan Horse has not gone away. Those of us who were involved, we knew it was the tip of the iceberg. We still have dead animals hung on the gates of schools, dismembered cats on playgrounds. We have petitions outside schools, objecting to teachers teaching against homophobia.' She had also been sent a message via social media that 'any headteacher who teaches my children it's alright to be gay will be at the end of my shotgun'.

Ninth, not only were children failed by the education system, a horrifying number of young English girls were failed by the legal system and the social services. A report written by Professor Alexis Jay into child abuse in Rotherham, found that a 'conservative' estimate of 1,400 girls as young as 11 were abused, raped, and trafficked by Asian gangs while the authorities turned a blind eye. The abuse had been believed to have been going on for at least 16 years. The victims were often referred to as 'white trash' by the paedophiles. The police estimate that there were as many as 5,000 victims across Britain.

The police regarded the children as being 'undesirable' and 'out of control' and deemed the girls to be having consensual sex. When the fathers of two abducted girls managed to find them and tried to remove them from where the girls were being held and abused, the police arrested the fathers. The Labour-run Rotherham council was determined to 'sweep the problem under the carpet'. The council 'suppressed' the scale of the abuse with managers giving 'clear direction' to staff that they should downplay the ethnic dimension. The report condemned the council for being 'at best naive, and at worst ignoring a politically incorrect truth'. Those council employees who complained about the paedophile gangs risked losing their jobs. Louise Casey, a government advisor who carried out an investigation into Rotherham council, said: 'Rotherham [council] … was repeatedly told by its own youth service what was happening and it chose, not only to not act, but to close that service down.' In her report, Louise Casey highlighted that the issue was considered 'taboo' because of political correctness. A former police officer said: 'They were running scared of the race issue … there is no doubt that in Rotherham, this has been a problem with Pakistani men for years and years. People were scared of being called racist.'

The Asian gangs, mostly of Pakistani origin, threatened both their victims and their families with violence if they went to the police. Some children were 'doused in petrol and threatened with being set alight, threatened with guns, made to witness brutally violent rapes and threatened they would be next if they told anyone'. Some of the victims tried to commit suicide. The responsible authorities positively obstructed efforts to help the victims. The Criminal Prosecution Service showed a distinct 'unwillingness to charge alleged perpetrators', which was 'the main reason so few prosecutions were pursued', according to the police. A mother who was concerned that her 14-year-old daughter was being abused was condemned by a social worker as being 'not able to accept' that her child was 'growing up'.

One girl who agreed to give evidence against the paedophiles received a text message telling her that they had her younger sister and 'the choice of what happened next was up to her'. The girl withdrew her evidence. Families of victims were also in danger of attack. Windows of their homes would be broken, there were abusive and threatening phone calls, and the paedophiles would sit in cars outside families' homes. One girl's brother was hospitalized after being beaten. One girl, who had been raped as a gang looked on and laughed, was threatened that if she complained then 'They said they would firebomb my home with my parents inside, shoot me with a pistol, rape my mother and kill my older brother if I told anyone about the rape.'

Some victims developed drink and drug addictions. One victim told the BBC: 'Police were aware, social services were aware and they still didn't stop him. It almost became like a game to him. He was untouchable.' Another victim told ITV: 'The authorities knew how old I was. They knew my abuser could be a danger to other children as well. They had full knowledge of it. They just never did anything. The authorities should get the same punishment as the men who did this to me.'

Even local charities supposedly trying to help abused girls refused to reveal the ethnicity of the paedophiles. Journalists and others who did so were accused of racism. A youth worker stated that the paedophiles 'are laughing at the police. These men may get called into the police station for a dressing down, but so few are taken to court. They now think they are invincible, and, of course, they're not frightened of accusing the police of racism themselves if things get tricky for them. Then everything is dropped.'

In June 2015, it was revealed that there remained as many as 300 paedophile suspects in Rotherham.

The practice of Asian paedophile gangs blighted not only Rotherham, but also Rochdale, Derby, Oldham, Oxford, Stockport, and Peterborough. A report published in October 2014 by the Greater Manchester Police was criticized as being a cover-up. The Coffey report stated that it would be 'wrong' to focus on Asian grooming gangs. Samantha Roberts, who had been raped by an Asian gang in Oldham when she was 12 years-old said: 'This report makes very depressing reading when I've done so much work campaigning against child sexual exploitation ... The report makes a valid point that not all grooming gangs across the country are Asian but it's very clear that in Greater Manchester there's an issue of girls being targeted by men from Pakistan and Bangladesh in particular.'

A report into paedophile gangs in Oxford found that the NHS even supplied the child victims with condoms. The abuse was on 'an industrial scale'.

Tenth, political correctness acts like a political version of Aids. It weakens a society's culture, identity, and its ability to defend itself, thereby allowing any opportunistic, hostile entity to attack. The undermining of British culture – especially English culture – is as unremitting as are the intended consequences.

On occasion, the anti-British sentiment of the ruling class can seem mild, such as when Suzy Klein accused those who complained at the inclusion of an Ibiza-style club music in the Proms – a classical music festival – of being snobs, saying: 'These self-elected snobs and scaremongers are not there to fight for the universal power that great music unleashes – what they want is to "protect" classical music ... from the onslaught of mass entertainment.' Miss Klein is a presenter on BBC Radio 3, which survives courtesy of licence fee payer's money and which has been eclipsed by the independent Classic FM.

The Last Night of the Proms has been a target for the politically correct for some time. The Parekh Report included the following 'presentation to the commission':

> 'The Rule Britannia mindset, given the full-blown expression at the Last Night of the Proms and until recently at the start of programming each day on BBC Radio 4, is a major part of the problem of Britain. In the same way that it continues to fight the Second World War ... Britain seems incapable of shaking off its imperialist identity. The Brits do appear to believe that "Britons never, never, never shall be slaves" ... [But] it is impossible to colonise three-fifths of the world ... without enslaving oneself. Our problem has been that Britain has never understood itself and has steadfastly refused to see and understand itself through the prism of our experience of it, here and in its coloniser mode.'

At the 2015 Last Night of the Proms, traditionally a rousing patriotic event, the conductor, the American Marin Alsop, included in her speech a call to tackle 'gender, racial, economic and ethnic inequality'. Such comments are remarkable given that during the election campaign, at a Labour Party election rally in Birmingham in May 2015, the audience was segregated between men and women. Labour insisted that both sexes were 'treated equally'.

Another example is when, in February 2015, Justin Welby, the Archbishop of Canterbury, told a German audience of his 'profound feeling of regret and deep sorrow' over the bombing of Dresden in WWII, which he said 'diminished all our humanity'. Angela Merkel did not apologize for the Blitz. Another is when Travelodge removed bibles from its rooms in August 2014, citing a desire not to offend non-Christians. This was despite never receiving any complaints from guests.

Amazon decreed that Tom and Jerry should carry a warning that 'they contain some ethnic and racial prejudices that were once commonplace in American society'. The book *Tintin in The Congo*, written in 1930, has been withdrawn from libraries and bookshops because it portrays Africans as being primitive and ignorant. In November 2014, the singer Ellie Goulding was accused of racism for wearing a Red Indian costume for a Halloween party. In November 2014, a re-release of the Band Aid single was accused of being 'patronising' and of perpetuating negative images of Africa. This was entirely in keeping with the rejection of charity contained within *The Authoritarian Personality*. To his credit, Bob Geldof was unmoved.

More controversially, In November 2014 during a by-election, the Labour Shadow Attorney General, Emily Thornberry, was forced to apologise and was then sacked following a Tweet with a picture in which she mocked a man because he had hung some English flags outside his home. The MP later said that she made the Tweet because she had 'never seen anything like it'. In the internet furore that followed, one writer described Labour as being 'vacuum-packed lefty snobs'. The person Thornberry was sneering at said: 'She's a snob. What's she got, a three-storey townhouse in Islington? These flags can be found anywhere you look.' Thornberry is the wife of a High Court judge and lives in a house worth more than £2million. She claimed to be a victim of a 'prejudiced attitude towards Islington'.

Also controversially, the BBC children's programme *Horrible Histories* had a sketch in which the Jamaican-born Mary Seacole was prevented from becoming a nurse during the Crimean War by Florence Nightingale, who held in the sketch that the role was 'only for British girls'. In the sketch, Seacole said: 'Four times me tried to join Old Lamp-Face's nurses in the Crimean War, and four times she said no.' Although Seacole is depicted as black, she was, in fact, three-quarters white. She was proud of her Scottish heritage and considered herself to be white and Scottish.

This sketch was a complete lie and an invention. Seacole never applied for a job with Florence Nightingale and was not even medically qualified. However, a spokesman for BBC's children's television claimed that the aim had been 'to open up a discussion about some of the attitudes of the time'. If such were the 'attitudes of the time', one wonders why the BBC had to invent lies about it. Eventually, even the BBC Trust admitted that the sketch was 'materially inaccurate'.

In fact, Seacole travelled to Crimea to set up what might be described as a restaurant and bar selling food and wine to officers. On arrival, she sought out Florence Nightingale and, according to Seacole's own memoirs, Florence Nightingale greeted her saying: 'What do you want, Mrs Seacole? Anything we can do for you? If it lies in my power, I shall be very happy.' Seacole wanted and was given a bed for the night before she continued on her journey to Balaclava.

Schoolchildren are even required to repeat the lies about Seacole to pass exams. For example, one GCSE paper required pupils to 'briefly describe the career of Mary Seacole'. To answer the question correctly, the pupils needed to lie. For example, Seacole's establishment was required to be described as a 'British hospital'. Furthermore, there are a number of children's books which completely misrepresent Seacole's status and activities.

But the Seacole saga did not end there. A Mary Seacole Memorial Statue Appeal, headed by Lord Clive Soley (a former Labour MP), determined to erect a large statue to Mary Seacole 'to facilitate a memorial statue to commemorate Mary Jane Seacole; nurse and heroine of the Crimean War', with further plans for a 'memorial garden'. As is often the case, the appeal was unable to raise sufficient funds and experienced 'soaring' construction costs. Even so, a site was cleared and even 'blessed'. The site chosen was none other than St Thomas' Hospital, where Florence Nightingale founded the first nurse training school in the world. The Seacole statue's dimensions were so large that it would dwarf the existing statue already at the hospital. The Seacole enterprise described Seacole as a 'Pioneer Nurse', which is something Seacole never claimed to be and was completely untrue.

Shamefully, Osborne, the Tory chancellor, stepped in with public monies to bail out the scheme. £240,000 was pledged. This is to peddle a lie. A letter from the Nightingale Society to Osborne pointed out:

> 'The massive grant to the Mary Seacole statue is misplaced in three important respects: (1) Seacole was not a nurse, let alone a 'Pioneer Nurse', nor ever claimed to be one (in her book, "nurses" are Nightingale and her nurses); (2) the place is wrong, as St Thomas' Hospital was for more than a century the home of the Nightingale School of Nursing, the first professional training school in the world, from which pioneers went out to bring the standards of the new profession to other countries. (3) It was Nightingale, not Seacole, who prepared briefs for committees, wrote and met with MPs and Cabinet ministers to press for reforms in nursing and health care.'

That someone such as Florence Nightingale, who did so much to save lives and develop the profession of nursing and who might normally be regarded as a true female role model, should be denigrated and smeared in this way demonstrates the malevolence and falsity of political correctness and those who practise it.

Meanwhile, a plaque dedicated to Cecil Rhodes (1853-1902), a dominant figure of the British Empire and South African statesman, at Oriel College in Oxford, was to be removed after some students branded it as racist. Those students also demanded that a statute likewise be removed. A so-called Rhodes Must Fall campaigner, Annie Teriba, had claimed that 'There's a violence to having to walk past the statue every day on the way to your lectures, there's a violence to having to sit with paintings of former slave holders whilst writing your exams.' Another organizer from that organisation, Ntokozo Qwabe alleged that African history had been written by European tourists and that the reading list for political sciences ignored African scholars: 'The list was dominated by white male Europeans and Americans.'

The campaign was supported by a leading human rights lawyer, Sir Geoffrey Bindman QC, who argued that to remove the statue would be 'no more than a symbolic and cost-free mark of disapproval of a man who manifested his racism in the commercial exploitation of those whom he considered inferior. The huge sum he gave to the college was its product.' Cecil Rhodes was a firm believer in the value of education and created a scheme whereby students would be funded to attend Oxford (Rhodes Scholarships) – the scheme was and remains open to all, no matter their ethnicity. The above mentioned Ntokozo Qwabe, a Zulu from South Africa, was himself a Rhodes Scholar – a fact that attracted some comment, leading Qwabe to proclaim that he was 'no beneficiary of Rhodes' but 'a beneficiary of the resources and labour of my people which Rhodes pillaged and slaved'. It is to be noted that Bindman refers to Rhodes' alleged 'commercial exploitation' – a term that any Leninist would happily use.

The fact that Rhodesia, even under Ian Smith after declaring UDI, was the breadbasket of southern Africa and that South Africa experienced significant immigration even under Apartheid, whereas Zimbabwe became a typical communist basket case under Mugabe (whose power stemmed from rigged elections) with Britain continuing to receive asylum applications from Africans from Zimbabwe, requires no further comment.

The attack on Rhodes was merely a sideshow of a larger campaign, run by the Oxford Campaign for Racial Awareness and Equality, the co-chair of which, Chi Chi Shi, announced: 'It is very important to see the statue as a symbol of Oxford's colonial past and history but also how that relates to the experience of BME [black and minority ethnic] students, especially in terms of the whiteness of the curriculum and Eurocentricity ... Challenging the narrative that the West discovered science ... rather than seeing it as a collaborative process in which Islamic science is fundamental.'

Schools have been a particular target, even over innocent matters such as nursery rhymes and singing. For example, in 2006, nursery school children at two centres in Abingdon and Oxford were banned from singing 'Baa Baa Black Sheep'. Instead, they are being compelled to sing 'Baa Baa Rainbow Sheep'. Stuart Chamberlain of the Oxford Sure Start Centre in Sutton Courtenay said: 'Basically we have taken the equal opportunities approach to everything we do. This is fairly standard across nurseries. We are following stringent equal opportunities rules. No one should feel pointed out because of their race, gender or anything else.'

This was not the first time that race zealots tried to ban or tamper with the nursery rhyme. Previously, attempts have been made to change it to 'green' or 'happy' sheep. In 1999, the Birmingham City Council banned the rhyme on the basis that it was racially negative and likely to cause offence. In fact, the rhyme has nothing to do with race and is believed to have originated from the Middle Ages and relates to a tax imposed by the king on wool.

Also, dealing with children's toys, albeit with a certain nostalgic appeal to some adults, the West Mercia police seized three golliwogs from a display in a shop window at Pettifer's gift shop in Bromyard. The shop owner, Donald Reynolds, was told that the police were acting on a complaint that the golliwogs were offensive. The police stated that they were acting under Section 5 of the Public Order Act, which outlawed the display of offensive material that was likely to cause alarm, harassment, or distress.

However, after a two-week investigation and consultation with the Crown Prosecution Service, Mr Reynolds was told that he would not be prosecuted and that the golliwogs would be returned to him. But the police further warned that they would be giving Mr Reynolds 'suitable advice about the sensitivities of placing such items on display'. Mr Reynolds said: 'I thought they would be good sellers and they were. Within ten minutes of putting them out I sold two of them.'

All of this has a cumulative effect, as is evidenced when in April 2014, in a survey by NatCen Social Research, it was revealed that only 35% of people felt 'very proud' to be British. This is a fall from 43% a decade ago. For those between 18 and 24, those who felt 'very proud' was only 20%. This fading of patriotism is what the politically correct want. Dr Wayne Mapp also warned of the danger 'of people losing faith in the institutions of government'.

Ultimately, things become much more dangerous. In August 2014, an estimated 200,000 Muslims participated in anti-Israel demonstrations in Manchester and London. There are no such protests against IS – not even after their grotesque atrocities such as the terrorist attacks in Paris in November 2015. In April 2014, a 12-year-old girl was openly flying a jihadi flag at a street protest in London. In August 2014, a nun pulled down a jihadi flag that was being flown over a housing estate in East London. Sister Christine, 77, climbed a ladder to remove the flag because she feared it could create 'community tension'.

In December 2014, to avoid terror attacks, not only were soldiers warned not to wear their uniforms in public, but children in cadet forces were likewise warned. They were also instructed to carry out searches of accommodation and training areas prior to setting up camp. This followed increased internet activity among jihadists, who were wanting to carry out a high-profile attack or beheading of a soldier. In June 2015, off-duty police officers were warned not to wear their uniforms in public.

A memorial to the victims of the 7/7 terrorist bombings was defaced with slogans describing the terrorists as '4 innocent Muslims' and that '7/7 was an inside job'. The vandalism was done overnight, just before relatives were due to attend the memorial to commemorate the ninth anniversary of the bombings.

In June 2014, the security services expressed concern that around 300 IS jihadists had re-entered Britain. A former director of MI6 described the task of tracking these extremists as 'impossible'. Some had been believed to have faked their own deaths to better enable them to sneak back. By November 2015, the number was estimated to have reached 450 jihadists who had returned. A government determined to defend British people from IS terrorism, as barbaric as it is, would not allow this, and those leaving to join IS would forfeit their British citizenship. That, of course, would fall foul of a variety of supposed human rights laws and would be discriminatory. But it is meaningless to speak of defending Britain when so many are able to move back and forth, and it is not as if when in Syria they sit around a camp fire singing Ging Gang Goolie. They know perfectly well what they are doing and wish to participate in what Tony Abbott described (see above) as 'a caliphate seeking to export its apocalyptic version of Islam right around the world', and that 'everywhere [IS] gains a foothold' there are 'beheadings', 'crucifixions', 'mass executions', 'hurling off high buildings', 'sexual slavery', and 'its perverse allure across the globe'.

In August 2014, Dominic Grieve, the attorney general, rejected calls to strip those who went to Syria to join IS of their British citizenship, saying that such a move might leave them stateless and hence would break UN conventions. The thought of it! Once again, abstract theories and allegiance to international bureaucracies takes priority over common sense or the national interest.

In February 2015, in reference to IS supporters, counter-terrorism chief Mark Rowley explained in a television interview that 'we are making 35% more arrests now than we used to in counter-terrorism. It's nearly one arrest a day.' Estimates as to the number who have gone to Syria to join IS vary from hundreds to up to 2,000. Many have since re-entered Britain. Sir Bernard Hogan-Howe warned in October 2014 that at 'a minimum' five a week were travelling to join IS. The numbers of terrorists arrested has increased by 70% over the previous three years, and 218 suspects had been held so far that year. In September 2015, the police told how they believed that there are more than 3,000 British Muslim extremists willing to carry out terrorist acts in Britain. Sir John Sawers, the former head of MI6, demanded more powers for the security services as there were 'probably several thousand ... of concern and the numbers are rising as more people go to Syria and Iraq and are radicalised out there'.

This is a long-standing problem. Following 9/11, up to September 2005, there were three main acts of terrorism in England. There was the murder of PC Stephen Oake in 2003, the 7/7 suicide bombings, and the subsequent 21/7 failed attempted terrorist bombings. In addition, there have also been other terrorist activities by British Muslims abroad (e.g. two suicide bombers in Israel and the presence of British IS fighters in Syria and Iraq).

Stephen Oake was stabbed eight times in the chest as he wrestled with a terror suspect, the Algerian Kamel Bourgass, in a flat in Manchester. Another two men were found at the flat, and another surrendered himself to the police shortly afterwards in connection with the murder. All four of these men were so-called asylum seekers. The police believed that they were Algerian Muslim extremists.

Bourgass had exploited the facilities of the infamous Finsbury Park Mosque. Even after he had had his asylum application rejected twice, and after he had commenced his terrorist activities, he was arrested by police for shoplifting. The police making the arrest suspected he was an illegal immigrant, knew that he was using aliases, and had contacted the Immigration Service, who did nothing. Bourgass was fined for shoplifting and then walked free.

The flat in which he was finally arrested and in which the murder took place had been provided by the Islington Council's Asylum Team. The total cost of his illegal entry into the UK, including the trials of him and his co-defendants and the police investigation, was estimated to be in excess of £40million. The cost of keeping him in jail continues. Bourgass's accomplices were all so-called asylum seekers, and many were using false passports and aliases. The tenant of the flat had had his application for asylum refused but had not been deported. Instead, after he had been on the run for four years, he was finally caught but was then granted exceptional leave to remain because it was alleged that he would be in danger if he were returned to Algeria. Up to 3,000 GIA Algerian Muslim extremists were let into the country by the Tories in the 1990s. The GIA were conducting a terrorist campaign in Algeria. Melanie Phillips wrote:

'For Islamist terrorists and jihadi ideologues, London during the 1980s and 1990s was the place to be. Kicked out of or repressed within their own countries, they streamed in their thousands to the British capital because they found it to be more hospitable and tolerant than any other place on the globe.

A more brutal way of putting it, however, is that British entry procedures were the most lax and sloppy in the developed world – a system which asked no questions, required no identity papers, and instead showered newcomers with a galaxy of welfare benefits, free education and free health care regardless of their behaviour, beliefs or circumstances. To state it more brutally still, during the 1990s Britain simply lost control of its borders altogether because of the gross abuse and total breakdown of its asylum system. Of the thousands of asylum seekers who arrive every year, most have no legal entitlement to remain in Britain. Yet only a very small minority are sent home, and the remainder melt into British society. The reason so many are attracted is largely because illegal immigrants can simply disappear with no questions asked.

It was hardly surprising, therefore, that so many Islamist terrorists and extremists found Britain to be such a delightful and agreeable destination. As the counterterrorism analyst Robert Leiken has pointed out, al Qaeda and its affiliates depend on immigration to get into the West to carry out their terrorist plots, and to that end they use – or abuse – every immigration category to infiltrate Western countries. According to Imam Abu Baseer, one of the leading religious supporters of al Qaeda: "One of the goals of immigration is the revival of the duty of jihad and enforcement of their power over the infidels. Immigration and jihad go together. One is the consequence of the other and dependent upon it. The continuance of the one is dependent upon the continuance of the other." The asylum shambles thus provided cover for the influx of large numbers of people into Britain who posed a direct threat to the state from without.'[585]

Of the four 7/7 suicide bombers, Mohammed Khan, Hasib Hussein, and Shehzad Tanweer were born in Britain. Germaine Lindsay was born in Jamaica, although he immigrated to the UK as a young child. Of the five 21/7 terrorists (including the man believed to be responsible for the discarded bomb subsequently found), Maktar Ibraihim, Yasin Omar, Osman Hussein, Manfo Kwaku Asiedu, and Ramzi Mohamed, at least four were immigrants. Details of Ramzi Mohamed's background were not released by the police.

Asiedu is Ghanian and needed an interpreter for his court appearance. Ibraihim is Eritrean, Hussein is Ethiopian, and Omar is Somalian. Hussein was granted a British passport as an act of fraud, claiming to be an asylum seeker, which he was not. He also went by, and has another passport in the name of, Hamdi Issac.   Ibrahim also managed to obtain a British passport, despite his criminal past which included shoplifting, the targeting of whites for mugging, his drug use, and serving half of a five-year prison sentence during which he participated in a riot in which several prison officers were injured. He also used aliases and at times claimed to be Sudanese.

There were of course others who had been detained and charged for assisting the terrorists, and those who had entered and fled the country who were believed to have been involved. Of the 13 people who were in the forefront of the terrorist campaign, at least nine were immigrants of various descriptions. Some had been allowed to stay in Britain, or even given British passports, despite clear criminal activity. Without continued immigration, it would have been very difficult for Al-Qaeda to have carried out its acts of terrorism. Certainly, its activities would have been much reduced.

The government response to the terror threat was steeped in political correctness and a desire not to offend Muslims. In a Prevent counter-terrorism training programme, in six invented case studies, participants are trained how to spot likely terrorists. Three of the case studies involve possible jihadis, two involve right-wing extremists, and one involves an ex-army serviceman who becomes mentally ill following cuts to his benefits. With one of the suspected jihadis, the correct procedure was apparently to invite the suspect to an Afghan community centre to discuss his asylum claim.

A BBC ComRes opinion poll following the Charlie Hebdo killings in France, where a satirical magazine's offices were invaded by Muslim terrorists who murdered 12 occupants, found that 27% of Muslims had sympathy for the motives for the murders. 24% believed that violence against those who published pictures of Mohammed could be justified, with 11% having sympathy for those who wanted to fight against the West. 20% believed that Western liberal society was incompatible with

Islam. 45% believed that those Muslim preachers who advocated violence against the West were not 'out of touch' with mainstream Muslim opinion. However, the BBC presented the findings very differently. The BBC presented the poll as being positive and highlighted that the majority of Muslims opposed violence against those who published pictures of Mohammed.

This opinion poll might be regarded as an improvement from October 2001, when an opinion poll by an Asian radio station, Sunrise, showed that 98% of Muslims in London under the age of 45 would not fight for Britain, while 48% said they would take up arms for Osama Bin Laden. The Sunrise opinion poll was not the only one at that time (just after 9/11) which highlighted the extent of anti-British hostility in the Muslim population. An opinion poll in the Sunday Times revealed that 40% of Muslims believed that Bin Laden was justified in fighting a war against the USA, and a similar percentage believed that those British Muslims who chose to fight with the Taliban were right to do so. A subsequent opinion poll by ICM revealed that 57% of Muslims disagreed with Tony Blair's assertion that the war was not a war against Islam, and 80% opposed the war in Afghanistan.

Such anti-British views were not confined to the opinion polls. One extremist, Abdul Haq, who spoke on behalf of the Al-Muhajiroun organisation on the Jimmy Young Show, stated that 'When you are bombing the people of Afghanistan, you are attacking my land and my brothers and my sisters. If I was capable of fighting I would like to go.' He further stated: 'What the West have failed to realise is that our identities are not based on nationality, they are based on belief.' He dismissed democracy as 'just the civilised face of dictatorship'. Haq was quite open that his aim was to bring about a world Islamic state, and he intended to see the Islamic flag flying over Downing Street.

Ten days after the 9/11 attacks, 17-year-old Ross Parker was attacked and killed by three Asian thugs in Peterborough for no other reason than he was white. He was unknown to his attackers. The ringleader, having attacked Ross Parker so violently that he had almost been decapitated, then held up the knife and said: 'Look at this. Cherish the blood.' The three Asians were convicted of murder. Peterborough, like Oldham, has anti-white, no-go areas.

In June 2005, Sheikh Omar Bakri Mohammed urged Muslims to kill kaffirs (non-Muslims). In reference to the US embassy, he said: 'We're going to incite people to do jihad, incite people to hate the new pharaoh [President Bush]. Why not do more? Maybe take over the embassy.' In reference to kaffirs, Bakri said: 'Wherever they are killed I feel happy.'

It is against this background that Labour decided to press ahead with its new law outlawing incitement to religious hatred. This law had been promised to the Muslim pressure groups in an attempt to get votes from those Muslims disenchanted with Labour as a result of the Iraq war.

In July 2015, Nicky Morgan the Education Secretary alleged that children making homophobic remarks could be a sign of radicalization. This equates a child's playground comments with the hostility to homosexuality from fundamentalist Muslims.

Anjem Choudary, a British Muslim extremist, said: 'By 2050, Britain will be a majority Muslim country. It will be the end of freedom and democracy.' The BBC's Home Editor, Mark Easton, comparing Choudary to Gandhi and Nelson Mandela said: 'History tells us that extreme views are sometimes needed to challenge very establish values.' Choudary said: 'The comparisons with Mandela and Gandhi are false. They are kuffar going to hellfire whilst I am a Muslim.'

Choudary is not a lone Muslim voice. In 2005, a spokesman for Hizb ut-Tahrir organisation stated: 'I think Muslims in this country need to take a long, hard look at themselves and decide what is their identity. Are they British or are they Muslim? I am a Muslim. Where I live, is irrelevant.' More prominently, in 2006, Yasmin Alibhai-Brown, a Ugandan Asian refugee and Muslim who immigrated into this country in 1972, launched into another of her attacks on the English (most Ugandan Asians have, thankfully, integrated far better than Alibhai-Brown). This time it was the white working class who came under attack in an article entitled 'Migrant Pride and Prejudice'. She began her article with a sneer at those who are opposed to mass immigration: 'From the day the Windrush arrived from the Caribbean in June 1948 has there been a time when the indigenous population has not panicked over outsiders raiding their blessed islands? When was the national conversation over this issue benign and temperate? The latest outbreak of hysteria is over Eastern Europeans, many more of whom have landed since the EU expanded to include their countries. The situation is said to be "unprecedented".' Alibhai-Brown then complained of people objecting to the current levels of immigration:

> 'One of the contagious whinges of the anti-immigrant lobby is that that they are not "allowed" to debate immigration when they know the subject has been churned around forever and ever and always irrationally. It lies at the core of our national identity. Our citizenship test should ask: "Are you British enough to loathe all future incomers who may well compete with you?"
>
> What has changed is not the hostility but the liberal consensus which was once progressive, egalitarian anti-imperialist and pro-immigration. Immigration is now opposed by influential individuals of the centre left and some settled

immigrants too who really should know better ... Some middle glass bigots claim they are against immigration because they care deeply for the poor workless classes who are driven out by low migrant wages. Is this why most employ Poles to do all their building and domestic work?'

It is to be noted, that Alibhai-Brown casually used the term 'middle class bigots' to describe those who oppose immigration. She continued:

'Xenophobic tabloids now have their arguments made by the Today Programme (which has turned vigilante and even finds illegal workers so they can be deported) and by tight little nationalists like Frank Fields. There is a campaign to convince Britons we are about to be overcome by a flood of garlicky strangers. And once again inconvenient truths are shunned. New migrants come to work. Can't have that even if our buoyant economy demands it. Only 7% claim benefits. Others live in cramped accommodation, earn, pay taxes and return home.'

The idea that the Today Programme puts forward xenophobic arguments is laughable. To speak of only 7% claiming benefits is tripe. The new immigrants from Eastern Europe were not allowed to claim benefits at once, although many were sending welfare benefits to their families back home. To describe Frank Field as a 'tight little nationalist' is presumably a response to his articles expressing concern as to the level of immigration. Alibhai-Brown can only resort to idiotic abuse rather than an intellectual argument. But she saved her main venom until the end:

'And all because of prejudice and envy. Young Poles and Lithuanians can find work and make something of their lives while our own people are either too lazy or expensive to compete. Tax paying immigrants past and present keep indolent British scroungers on their couches drinking beer and watching daytime TV. I resent that. We are despised because we seize opportunities which these slobs don't want. Two fit white British men loiter outside my local bank. They beg. I asked if they wanted to clear out my back garden for a fair wage. They said I was one crazy lady. Andrew, Polish and obliging did the job cheerfully and efficiently. God bless bloody foreigners who do our dirty work and are then damned by an ungrateful, obtuse nation.'

So, the great Marxist herself is suddenly a believer in an international free market for labour when it is damaging to the interests of the English. Given the backward status of the former communist East European countries, it is nonsense to pretend that there is one single European market in anything – no matter how much the EU might like to pretend otherwise. Those who find themselves pushed out of employment by immigrants have every right to complain. There is no reason for them to be insulted for having their own opinions either. Yet Alibhai-Brown condemns them as 'too lazy or expensive', 'indolent British scroungers on their couches drinking beer' and 'slobs', and the British as a whole as being 'an ungrateful, obtuse nation'. An English or white person would be prosecuted for making such insulting comments about an ethnic minority. Alibhai-Brown is another of those responsible for the Parekh report and someone who endlessly claims to be a victim of racism.

In fact, at the time, according to the Office of National Statistics, 35% of Muslim households had no adult in employment, which is more than twice the national average. The Muslim Alibhai-Brown makes no mention of that. But it got worse. In a subsequent article entitled 'Muslims are a much misunderstood community', she drew a moral equivalence between British soldiers and Muslim suicide bombers:

> 'Those who wanted a war in Iraq have also become inadvertent propagandists for terrorist cells in Britain. I have never understood why suicide bombers are more heinous than our soldiers who rip up civilians with cluster bombs used from a distance so you cannot see the havoc. Contrition and apologies for these acts would disarm Islamist mobilisers of their best weapons. But the British state, as we know, never says sorry.'

There have never been reports of any occurrence of British soldiers bombing civilians with cluster bombs – even by mistake. Suicide bombers do of course deliberately target civilians in order to spread terror. There is no moral equivalence. Nor even is any casualty incurred on a battlefield an excuse for suicide attacks, or any other form of terrorism, either in Britain or elsewhere. Alibhai-Brown is simply an apologist for Muslim terrorism. It is she who is the 'propagandist' for terrorist cells in Britain.

One should also compare the tolerance of Alibhai-Brown's articles in a national newspaper (*The Independent*) with the intolerance of others who have been victims of the British Inquisition for writing in local newspapers criticising immigration (e.g. Alan Buchan, the editor of a local paper called North East Weekly, was charged with inciting racial hatred as a result of an article he wrote opposing the construction of a prison and asylum centre in his area – the article attracted one complaint to the police), or making jokes or statements deemed politically incorrect. Tony Blair's concept of the battle of ideology counted for little at *The Independent*, which was more than happy to fund and promote terrorist apologists.

Alibhai-Brown has been quoted as previously making the following comments: 'Once, as a rabid anti-imperialist (which I still am), I would have applauded anybody who publicly humiliated the English. If it was done cleverly and with panache it was even more satisfying. Like other nationals who had been subjugated for so long, these small affronts were liberating, a way of confronting that arrogance of Englanders. But these days I feel more disquiet than wicked delight when the English are gratuitously slagged off.'

In 2005, Alibhai-Brown wrote an introduction to a British Council exhibition which was touring the Middle East in which she said: 'Too many young Muslims are emotionally homeless. Racism makes them believe they cannot belong in Britain.' At a time when British troops were in Iraq and when we were supposed to be fighting a war on terror, such comments could do nothing other than encourage anti-British hatred amongst Muslims, could only be helpful to Al Qaeda, and other anti-Western terrorist groups and their supporters, and could be no other than damaging to Britain and the safety of British soldiers and citizens. Shortly after 7/7, she held to this view when she wrote in the Daily Mail and repeated the above quote verbatim.

In an article for *The Independent* entitled 'My hopes of progress are turning to ashes', Alibhai-Brown complained about the sense of pride and patriotism flowing from the impending Ashes victory for England's cricket team. She wrote that devolution had weakened England and that, unlike with the ethnic minorities, there was 'something shameful and ridiculous in proclaiming your Englishness'. She advocated the teaching of English history and claimed that the English were: 'The most adventurous, open and promiscuous, wilfully and joyously appropriating, replicating and incorporating different cultures and ideas and peoples from the world.' She then continued:

> 'Yet today's understandings pull in the opposite direction. Currently the most ardent advocates for England want to tame these wild and defining characteristics of Englishness. They want to remake Jerusalem. They want green and pleasant villages and church spires and cricket greens where no impertinent outsiders will be admitted, as they have under the messy and inclusive

British flag. Reading between the lines, these calls for purity are pitched by cricket pundits imagining the England they want – an England unsullied by the likes of us or gypsies or Albanians, I reckon. ' And: 'Yes folks, there is white flight into Englishness, and it seems unstoppable. And if the Ashes are won, I reckon this purification and reclamation project will be boosted immeasurably. And many more white Britons will give up on Britain and take refuge in England.'

She then managed to turn the article around to the 7/7 terrorist bombings:

> 'And if this disengagement carries on, will Britishness be like an inner-city area, a dejected, hopeless place for poor blacks left behind with nowhere to go? When I think the four British born Muslim men who blew up London, I fret about their lack of connection to this country. Did they feel homeless? Their own people probably told them never to become too English, and some must have been rejected by indigenous locals who hate Pakis.
>
> It isn't to excuse their acts, which will remain unforgiven. But if even I can feel forlorn and bitter about the different ways my countrymen can make me feel unwanted by drawing up bridges using the arsenal of abuse, how must it be for black and Asian men with no opportunities to make themselves matter to themselves and others?'

As a matter of fact, one of the bombers was born in Jamaica – only three were born in England. She concluded: 'Britain could carry on becoming a modern, confident internationalist nation or a sadly balkanised one, progressive hopes turned to ash. The ball is in England's court.'

Alibhai-Brown is a longstanding opponent of devolution in general, and an English parliament in particular. The thrust of her article is an attack upon English nationalism. Devolution resulted in a constitutional problem with Scots and Welsh continuing to vote on English affairs, despite having home rule for themselves, and England has been required to give extra subsidies to Scotland in particular. An English parliament is the only credible and fair solution to that, which gives rise to English nationalism.

Alibhai-Brown caricatures the English as being 'open and promiscuous' etc. and then invents another caricature of the English nationalists as being, in effect, white supremacists and racial purists. She then talks of 'white Britons' giving up on Britain and taking 'refuge in England'. The number of Scots and Welsh (also white Britons) who Alibhai-Brown avers intend to 'take refuge in England' is not quantified.

The end of Alibhai-Brown's article is as silly as it is nasty. She tries to portray the suicide bombers as victims of English racism and implies that the terrorists were driven to their terrorism because they '*must have been rejected by indigenous locals who hate Pakis*' – note the objectivity – and possibly felt 'homeless'. This is a nasty little trick to try and perpetuate the notion of the victim status of immigrants and to make the English responsible for the actions of Jihadist terrorism. Racism did not play any part in the terrorist bombings at all. We know so because one of the terrorists told us so in his pre-recorded video, in which he said:

> 'Our words have no impact on you therefore I am going to speak to you in a language you understand. Our words are dead until we give them life with our blood ... I and thousands like me have forsaken everything for what we believe. Our drive and motivation does not come from tangible commodities from what the world has to offer. Our religion is Islam.
>
> What we have is obedience to the one true God and following in the footsteps of the final prophet and messenger Mohammed. This is how our ethical stances are dictated.
>
> While your democratically elected Government continually perpetuate atrocities against my people all over the world your support for them makes you responsible. Just as I am directly responsible for protecting and avenging my Muslim brothers and sisters, now you will taste the reality of this situation.
>
> Until we feel security you will be our targets and until you stop the bombing, gassing and torture and imprisonment of my people we will not stop. We are at war and I am a soldier.'

Mohammed Khan was clear enough. This was someone who had been globetrotting to Pakistan and whitewater rafting in Wales. He had a good job and had even visited the House of Commons as a guest of the Labour MP Jon Trickett, with whom he had been on friendly terms for 17 years and was considered a family friend. Khan's motives were religious, including the concept of *Jihad*. He was a Muslim fundamentalist. His loyalty was to the Muslim *Ummah*. He did not regard himself as English at all. He was not a victim of English racism.

The fight against IS and other extremist groups requires not only an intolerance of Islamic hate preachers, but also an intolerance of politically correct hate preachers. The Frankfurt School, as has been shown above, have corrupted the original intention of constitutional patriotism. In reference to Germany, Sternberger advocated a 'militant democracy', and Loewenstein argued that democracy needed to be prepared to fight fire with fire when dealing with anti-democratic forces. To put it another way, British culture, English culture in particular, needs to be defended and positively promoted. Political correctness, acting like a political version of Aids, has disabled the national defence mechanisms.

Eleventh, dealing with the above problems is undermined, as is the intention, by the forceful denial of the freedom of speech. This is a high profile aspect of political correctness. Ordinary people are not allowed to express politically incorrect opinions or use politically incorrect language. This is a long-standing hallmark of political correctness and a key part of the British Inquisition.

Even tongue in cheek comments are to be prosecuted, as the hapless Robin Page discovered when he made the following remark at a country fair some years ago: 'If there is a black, vegetarian, Muslim, asylum-seeking, one-legged, lesbian lorry driver present, then you may be offended at what I am going to say, as I want the same rights that you have got already.' For daring to make this joke, the police even advertised that they would 'like to hear from anyone who was upset by the commentary'. In this case, the charges were ultimately dropped.

Even a spat between neighbours can lead to police prosecution, *unless you are deemed to belong to a victim group*. Not long after the 9/11 attacks, two neighbours got into an argument in Exeter. One of those, Alistair Scott was arrested, charged, and convicted on three counts of religiously aggravated threatening behaviour as a result of a complaint from Mohammed Hudaib. Both men had been abusive, and Mr Hudaib had shouted that 9/11 had been a great day, that Osama Bin Laden was a great man, and that all Americans deserved to die. Mr Hudaib admitted that he 'could have said that Osama Bin Laden was a great man and that all Americans deserved to die and are stupid'. Mr Hudaib was neither arrested nor charged.

More recently, in October 2015, Germaine Greer, the 76-year-old arch-feminist writer and academic, withdrew from a debate at Cardiff University after being branded 'transphobic' by students who tried to have her banned. Greer's offence was that she had reiterated her view that even if a man were to be castrated then he still would not look, sound, or behave like a woman and that 'a great many women [think] male to female transgender people [do not] look like, sound like or behave like women'.

Another feminist, Julie Bindell, was likewise banned from speaking by the University of Manchester due to some articles she had written previously about transexuality that were deemed 'offensive'. In 2004, Bindell had written: 'I don't have a problem with men disposing of their genitals, but it does not make them women, in the same way that shoving a bit of vacuum hose down your 501s [jeans] does not make you a man.'

The Iranian human rights campaigner and opponent of Sharia, Maryam Namazie, was banned from speaking by the University of Warwick students' union on the grounds of 'the right of Mulsim students not to feel intimidated or discriminated against'. Namazie responded: 'If *anyone* is inciting hatred, it is the Islamists who are threatening people like me ... just because we don't want to toe the line.' Following a public backlash, the ban was withdrawn.

At Warwick University, one 19-year-old student, who had dared to write on a blog that he found it 'incredibly hurtful' to be invited to a 'consent workshop' and that the vast majority 'don't have to be taught to not be a rapist', was subjected to abuse and bullying, and was branded a 'rapist' and a 'misogynist'. The abuse was so bad that he stopped attending lectures.

The twelfth and final example of the impact of political correctness, often overlooked, is the adverse economic consequences of it. One can see the plight of the eurozone as the pursuit of civic nationalism takes its toll. The impact of that in Britain is ignored, and the consequences of other aspects of civic nationalism, such as immigration, is likewise ignored and suppressed under a deluge of false allegations and name calling. But the economic consequences are profound. (A rejection of patriotism and an unwillingness to defend the national interest means that national economic problems are not managed; see *The Ponzi Class,* chapters 11 and 12.) The thrust of the arguments in *The Ponzi Class* are not in dispute. That Osborne was planning on a net immigration rate of at least 185,000 per year was disclosed in the small print of his autumn statement in November 2015. The pro-immigration OBR also anticipated an increase in the size of the working population of 1.1million between 2015 and 2020; the OBR stated 'about three-quarters of that would arise from migration'. No provision has been made for the costs of this ongoing immigration, such as the health, social care, housing, or educational costs. The government simply pockets the expected tax revenues and leaves the costs unpaid as a strain on public services. Nor has there been any provision for the future costs, such as pensions, for those immigrants. The Ponzi class simply assumes that there will be yet more immigrants whose money can be pocketed to pay for those costs. This is Ponzi economics, and it is a fraud. Even then, it was disclosed in December 2015 that the 'growth' that the Tories boasted of could only be achieved by a massive rise in consumer debt of no less than

£40billion in 2015, and that this debt-fuelled spending – beyond what families were earning – was forecast to continue indefinitely and actually increase, meaning that the growth rate forecast was entirely accounted for by the amount consumers were prepared to borrow to spend beyond their incomes.

The political correctness continued, following the Tory victory in the 2015 general election, as was evidenced in the leaders' speeches of both the previous coalition partners. In his conference speech, Tim Farron, who replaced Nick Clegg as the Liberal Democrat leader, focused on housing. He told how he had been influenced by a play called *Cathy Come Home*, from the 1960s, and how '*Cathy Come Home* lit a spark in me – it made me angry, it energised me, it made me want to get up and get involved. And so I did, and I haven't stopped. I meet Cathys in my surgery most weeks – people in housing need, desperate for a home, desperate to be settled, desperate for dignity. Maybe some in politics can look at this desperation and shrug it off, or ignore it, rationalise it, or tolerate it. Well I can't.' Instead, Farron announced: 'Liberal Democrats have a target of building 300,000 homes a year – a massive challenge, but we must be prepared to meet it. And this means bold choices. We will give councils the freedom and power to borrow so they can start building again. We will create 10 new garden cities with the infrastructure they need to thrive. We will create a housing investment bank to bring in much more cash and give the industry the support and security it needs.'

This is all very moving stuff, save for the fact that Farron is not reacting to a housing shortage created by some uncompassionate system that leaves innocent young women clutching their children on the street, waiting for white wet liberals like him to come dashing to the rescue. No, the housing shortage is created by people like him, who demand ever more immigration, and he was even at it in the same conference speech:

> 'During the summer, I went to Calais. I went because I wanted to see what was going on for myself and because my liberal instinct told me to be suspicious when the establishment started pointing the finger at outsiders. I wanted to gauge the scale of the problem, to see whether we were being told the truth, I wanted to see the people and not the label. So I met with people and heard their stories of harrowing risks, dangers fled and desperation for their children.
>
> I have to tell you, not a single one of them mentioned coming to Britain to draw benefits. Indeed, more than that. Not a single one of them had ever heard of Britain's benefits system. They

wanted to come to Britain to be safe, to work, to contribute. They see our country as a place of opportunity, a place where you can make the most of yourself, a place where you can be the best you can be – a liberal place. So I am calling on our Government to opt in now to the EU plan to take our share of the refugees to be relocated throughout the continent.'

This is a truly unbelievable piece of self-indulgent sanctimony. At a time when IS are people smuggling vast numbers into the EU, and when they are openly bragging as to how they wish to kill Europeans, Farron actually believes that he can wander around the tents at the immigrant camp at Calais, speak to the illegal immigrants (clutching his handkerchief, no doubt), treat all their stories as proven fact, and make the above comment in all seriousness. No doubt none of those he spoke to had heard of IS either. What Farron is doing is parading his own sense of moral righteousness by his commitment to running up the national debt and spending other people's money on building houses for immigrants, and he is prepared to sacrifice the safety of British citizens in that aim.

In his conference speech, Cameron made great play in what he saw as the Tory Leftie credentials: 'It wasn't just me who put social justice, equality for gay people, tackling climate change, and helping the world's poorest at the centre of the Conservative Party's mission – we all did.' He continued to highlight the number of those from immigrant communities around the Cabinet table. Cameron continued:

'Picture this. You've graduated with a good degree. You send out your CV far and wide. But you get rejection after rejection. What's wrong? It's not the qualifications or the previous experience. It's just two words at the top: first name, surname. Do you know that in our country today: even if they have exactly the same qualifications, people with white-sounding names are nearly twice as likely to get call backs for jobs than people with ethnic-sounding names? This is a true story. One young black girl had to change her name to Elizabeth before she got any calls to interviews. That, in 21^s century Britain, is disgraceful.

We can talk all we want about opportunity, but it's meaningless unless people are really judged equally. Think about it like this. Opportunity doesn't mean much to a British Muslim if he walks down the street and is abused for his faith. Opportunity doesn't mean much to a black person constantly stopped and searched by the police because of the colour of their skin. Opportunity doesn't mean much to a gay person rejected for a job because of the person they love. It doesn't mean much to a disabled person prevented from doing what they're good at because of who they are. I'm a dad of two daughters – opportunity won't mean anything to them if they grow up in a country where they get paid less because of their gender rather than how good they are at their work.'

Regarding social cohesion, Cameron made much of those who are supportive of IS terrorism and of the need to tackle it. He drew no difference between those terrorist sympathizers in Britain and those abroad, saying, 'This ideology, this diseased view of the world, has become an epidemic – infecting minds from the mosques of Mogadishu to the bedrooms of Birmingham,' before setting out three solutions. The first solution was to oppose the 'narrative' that the Muslims are victims. The second was to ' take on extremism in all its forms, the violent and non-violent'. And the third:

'We need to tackle segregation. There are parts of Britain today where you can get by without ever speaking English or meeting anyone from another culture. Zoom in and you'll see some institutions that actually help incubate these divisions. Did you know, in our country, there are some children who spend several hours each day at a Madrassa? Let me be clear: there is nothing wrong with children learning about their faith, whether it's at Madrassas, Sunday Schools or Jewish Yeshivas. But in some Madrassas we've got children being taught that they shouldn't mix with people of other religions; being beaten; swallowing conspiracy theories about Jewish people. These children should be having their minds opened, their horizons broadened...not having their heads filled with poison and their hearts filled with hate.

So I can announce this today: If an institution is teaching children intensively, then whatever its religion, we will, like any other school, make it register so it can be inspected. And be in no doubt: if you are teaching intolerance, we will shut you down.'

This third solution sits uneasily with the speech given by the Home Secretary Theresa May earlier at the conference, when she said:

'When immigration is too high, when the pace of change is too fast, it's impossible to build a cohesive society. It's difficult for

181

schools and hospitals and core infrastructure like housing and transport to cope. And we know that for people in low-paid jobs, wages are forced down even further while some people are forced out of work altogether.'

Theresa May's speech attracted widespread derision, partly because she had dared to contradict the politically correct mantra that mass immigration is good and partly because, as Home Secretary, she was responsible for it. Looking at what Theresa May said, it is clear that she offered no real solution to mass immigration, and the sentiments expressed were little more than flannel. Instead of making speeches, she needs to govern. Neither has she said anything new. The difficulty of integrating large numbers of immigrants was explained by the Conservative MP Enoch Powell in 1968:

'The other dangerous delusion from which those who are wilfully or otherwise blind to realities suffer, is summed up in the word "integration". To be integrated into a population means to become for all practical purposes indistinguishable from its other members. Now, at all times, where there are marked physical differences, especially of colour, integration is difficult though, over a period, not impossible. There are among the Commonwealth immigrants who have come to live here in the last 15 years many thousands whose wish and purpose is to be integrated and whose every thought and endeavour is bent in that direction. But to imagine that such a thing enters the heads of a great and growing majority of immigrants and their descendants is a ludicrous misconception, and a dangerous one.

We are on the verge here of a change. Hitherto it has been force of circumstance and of background which has rendered the very idea of integration inaccessible to the greater part of the immigrant population – that they never conceived or intended such a thing, and that their numbers and physical concentration meant the pressures towards integration which normally bear upon any small minority did not operate. Now we are seeing the growth of positive forces acting against integration, of vested interests in the preservation and sharpening of racial and religious differences, with a view to the exercise of actual domination, first over fellow-immigrants and then over the rest of the population. The cloud no bigger than a man's hand, that can so rapidly overcast the sky, has been visible recently in Wolverhampton and has shown signs of spreading quickly.'

More recently, Rear Admiral Chris Parry, a British military strategist, warned of the danger of a 'Rome Scenario', that Western civilization is faced with a threat comparable with the barbarian invasions that destroyed the Roman Empire: 'Globalisation makes assimilation seem redundant and old-fashioned ... [the process] acts as a sort of reverse colonisation, where groups of people are self-contained, going back and forth between their countries, exploiting sophisticated networks and using instant communication on phones and the internet.'[586] If the immigration is on a large enough scale then the immigrants do not have to integrate but can form a society of themselves in an area. They can speak their own language, retain their own customs, and take advantage of the communications revolution to keep in contact with their homelands by internet, smart phones, and satellite TV. The issues raised by Enoch Powell therefore apply with even greater force. The problem is not that the issues are not recognised, but that the ruling class, of whatever political party, refuses to respect the views of ordinary people and refuses to tackle the situation. Mass immigration continues uninterrupted and on an ever-increasing scale.

Cameron's conference speech was revealing in its political correctness and dishonesty. Cameron is proud to be politically correct, as he revealed at a hustings meeting during his campaign to become Tory leader. At the meeting, according to one member of the audience, Simon Whelband: 'There were a few eyebrows raised when Mr Cameron said political correctness was good because it encouraged people to be more polite to each other.' This is the mentality of the British Prime Minister; as has been set out above, political correctness has a far more evil intent than a concern for politeness. To quote Jaques Barzun: 'Political correctness does not legislate tolerance; it only organizes hatred.'

Despite Cameron's commitment to politeness, his conference speech engaged in stirring up a hatred of society and the English. It is not the case that immigrants are victims of English racism. In the jobs market, immigrants are taking the majority of jobs and have pushed English people out of work. Of course, it might be possible to tell a story of how one immigrant name put off some employers, but that is not typical of the jobs market as a whole (see The Ponzi Class, page 313). So far as education is concerned, it is the poor English who are losing out – as detailed above. Furthermore, it was reported in November 2015 by the Institute for Fiscal Studies that white British pupils were now less likely to go to university than those from ethnic minorities. It was found that 'All ethnic minority groups are now, on average, more likely to go to university than their white British peers.' Researchers discovered that 32.6% of white British pupils go to university, and the figures for others are: Black/Caribbean 37.4%; Pakistani 44.7%; Bangladeshi 48.89%; Indian 67.4%; and Chinese 75.4%. The poorest Chinese families are five times more likely to go to university than poor white British.

Cameron was dishonest to imply that his daughters would be 'paid less because of their gender'. After the conference Cameron announced that public sector organizations, including the NHS, schools, the BBC, councils, and the civil service, will not see the name of applicants when examining job applications. Furthermore, the government announced that it would force firms employing more than 250 workers to publicize an audit of their 'gender pay gap'. David Cameron said: 'I said in my conference speech that I want us to end discrimination and finish the fight for real equality in our country today.' Nicky Morgan, the Equalities Minister, said on Radio 5 Live: 'If you read any of the articles on this, you will find that actually when women ask the question about bonuses, they'll find that their male colleagues have been paid more in bonuses than they have. We think that this is unacceptable.' Mrs Morgan further said: 'The thing about the gender pay gap is understanding why does it happen, often it's women aren't in high enough pay and careers, they don't get to stay in longer before they take time out, it's all those things, it's building that pipeline of talent.'

In education, Girls are more likely to get five good GCSEs than boys. Only a quarter of white boys qualifying for free school meals get five or more good GCSEs. Only a quarter of males go to university, whereas one-third of girls do. Females are more likely to graduate with a 2:1 degree or a First. 55% of those enrolling in medicine and dentistry courses were female, as were 62% of those studying law. Women under 40 earn more than men.

In fact, women find it easier to gain employment, and their pay is more likely to be affected by motherhood rather than sexism. In August 2015, figures from the ONS disclosed that boys earn more than girls up until 21 (possibly due to more girls going to university), that, between the ages of 22 and 39, women earn more than men, and that it is only above the age of 40 that men earn more than women. Figures from the Press Association showed that, in 2013, women in their twenties typically earned £1,111 more than men annually. Patricia Morgan, a researcher on the family, said: 'If the pay gap in the 20s and 30s was the other way around there would be bucketloads of experts jumping up and down demanding that we act to address this dreadful inequality. No one seems to worry about being unfair to men. This is about women and their ability to choose to have children, and to look after them themselves. There is a smack of totalitarianism about the attitude which says women cannot choose to bring up their own children rather than pursue careers.'

Cameron further announced that the police recording of so-called hate crimes against Muslims would be kept separate, the rationale being that Muslims were likely to be facing the consequences from issues such as terrorism and the paedophile gangs. Figures for 2013-14 showed a 45% increase in such crimes following the beheading of Fusilier Lee Rigby in May 2013. More recent figures show that, although there was a large increase in such incidents following the Charlie Hebdo murders in Paris, overall, the figures have since fallen from the 2013-14 level.

This announcement, again, is an attempt to foster a sense of grievance against the English. In fact, it is the ethnic minorities who are responsible for most of the racial violence. For example, this was demonstrated in the 2002-03 British Crime Survey, which revealed that 2% of blacks claimed to have suffered a racially motivated crime, 3% of Asians, and less than 1% whites. Of course 1% of whites, given that they are the overwhelming majority, constitutes a far greater number than 2-3% of an ethnic minority. Nor should it be overlooked that there is interracial violence between the ethnic minorities themselves.

It is hardly surprising that there is hostility towards Muslims from some. The beheadings, the steady flow of volunteers for the barbaric IS, the terrorism, the paedophile gangs, and the overt hostility to Western society – and the extent of the sympathy for such acts from within the Muslim population – is bound to create hostility. The solution is not to demonise the English as being racist, or Western society as anti-Muslim, but to roundly oppose those acts that are unacceptable and for Muslims to make real efforts to integrate into society and accept the values and culture of that society.

Further to his speech about extremism and the Paris attacks by IS, Cameron announced that the numbers employed by the security services would be significantly increased. What he did not do was announce that there would be an increase in border controls. Jihadists could come back and forth just the same as anyone else. Nor did the government show any inclination to take other measures to stem the growth of Muslim extremism. For example, there was increasing concern as to the extent to which Saudi and Qatari money funds Wahhabi-ist mosques across Britain and that such was a contributory factor in the rise of extremism. The literature made available, paid for with Saudi money, was extremist and included DVDs and journals with material advocating that 'homosexuals should be burnt, stoned or thrown from mountains or tall buildings (and then stoned where they fell just to be on the safe side). Those who changed their religion or committed adultery should experience a similar fate.' The Saudis were believed to be spending up to $6billion per annum on Wahhabi-ist propaganda.

The number of Wahhabi-ist (aka Salafi-ist) mosques increased by around 20% in the eight years to 2015, to around 1,850, of which around 110 are thought to be under Wahhabi/Salafi control and in receipt of Saudi funding. Despite the growth in this extremist sect, and the overseas funding of it, the Tories did not act.

Austria, by comparison, banned overseas funding for mosques (only one-off donations being allowed) with a view to help Islam develop within Austrian society to adopt European values. The Austrian Foreign Minister Sebastian Kurz said: 'We have different laws for every single religious community in Austria. There is a special law for the Jewish community, a special law for the orthodox, and a special law for the Muslim community ... the influence of foreign countries is a problem we only have in the Muslim community. We do not have this problem in the other religious communities.' The Austrians have been prepared to adopt laws to deal with a specific problem with a specific group of people, without having to make allegations against other people to avoid being called racist. The Tories are too are in the grip of political correctness to do the same.

SUMMARY

Political correctness was the insurgent political creed of the late 20th century. By the 21st century it has become the establishment political creed. It dominates Western societies. The contempt for ordinary people and for patriotism that the politically correct have is unconcealed. They have successfully infiltrated, as Dr Mapp rightly set out, public institutions from where they can enforce their creed on everyone else. Importantly, they also have access to public monies. As has been set out by the above examples, the consequences are far reaching.

There is an economic concept known as 'producer capture'. This applies where there is a monopoly. Instead of the monopoly responding to customers and producing goods that the customers want, the monopoly produces what it likes, and the consumers are trapped into buying whatever is produced. For example, in a car market, customers may want cars with sunroofs. In a competitive market with a choice of producers, those producers that make cars with sunroofs will sell more cars. However, with a monopoly, if the producer cannot be bothered to manufacture cars with sunroofs, since the customers can go nowhere else then cars without sunroofs will continue to be bought. The monopoly does as it likes.

The same concept applies with the capture of public institutions by the politically correct. For example, would parents normally pay people to teach their children to say, 'Peace Be Upon Him', after saying, 'Mohammed'? Normally they would not – but they are. In December 2015, it was revealed that, at a Christian state school in Worcester, children have been taught to do this in the Religious Education lessons. This, in a predominantly white school, did not arise because parents wanted to pay for teachers to teach this but because the politically correct school decided to do so. The same ethos applies across a range of public institutions. Not only do they do as they like, but go so far as to sincerely believe that they are morally superior in their political correctness. Ordinary people should be grateful for paying up. The politically correct are entitled to be well paid with public monies for showing ordinary plebs how racist etc. those plebs are. The capture of public institutions enables the politically correct to get money via the tax system. Ordinary people have to pay up.

As can be seen from the above examples, Britain has become a less tolerant, less prosperous, and more totalitarian society. There is worse to come. Democracy is steadily hijacked by politically correct institutions. Britain has become a beds in sheds lawyers' dictatorship. Ordinary people are persecuted. Even children are persecuted. Free speech is eroded and lying propaganda promoted. The defensive mechanisms of society have been disabled, thus allowing opportunistic criminals and political extremists to flourish. Patriotism is denigrated and hatred encouraged.

One can consider the above examples from the different perspectives set out earlier in this book. The hatred of Rhodes and his statue can be seen from a genuinely Conservative or ethnic nationalist perspective as a desecration, from a wet liberal, civic nationalist perspective as an attempt to unify by challenging historical wrongs, or from a communist or Habermasian perspective as a means of fomenting radical change (i.e. a communist revolution). There is also Habermas's doctrine that heritage needed to be challenged (i.e. debunked).

Likewise, one can consider the practice of the British Inquisition and its targeting of schoolchildren. A genuine Conservative or ethnic nationalist would object. A wet Liberal would believe that this enables the achievement of national unity by shared ideals of human rights and civic patriotism. A communist view would support the crushing of independent thought, the promotion of a hatred of the English, and the fact that plebs were being politically educated and radicalised.

The drive towards a United States of Europe would, likewise, be opposed by those who are patriotic but supported by those who are keen on international institutions (as per civic nationalism/constitutional patriotism), especially the communists who wish to undermine any concept of national identity and unity. One can examine the other examples cited, as well as many others, in a similar way.

Although the rationale of political correctness has been examined, one should not overthink the communist mindset and try to explain why communists hate so many, spread hatred, and kill so many if given the opportunity. One could just as easily ask why an internet troll posts insults on the internet, why a yobbo lobs a brick through a window, why a vandal sprays graffiti on walls, why a peeping tom can be found hiding in bushes, why dirty old men wear mackintoshes, or why sickos write rude words on lavatory walls. They do so because they are trolls, yobbos, vandals, peeping toms, dirty old men, and sickos. Communists hate, spread hatred, and commit genocide because they are communists. It is what communists do.

One of the above 12 examples stands out in its evil depravity and sets Britain apart from other Western countries. It is a trademark of political correctness that reporting of the news has to be manipulated to hide inconvenient facts. A deviation from this can lead to allegations of racism; for example, if a criminal's immigration status is revealed. Ann Coulter gives a detailed account of how the media in the USA withholds details of illegal immigrant criminality (including rape, paedophila, and murder) from the general public.[587] No doubt, other countries will have their own experiences. In January 2016, there were widespread reports of sex assaults by immigrants on New Year's Eve across Germany, and further reports that such assaults had been taking place elsewhere in Europe, particularly in Sweden. In Cologne 120 women complained; in Hamburg the number was 50. The reports had a common theme of there being large gangs of immigrants involved and of the police refusing to take action.

With the Asian paedophile gangs in Britain, however, the political correctness went far further than that. The authorities (including the police, social workers, and politicians) did not simply try to hide the ethnic backgrounds of the paedophiles; they actively hid the ongoing child abuse itself. They allowed the paedophiles to continue to abuse English children. The authorities were too politically correct to stop paedophila by Asian gangs. They were so snobbish that they themselves reverted to barbarity.

CONCLUSION

The development of civilization requires cooperation and a common commitment to enhance society. The evolution of Western nations has facilitated a more advanced civilization than elsewhere with the attendant higher standards of living. Welfare provision, healthcare, pensions, the rule of law, and democracy have all flourished in the West – albeit not to absolute perfection, but then nothing ever is, and even the best of today's society can be improved upon with steady advance, both socially and economically.

A developed society, politically stable with a prosperous economy, can afford to tolerate alternative lifestyles, atypical activities, and dissent. This does not alter the fact that society did not progress and will not progress by people living in a hippy commune, for example. There needs to be a critical mass of those who are committed to patriotism and the advancement of civilization. No matter how disgruntled some might be at the imperfections of society, they should be on their guard against being used by others to promote dissent; and they should be alert to the consequences of a revolution that might transform Western democracy into, for example, a Sharia state or simply anarchy. Members of a minority should not acquiesce to pressure groups of zealots, corrupted by the receipt of public monies, to agitate endlessly on their behalf. The development of civilization is in the interests of all those who seek a better life.

Collingwood developed the concept of the barbarist, someone who wishes to barbarize civilization. This goes beyond being what Thatcher once described as being a wrecker. A wrecker, often a communist, wants to wreck, and in the 1970s in Britain, many communist trade unionists did wreck much of British industry with restrictive practices and strikes. But the barbarist seeks to totally destroy the targeted civilization. Where Collingwood is wrong is that the barbarist can succeed. Civilization can be destroyed.

William Lind is correct in describing political correctness as cultural Marxism and correct in holding the Frankfurt School responsible for the creed's development. Of course others, such as Gramsci, have also reworked Marxism. But the Frankfurt School's output and dominance of Leftist thought render it the central culprit. The Frankfurt School was neo-Marxist from its very inception, and it remained so.

The three Frankfurt School items were chosen to demonstrate the key points in the attack on the West, and each has a key purpose. Of course, others may decide that other essays and books are of greater importance and that the development of political correctness owes little to the three items chosen. As critical theorists, they are bound to allege that, and no doubt it will be alleged that political correctness does not exist and is simply a term of abuse used by right-wing extremists. But it does exist, as the extent of the denial of its existence demonstrates. Like vampires, communists lurk in dark places away from the sunlight of public awareness. For them to succeed, it is important that their activities are not recognised until it is too late. So they crawl about various government, charity, and other public organizations, feeding off ordinary peoples' monies.

A key reason for the advance of political correctness is that its advocates do not face the financial consequences of their actions. They can carry out their activities on the public payroll. As Dr Mapp has identified, the politically correct have infiltrated public institutions and thus acquired a legislative base with coercive powers – and all the funding that goes with that. The taxpayer funds them, and they have almost unrestricted access to public monies. The West's success thereby becomes its weakness. It is other people, ordinary families, who end up bearing the cost. This issue overlaps the damage caused by the Ponzi class. (see *The Ponzi Class*, which details the costs of the Ponzi economics and globalization that are being dumped onto ordinary people and which advocates a Solidarity Tax to help pay those costs.) Ordinary families have already had to pay their share for Ponzi economics, of which the funding of political correctness is a part, be it in the form of lower pensions, university tuition fees, the seizure of old people's homes, lower wages, the inability to get social housing, etc. Meanwhile, the Ponzi class, including the politically correct, lead the high life with their incomes and assets untouched by the financial calamity they happily cause.

Mrs Thatcher remarked in 1976 that 'Socialist governments traditionally do make a financial mess. They always run out of other people's money. It's quite a characteristic of theirs.' This is a telling point even if it is not quite the whole truth. Socialists rarely run out of money altogether because, when they get a bit low, they go off and start printing it. Nonetheless, Thatcher made an important point that remains relevant especially with respect to the 'We' argument. Time and again on television, and during the 2015 general election campaign in Britain, ordinary people were presented with the 'We' argument: 'we' should be more generous in foreign aid; 'we' should accommodate more immigrants; 'we' should be more compassionate; 'we' should build more houses; etc. Who is 'we'?

In everyday life, when someone is walking down a street and is greeted with an appeal to put money into a bucket for charity, then that someone takes a fiver, say, out of their pocket and puts it in the bucket. That someone is £5 poorer, and the charity gains £5 for its cause. But when it comes to public monies, a different rule applies. Again and again, television studios are full of those (human rights activists, lawyers, politicians, journalists, members of pressure groups, and quangos) who happily demand that 'we' should be doing all sorts of things and donating all kinds of monies without the slightest intention of forking out themselves. (Indeed, many are in receipt of public monies and have a vested interest in more being spent.) No one is stopping these assorted worthies from donating money to whatever cause they are pontificating about if they want to do so. However, they have a far better idea. They have their eyes set on a big pile of cash known as taxpayer's monies. It is that which they wish to dip into. Even the general public can be suckered into this notion and involve themselves in discussion programmes as to how 'we' should be spending more money on all sorts of things. But where does the money come from?

In Britain during the general election campaign of 2015, even the Scottish and Welsh nationalists were very aggressive in their demands that 'we' should let in more immigrants and as to how proud they were that 'we' were giving so much in foreign aid. The Scottish nationalists have been very loud that 'we' should be more generous to Syrians in 2015 and condemned the government's refusal to participate in the EU quota scheme for asylum seekers. The overwhelming majority of immigrants settle in England, London in particular. Scotland and Wales are both dependent upon very large English subsidies to make ends meet. Those Scottish and Welsh nationalists had not the slightest intention of paying so much as twopence. What they were loudly demanding, as with the rest of those advancing the 'we' argument, was that English taxpayer's monies should be spent – not theirs. They were being very generous with somebody else's monies. The free access to (English) taxpayer's monies is a corrupting influence that takes away responsibility and encourages wanton profligacy. The buck stops nowhere.

(The same problem applies to the admission of immigrants into the EU. The Marxist government in Greece, in particular, is happy to watch immigrants pour into Greece, happy in the knowledge that those immigrants will be moving north. Greece does not secure its borders because they do not face the full consequences of the immigration.)

In fairness, many of those advocating political correctness could well be very keen to pay more tax. A Solidarity Tax is the means to allow them to do so. Such a tax could be levied at either 10% or 20% on targeted incomes such as television advertising, the BBC licence fee, union subscriptions, subscriptions to business organizations, charity donations received for those charities promoting and engaged in political correctness, MPs salaries, the salaries of senior civil servants, the salaries of senior executives of public bodies, the pensions of MPs and senior civil servants, the block grant to Scotland and Wales, the salaries and pensions of others who have advocated political correctness (in particular called for mass immigration), the salaries of union officials, all those high-minded judges with their lavish salaries and pensions, etc. Finally, there would be a need to impose a cost on those businesses employing immigrants to fully compensate for the additional costs to the country of those immigrants. A solidarity audit could be performed, with those firms employing immigrants being required to pay a sum equal to the cost of a house for each immigrant they have employed. The same could apply to universities and colleges for their students.

Currently, there are those businesses which happily employ immigrants, sometimes in preference to available local people, paying lower wages and benefiting from the extra output with the increased profits that such employment entails. Yet the cost of housing the immigrants is dumped onto the general public and the taxpayer. Many businessmen think that this is a good thing, as well they might.

It was disclosed in a report by the Migration Advisory Committee in January 2016, that many hospitals and schools were hiring immigrants to 'undercut' British staff by paying the immigrants 'significantly less' – with salaries being up to £6,000 a year less than an equivalent British worker. This 'saving' is not a saving to the taxpayer who has to provide housing for these immigrants, nor to the British people who find that their salaries are forced down at the same time as they have to cope with the increased housing shortage.

Likewise, universities and colleges enrol overseas students and pocket the fees while expecting the general public and the taxpayer to foot the bill for housing those overseas students, many of whom do not return to their own countries once their courses are completed. Likewise, the university and college staff think that this is a good thing and enjoy the extra income, as one can imagine. Those businesses, many of which are involved in a variety of tax dodging escapades (especially the multinationals), and those universities and colleges are benefiting from the extra income by exploiting immigration, and they should be expected to pay the bills for that immigration including the housing costs, rather than, as is currently the case, expecting a whopping great subsidy. The extent of that subsidy should not be underestimated given that, according to Nationwide in December 2015, the average house price had reached £456,229 in Central London, or £146,086 in the North West, for example, and especially given the number of immigrants.

Substantial funds could be raised by insisting that those organizations that promote mass immigration pay for the costs of that immigration.

If sufficient revenues are raised, then it may be possible to compensate those British nationals who have been denied social housing, either in the form of a cash payment or in the form of a newly built house.

To put it into language that might appeal to the Left, what is needed is an irreversible transfer of wealth from those who advocate political correctness to the victims of political correctness. A Solidarity Tax is a means by which such transfer might be achieved.

Thus far, political correctness has advanced remorselessly, without any democratic legitimacy, and there has been no push back. Even supposed centre-right parties across the West have gone along with its strictures. Laws passed relating to immigration, equality, human rights, etc., are deemed sacrosanct. There is no effort to reverse them. But, in 2015, there were signs of increasing public discontent. Merkel's irresponsible offer for Germany to accept unlimited numbers of Syrians proved popular in that country for a few weeks until the sheer scale of the lunacy that she had unleashed became clear and her popularity plummeted. Hungary defended its borders against the immigrant invasion despite what the EU bureaucrats thought.

In the USA, Donald Trump has led the polls to be the Republican Party candidate for the presidency, despite attacks from a whole host of politically correct entities and from within the Republican Party itself. Should he win the presidency and follow through, then the USA will experience a sharp U-turn regarding immigration. In Britain, the Tory renegotiation of Britain's membership of the EU has been revealed as a sham conducted by charlatans (one cannot be too contemptuous of the phoney renegotiation process given the petty nature of the alleged major reforms). Britain might just vote to leave the EU despite the government intention of manipulating the vote.

In France, the Front National was beaten in elections only by the other parties combining to exploit tactical voting. It was a case of the Front National against the rest. Marine Le Pen remarked: 'This election has shown that there are only two forces in the country. The forces of globalization which want to sink France in some kind of internationalist mess, and the forces of patriotism and national identity.' This analysis is close to that voiced by George Wyndham (1863-1913), Conservative MP, when he said that England faced a choice between 'Imperialism which demands Unity at Home between classes, and Unity throughout the Empire' and 'Insular Socialism, and Class Antagonism ...'. He believed that 'Between these two ideals a great battle will be fought ... If Imperialism wins, we shall go on and be a great Empire. If Socialism wins we shall cease to be. The rich will be plundered. The poor will suffer. We shall perish with Babylon, Rome and Constantinople' (*The Ponzi Class*, page 33). In fact, the outcome was in favour of Imperialism when Britain finally introduced Tariff Reform in 1932, but then that decision was overturned with the election of a Labour government in 1945. The British Empire did fall and class antagonism reigned, before giving way to race war politics. That outcome needs to be revisited with patriotism once again becoming the dominant philosophy.

There needs to be a de-Marxification programme to root out the politically correct and consign them to the dustbin of history. In the fight against Muslim extremists such as IS and Al-Qaeda, it is not only necessary to deal with the Islamist hate preachers; it is also necessary to tackle the politically correct hate preachers.

The politically correct can be divided into three groups. First, there are the doctrinaire communists, such as the Frankfurt School. They use high-minded, pompous, and flowery language to mask their true intentions. They aim to bring about a communist revolution with all the attendant destruction and bloodshed. Second, there are the wet liberals, who actually *believe* in the high-minded, pompous and flowery language; they actually *believe* that political correctness is about encouraging politeness and redressing all kinds of social wrongs. For the wet liberals, their vanity, their desire to look good and be morally superior is clouding their judgement; they are snobs, and political correctness is highly appealing to their snobbery. Third, there are those whom Lenin described as useful idiots, and for whom further comment is unnecessary.

As can be seen from the examination of the Frankfurt School, they are hardened communists. Their every word is tailored to foment revolution, anarchy, division, and strife. The failure of the proletariat to do what Marx predicted led to a whole new set of oppressed groups being identified. Class war politics has given way to race war politics. This is a telling point. Instead of conceding that capitalism evolved in a way unforeseen by Marx and welcoming the higher standards of living and better quality of life that the proletariat enjoys, the communists dismiss the views of ordinary people as being false consciousness and then embark on trying to find new excuses for revolution. If class war politics is insufficient to trigger a revolution, then race war politics, with all the danger and hatred which that involves, is to be promoted. For communists, their hatred of society is all consuming. Their motive is hatred and nothing more. They wish to destroy, no matter how bloodily, Western civilization. They are barbarists.

Political correctness is a false morality. It does not increase human rights, equality, or fairness. Mass immigration and multiculturalization are not about enrichment, but about confrontation and conflict. Political correctness is the organization of hatred. It is evil. Those who spout political correctness are not morally superior. They are degenerate. They are snobs. The emperor has no clothes on.

1   JS Mill, *Dissertations and Discussions*, volume 1, second edition, Longmans, Green, Reader, and Dyer, London, page 160

2   JS Mill, *Dissertations and Discussions*, volume 1, second edition, Longmans, Green, Reader, and Dyer, London, page 160

3   JS Mill, *Dissertations and Discussions*, volume 1, second edition, Longmans, Green, Reader, and Dyer, London, page 161

4   JS Mill, *Dissertations and Discussions*, volume 1, second edition, Longmans, Green, Reader, and Dyer, London, page 162

5   JS Mill, *Dissertations and Discussions*, volume 1, second edition, Longmans, Green, Reader, and Dyer, London, page 162

6   JS Mill, *Dissertations and Discussions*, volume 1, second edition, Longmans, Green, Reader, and Dyer, London, page 162

7   JS Mill, *Dissertations and Discussions*, volume 1, second edition, Longmans, Green, Reader, and Dyer, London, page 168

8   JS Mill, *Dissertations and Discussions*, volume 1, second edition, Longmans, Green, Reader, and Dyer, London, page 165

9   JS Mill, *Dissertations and Discussions*, volume 1, second edition, Longmans, Green, Reader, and Dyer, London, page 166

10   JS Mill, *Dissertations and Discussions*, volume 1, second edition, Longmans, Green, Reader, and Dyer, London, page 167

11   JS Mill, *Dissertations and Discussions*, volume 1, second edition, Longmans, Green, Reader, and Dyer, London, page 180

12   JS Mill, *Dissertations and Discussions*, volume 1, second edition, Longmans, Green, Reader, and Dyer, London, page 184

13   JS Mill, *Dissertations and Discussions*, volume 1, second edition, Longmans, Green, Reader, and Dyer, London, page 196

14   JS Mill, *Dissertations and Discussions*, volume 1, second edition, Longmans, Green, Reader, and Dyer, London, page 193

15   JS Mill, *Dissertations and Discussions*, volume 1, second edition, Longmans, Green, Reader, and Dyer, London, page 199

16   JS Mill, *Dissertations and Discussions*, volume 1, second edition, Longmans, Green, Reader, and Dyer, London, page 196

17   JS Mill, *Dissertations and Discussions*, volume 1, second edition, Longmans, Green, Reader, and Dyer, London, page 200

18   JS Mill, *Dissertations and Discussions*, volume 1, second edition, Longmans, Green, Reader, and Dyer, London, page 193

19   Alexander Bain, *John Stuart Mill: A Criticism*, Longmans, Green and Co, London, 1882, page 48

20   RP Anshutz, *The Philosophy of JS Mill*, Oxford at the Clarendon Press, London, 1953, page 30

21   Alexander Bain, *John Stuart Mill: A Criticism*, Longmans, Green and Co, London, 1882, pages 30 and 37

22   Christopher Hibbert, *The French Revolution*, Penguin Books, England, 1982, page 216

23   JS Mill, *Liberty and Representative Government*, edited by RB McCallum, Basil Blackwell, Oxford, 1948, On Liberty, page 3

24   RB McCallum writing his introduction to JS Mill, *Liberty and Representative Government*, edited by RB McCallum, Basil Blackwell, Oxford, 1948, On Liberty, page xxvi

25   Beate Jahn, Barbarian Thoughts: Imperialism in the Philosophy of John Stuart Mill, *Review of International Studies*, 31:3 (2005), page 604

26   Beate Jahn, Barbarian Thoughts: Imperialism in the Philosophy of John Stuart Mill, *Review of International Studies*, 31:3 (2005), pages 603, 605 and 609: and JS Mill, *Liberty and Representative Government*, edited by RB McCallum, Basil Blackwell, Oxford, 1948, On Liberty, page 64

27   JS Mill, *Liberty and Representative Government*, edited by RB McCallum, Basil Blackwell, Oxford, 1948, On Liberty, page 610; and

JS Mill, *Dissertations and Discussions*, volume 1, second edition, Longmans, Green, Reader, and Dyer, London, page 188

28   Clark W Bouton, John Stuart Mill: On Liberty and History, *Western Political Quarterly*, volume 18, number 3, September 1965, pages 569-578

29   Carlos Santiso, Good Governance and Aid Effectiveness: The World Bank and Conditionality, *Georgetown Public Policy Review*, volume 7, number 1, Fall 2001, page 5

30   Arthur Ferrill, *The Fall of the Roman Empire: The Military Explanation*, Thames and Hudson, London, 1986, pages 26 and 29

31   Arthur Ferrill, *The Fall of the Roman Empire: The Military Explanation*, Thames and Hudson, London, 1986, page 129; and Edward Gibbon, *The Decline and Fall of the Roman Empire*, volume 3, Dent & Sons Ltd, Great Britain, 1981, page 182

32   Edward Gibbon, *The Decline and Fall of the Roman Empire*, volume 3, Dent & Sons Ltd, Great Britain, 1981, pages 125-135

33   Edward Gibbon, *The Decline and Fall of the Roman Empire*, volume 3, Dent & Sons Ltd, Great Britain, 1981, pages 201-210

34   Edward Gibbon, *The Decline and Fall of the Roman Empire*, volume 3, Dent & Sons Ltd, Great Britain, 1981, page 177

35   Correlli Barnett, *The Collapse of British Power*, Alan Sutton, Great Britain, 1984, pages 218-228

36   Sidney Pollard, *Britain's Prime and Britain's Decline: The British Economy 1870-1914*, Edward Arnold, Great Britain, 1989, page 169; EJ Hobsbawm, *Industry and Empire*, Penguin Books, Great Britain, 1985, page 169; and Correlli Barnett, *The Collapse of British Power*, Alan Sutton, Great Britain, 1984, page 96

37   Sidney Pollard, *Britain's Prime and Britain's Decline: The British Economy 1870-1914*, Edward Arnold, Great Britain, 1989, page 172

38   Sidney Pollard, *Britain's Prime and Britain's Decline: The British Economy 1870-1914*, Edward Arnold, Great Britain, 1989, page

39   Sidney Pollard, *Britain's Prime and Britain's Decline: The British Economy 1870-1914*, Edward Arnold, Great Britain, 1989, page 199

40   Correlli Barnett, *The Collapse of British Power*, Alan Sutton, Great Britain, 1984, page 94

41   Sidney Pollard, *Britain's Prime and Britain's Decline: The British Economy 1870-1914*, Edward Arnold, Great Britain, 1989, page 205

42   RG Collingwood, *The New Leviathan*, Oxford Univeristy Press, New York, 1992, page 485

43   RG Collingwood, *The New Leviathan*, Oxford Univeristy Press, New York, 1992, page 487

44   RG Collingwood, *The New Leviathan*, Oxford Univeristy Press, New York, 1992, page 487

45   RG Collingwood, *The New Leviathan*, Oxford Univeristy Press, New York, 1992, page 487

46   RG Collingwood, *The New Leviathan*, Oxford Univeristy Press, New York, 1992, page 488

47   RG Collingwood, *The New Leviathan*, Oxford Univeristy Press, New York, 1992, page 489

48   RG Collingwood, *The New Leviathan*, Oxford Univeristy Press, New York, 1992, page 489

49   RG Collingwood, *The New Leviathan*, Oxford Univeristy Press, New York, 1992, page 494

50   RG Collingwood, *The New Leviathan*, Oxford Univeristy Press, New York, 1992, page 501

51   RG Collingwood, *The New Leviathan*, Oxford Univeristy Press, New York, 1992, page 502

52   RG Collingwood, *The New Leviathan*, Oxford Univeristy Press, New York, 1992, page 342

53   RG Collingwood, *The New Leviathan*, Oxford Univeristy Press, New York, 1992, page 342

54   RG Collingwood, *The New Leviathan*, Oxford Univeristy Press, New York, 1992, page 342

55   RG Collingwood, *The New Leviathan*, Oxford Univeristy Press, New York, 1992, page 346

56   RG Collingwood, *The New Leviathan*, Oxford Univeristy Press, New York, 1992, page 347

57   RG Collingwood, *The New Leviathan*, Oxford Univeristy Press, New York, 1992, page 347

58   Tim Newark, The Barbarians; *Warriors and Wars of the Dark Ages*, Blandford Press, Poole, 1986, page 49

59   Arthur Ferrill, *The Fall of the Roman Empire: The Military Explanation*, Thames and Hudson, London, 1986, page 99; and Edward Gibbon, *The Decline and Fall of the Roman Empire*, volume 3, Dent & Sons Ltd, Great Britain, 1981, page 322

60   AHM Jones, The Later Roman Empire 284-602, Volume 1, Basil Blackwell, Padstow, 1986, page 183; and Edward Gibbon, *The Decline and Fall of the Roman Empire*, volume 3, Dent & Sons Ltd, Great Britain, 1981, pages 351, 358 and 373

61   RG Collingwood, *The New Leviathan*, Oxford Univeristy Press, New York, 1992, page 348

62   RG Collingwood, *The New Leviathan*, Oxford Univeristy Press, New York, 1992, page 350

63   RG Collingwood, *The New Leviathan*, Oxford Univeristy Press, New York, 1992, page 352

64   RG Collingwood, *The New Leviathan*, Oxford Univeristy Press, New York, 1992, page 352

65   RG Collingwood, *The New Leviathan*, Oxford Univeristy Press, New York, 1992, page 357

66   Tim Newark, The Barbarians; *Warriors and Wars of the Dark Ages*, Blandford Press, Poole, 1986, pages 96-98

67   RG Collingwood, *The New Leviathan*, Oxford Univeristy Press, New York, 1992, page 353

68   RG Collingwood, *The New Leviathan*, Oxford Univeristy Press, New York, 1992, pages 354 and 355

69   RG Collingwood, *The New Leviathan*, Oxford Univeristy Press, New York, 1992, page 356

70   RG Collingwood, *The New Leviathan*, Oxford Univeristy Press, New York, 1992, page 356

71   RG Collingwood, *The New Leviathan*, Oxford Univeristy Press, New York, 1992, page 357

72   RG Collingwood, *The New Leviathan*, Oxford Univeristy Press, New York, 1992, page 357

73   RG Collingwood, *The New Leviathan*, Oxford Univeristy Press, New York, 1992, page 359

74   RG Collingwood, *The New Leviathan*, Oxford Univeristy Press, New York, 1992, page 361

75   RG Collingwood, *The New Leviathan*, Oxford Univeristy Press, New York, 1992, page 363

76   RG Collingwood, *The New Leviathan*, Oxford Univeristy Press, New York, 1992, page 360

77   RG Collingwood, *The New Leviathan*, Oxford Univeristy Press, New York, 1992, page 360

78   RG Collingwood, *The New Leviathan*, Oxford Univeristy Press, New York, 1992, page 364

79   RG Collingwood, *The New Leviathan*, Oxford Univeristy Press, New York, 1992, page 365

80   RG Collingwood, *The New Leviathan*, Oxford Univeristy Press, New York, 1992, page 367

81   RG Collingwood, *The New Leviathan*, Oxford Univeristy Press, New York, 1992, page 367

82   RG Collingwood, *The New Leviathan*, Oxford Univeristy Press, New York, 1992, page 369

83   RG Collingwood, *The New Leviathan*, Oxford Univeristy Press, New York, 1992, page370

84   RG Collingwood, *The New Leviathan*, Oxford Univeristy Press, New York, 1992, page 371

85   RG Collingwood, *The New Leviathan*, Oxford Univeristy Press, New York, 1992, page 371

86   RG Collingwood, *The New Leviathan*, Oxford Univeristy Press, New York, 1992, page 372

87   RG Collingwood, *The New Leviathan*, Oxford Univeristy Press, New York, 1992, page 373

88   RG Collingwood, *The New Leviathan*, Oxford Univeristy Press, New York, 1992, page 374

89   RG Collingwood, *The New Leviathan*, Oxford Univeristy Press, New York, 1992, page 375

90   RG Collingwood, *The New Leviathan*, Oxford Univeristy Press, New York, 1992, page 375

91   RG Collingwood, *The New Leviathan*, Oxford Univeristy Press, New York, 1992, page 375

92   RG Collingwood, *The New Leviathan*, Oxford Univeristy Press, New York, 1992, page 376

93   RG Collingwood, *The New Leviathan*, Oxford Univeristy Press, New York, 1992, page 377

94   RG Collingwood, *The New Leviathan*, Oxford Univeristy Press, New York, 1992, page 379

95   RG Collingwood, *The New Leviathan*, Oxford Univeristy Press, New York, 1992, page 379

96   RG Collingwood, *The New Leviathan*, Oxford Univeristy Press, New York, 1992, page 380

97   RG Collingwood, *The New Leviathan*, Oxford Univeristy Press, New York, 1992, page 381

98   RG Collingwood, *The New Leviathan*, Oxford Univeristy Press, New York, 1992, page 381

99   RG Collingwood, *The New Leviathan*, Oxford Univeristy Press, New York, 1992, pages 381 and 382

100   RG Collingwood, *The New Leviathan*, Oxford Univeristy Press, New York, 1992, page 385

101   RG Collingwood, *The New Leviathan*, Oxford Univeristy Press, New York, 1992, page 385

102   RG Collingwood, *The New Leviathan*, Oxford Univeristy Press, New York, 1992, page 386

103   David Boucher, editor, *The New Leviathan*, Oxford Univeristy Press, New York, 1992, page xiii

104   *Catholic Encyclopedia*, http://www.newadvent.org/cathen/01267e.htm

105   Hilail Gildin, *Rousseau's Social Contract: the design of an argument*, Chicago, 1983, page 151

106   Hilail Gildin, *Rousseau's Social Contract: the design of an argument*, Chicago, 1983, page 152

107   Jean-Jacques Rousseau, *The Social Contract*, Book 3, chapter 11

108   Jean-Jacques Rousseau, *The Social Contract*, Book 3, chapter 11

109   Richard Murphy, *Collingwood and the Crisis of Western Civilization*, Imprint Academic, Exeter, 2008, page 2

110   RG Collingwood, *The New Leviathan*, Oxford Univeristy Press, New York, 1992, page 351

111   AHM Jones, *The Later Roman Empire 284-602, Volume II*, Basil Blackwell, Padstow, 1986, page 1026

112   AHM Jones, *The Later Roman Empire 284-602, Volume II*, Basil Blackwell, Padstow, 1986, pages 1030 and 1031

113   Correlli Barnett, *The Collapse of British Power*, Alan Sutton, Great Britain, 1984, page 107; and Sidney Pollard, *Britain's Prime and Britain's Decline: The British Economy 1870-1914*, Edward Arnold, Great Britain, 1989, page 235

114   Beate Jahn, Barbarian Thoughts: Imperialism in the Philosophy of John Stuart Mill, *Review of International Studies*, 31:3 (2005), page 609

115   AHM Jones, *The Later Roman Empire 284-602, Volume II*, Basil Blackwell, Padstow, 1986, page 1064

116   Tim Newark, The Barbarians; *Warriors and Wars of the Dark Ages*, Blandford Press, Poole, 1986, page 90

117   Tim Newark, The Barbarians; *Warriors and Wars of the Dark Ages*, Blandford Press, Poole, 1986, pages 52 and 53

118   RG Collingwood, *The New Leviathan*, Oxford Univeristy Press, New York, 1992, page 352

119   Arthur Ferrill, *The Fall of the Roman Empire: The Military Explanation*, Thames and Hudson, London, 1986, page 121; and Edward Gibbon, *The Decline and Fall of the Roman Empire*, volume 3, Dent & Sons Ltd, Great Britain, 1981, page 263

120   Edward Gibbon, *The Decline and Fall of the Roman Empire*, volume 3, Dent & Sons Ltd, Great Britain, 1981, page 377

121   *Collins English Dictionary*, Second Edition, Collins, Glasgow, 1986

122   AHM Jones, *The Later Roman Empire 284-602, Volume I*, Basil Blackwell, Padstow, 1986, page 185

123   Arthur Ferrill, *The Fall of the Roman Empire: The Military Explanation*, Thames and Hudson, London, 1986, page 124

124   Tim Newark, The Barbarians; *Warriors and Wars of the Dark Ages*, Blandford Press, Poole, 1986, page 62

125   Arthur Ferrill, *The Fall of the Roman Empire: The Military Explanation*, Thames and Hudson, London, 1986, page 154

126   Tim Newark, The Barbarians; *Warriors and Wars of the Dark Ages*, Blandford Press, Poole, 1986, page 62

127   RG Collingwood, *The New Leviathan*, Oxford Univeristy Press, New York, 1992, page 352

128   Edward Gibbon, *The Decline and Fall of the Roman Empire*, volume 3, Dent & Sons Ltd, Great Britain, 1981, pages 177 and 178

129   Edward Gibbon, *The Decline and Fall of the Roman Empire*, volume 3, Dent & Sons Ltd, Great Britain, 1981, page 251

130   Arthur Ferrill, *The Fall of the Roman Empire: The Military Explanation*, Thames and Hudson, London, 1986, page 146

131   Edward Gibbon, *The Decline and Fall of the Roman Empire*, volume 3, Dent & Sons Ltd, Great Britain, 1981, page 395

132   Tim Newark, The Barbarians; *Warriors and Wars of the Dark Ages*, Blandford Press, Poole, 1986, page 85

133   Tim Newark, The Barbarians; *Warriors and Wars of the Dark Ages*, Blandford Press, Poole, 1986, pages 90 and 98

134   Edward Gibbon, *The Decline and Fall of the Roman Empire*, volume 6, Dent & Sons Ltd, Great Britain, 1981, page 449

135   JS Mill, *Dissertations and Discussions*, volume 1, second edition, Longmans, Green, Reader, and Dyer, London, pages 165-168

136   RG Collingwood, *The New Leviathan*, Oxford Univeristy Press, New York, 1992, page 342

137   Correlli Barnett, *The Collapse of British Power*, Alan Sutton, Great Britain, 1984, pages 13,14 and 591

138   RG Collingwood, *The New Leviathan*, Oxford Univeristy Press, New York, 1992, page 376

139   Robert Massie, *Dreadnought: Britain, Germany, and the coming of the Great War*, Jonathan Cape, London, 1991, pages 57-65

140   Thomas Pakenham, *The Scramble for Africa*, Weidenfield and Nicholson, London, 1993, pages 206-217 and 239-241

141   John Eatwell, Whatever Happened to Britain?, Duckworth, London, 1982, pages 63-65; and Correlli Barnett, *The Collapse of British Power*, Alan Sutton, Great Britain, 1984, pages 84-88, 101 and 307

142   Stephen Tonge, A Web of English History, http://www.historyhome.co.uk/europe/bisdom.htm

143   Http://www.bbc.co.uk/history/worldwars/wwtwo/hitler_lebensraum

144   Correlli Barnett, *Bonaparte*, Wordsworth Editions Ltd, Chatham, 1998, pages 27 and 30

145   Christopher Hibbert, *The French Revolution*, Penguin Books, St Ives, England, 1982, page 225

146   Oswald Spengler, *The Decline of the West; Perspectives of World-History, Volume Two*, Allen & Unwin, London, 1928, page 454

147   William Lind, *The Origins of Political Correctness*, speech, 2000, page 1

148   Christopher Hibbert, *The French Revolution*, Penguin Books, St Ives, England, 1982, pages 29-41

149   Jean-Jacques Rousseau, *The Social Contract*, Book II, chapter 7

150   Jean-Jacques Rousseau, *The Social Contract*, Book II, chapter 3

151   William Sweet, *Bernard Bosenquet and the Development of Rousseau's Idea of the General Will, Man and Nature*, vol X, pages 179-197

152   Alexander Bain, *John Stuart Mill: A Criticism*, Longmans, Green and Co, London, 1882, pages 30 and 37

153   Christopher Hibbert, *The French Revolution*, Penguin Books, St Ives, England, 1982, page 216

154   William Sweet, Liberalism, *Bosanquet and the Theory of the State, Liberalism, Oppression and Empowerment*, Edwin Mellen Press, Lewiston NY, 1995, page 1; and Creagh McLean Cole, John Anderson, *Lectures on Political Theory 1941-45*, Sydney University Press, Sydney, 2007, page xii

155   JS Mill, *On Liberty*, The Library of Liberal Arts Edition, page 7, cited on: http:// www.serendipit.li/jsmill.htm

156   Beate Jahn, Barbarian Thoughts: Imperialism in the Philosophy of John Stuart Mill, *Review of International Studies*, 31:3 (2005), page 610

157   Clark W Bouton, John Stuart Mill: On Liberty and History, Western Political Quarterly, 18:3 (1965:Sept) pages 569 and 570

158   Bernard Bosanquet, *The Philosophical Theory of the State*, Mcmillan & Co, New York, 1965, page 114

159   Bernard Bosanquet, The Reality of the General Will, *International Journal of Ethics*, vol 4, no 3, page 316

160   William Sweet, *Bernard Bosenquet and the Development of Rousseau's Idea of the General Will, Man and Nature*, vol X, page 9

161   Hilail Gildin, *Rousseau's Social Contract: the design of an argument*, Chicago, 1983, page 151

162   William Sweet, *Bernard Bosenquet and the Development of Rousseau's Idea of the General Will, Man and Nature*, vol X, page 9

163   William Sweet, *Bernard Bosenquet and the Development of Rousseau's Idea of the General Will, Man and Nature*, vol X, page 10

164   William Sweet, *Bernard Bosenquet and the Development of Rousseau's Idea of the General Will, Man and Nature*, vol X, page 11

165   Bernard Bosanquet, *The Philosophical Theory of the State*, Mcmillan & Co, New York, 1965, page 142

166   Jeannie Morefield, Hegelian Organicism, British New Liberalism and the Return of the Family State, History of Political Thought, vol XXIII, No 1, Spring 2002, page 143

167   Stamatoula Panagakou, Defending Bosanquet's Philosophical Theory of the State: A Reassessment of the "Bosanquet-Hobhouse Controversy", *Political Studies Association*, Blackwell Publishing, Oxford, 2005, page 38

168   Hilail Gildin, *Rousseau's Social Contract: the design of an argument*, Chicago, 1983, page 35

169   Jean-Jacques Rouseau, *The Political Writings of Jean-Jacques Rousseau 1712-1778*, Blackwell, Oxford, 1962, page 52

170   Jean-Jacques Rousseau, *Oeuvres completes*, 5 volumes, Paris, 1959-95, edited by M Raymond and B Gagnebin, volume 1, page 388

171   Voltaire, *Correspondenc*e, volume xxvii, page 230

172   Colin Jones, *The Great Nation*, Penguin Books, London, 2003, page 192

173   Colin Jones, *The Great Nation*, Penguin Books, London, 2003, page 193

174   Colin Jones, *The Great Nation*, Penguin Books, London, 2003, page 193

175   Ruth Scarr, *Fatal Purity: Robespierre and the French Revolution*, Vintage, London, 2007, page 21

176   Colin Jones, *The Great Nation*, Penguin Books, London, 2003, page 195

177   Colin Jones, *The Great Nation*, Penguin Books, London, 2003, page 211

178   Author of *Memoires Secretes*, cited by Simon Shama, *Citizens: A Chronicle of the French Revolution*, Penguin Books, London, 2004, page 130

179   Simon Shama, *Citizens: A Chronicle of the French Revolution*, Penguin Books, London, 2004, page 130

180   Simon Shama, *Citizens: A Chronicle of the French Revolution*, Penguin Books, London, 2004, page 131

181   Simon Shama, *Citizens: A Chronicle of the French Revolution*, Penguin Books, London, 2004, page 131

182   Simon Shama, *Citizens: A Chronicle of the French Revolution*, Penguin Books, London, 2004, page 151

183   Robespierre, speech on 18 Floreal II, cited by MH Huet, *Mourning Glory: The Will of the French Revolution*, Philadelphia, 1997, page 27

184   Ruth Scarr, *Fatal Purity: Robespierre and the French Revolution*, Vintage, London, 2007, page 76

185   Ruth Scarr, *Fatal Purity: Robespierre and the French Revolution*, Vintage, London, 2007, page 210

186   Ruth Scarr, *Fatal Purity: Robespierre and the French Revolution*, Vintage, London, 2007, page 216

187   KM Baker, editor, *The Old Regime and the French Revolution*, University of Chicago, London and Chicago, 1987, page 355

188   Ruth Scarr, *Fatal Purity: Robespierre and the French Revolution*, Vintage, London, 2007, page 261

189   David Andress, *The Terror – Civil War in the French Revolution*, Abacus, Great Britain, 2010, page 235

190   David Andress, *The Terror – Civil War in the French Revolution*, Abacus, Great Britain, 2010, page 249

191   David Andress, *The Terror – Civil War in the French Revolution*, Abacus, Great Britain, 2010, page 249

192   KM Baker, editor, *The Old Regime and the French Revolution*, University of Chicago, London and Chicago, 1987, page 374

193   John Hardman, *Robespierre*, Routledge, London, 2000, page 107

194   David Andress, *The Terror – Civil War in the French Revolution*, Abacus, Great Britain, 2010, page 300

195   David Andress, *The Terror – Civil War in the French Revolution*, Abacus, Great Britain, 2010, page 311

196   Gill Hands, *Marx: A Beginners Guide*, Hodder & Stoughton, London, 2000, page 2

197   Gill Hands, *Marx: A Beginners Guide*, Hodder & Stoughton, London, 2000, page 3

198   Gill Hands, *Marx: A Beginners Guide*, Hodder & Stoughton, London, 2000, page 9

199   Gill Hands, *Marx: A Beginners Guide*, Hodder & Stoughton, London, 2000, page 17

200   Gill Hands, *Marx: A Beginners Guide*, Hodder & Stoughton, London, 2000, page 27

201   Gill Hands, *Marx: A Beginners Guide*, Hodder & Stoughton, London, 2000, page 32

202   Gill Hands, *Marx: A Beginners Guide*, Hodder & Stoughton, London, 2000, page 32

203   Karl Marx and Fredrerick Engels, *Manifesto of the Communist Party*, 1848, page 2

204   Gill Hands, *Marx: A Beginners Guide*, Hodder & Stoughton, London, 2000, page 35

205   Karl Marx and Fredrick Engels, *Manifesto of the Communist Party*, February 1848, page 14

206   Gill Hands, *Marx: A Beginners Guide*, Hodder & Stoughton, London, 2000, page 42

207   Karl Marx and Fredrerick Engels, *Manifesto of the Communist Party*, 1848, page 2

208   Gill Hands, *Marx: A Beginners Guide*, Hodder & Stoughton, London, 2000, page 43

209   Karl Marx and Fredrick Engels, *Manifesto of the Communist Party*, February 1848, page 22

210   Gill Hands, *Marx: A Beginners Guide*, Hodder & Stoughton, London, 2000, page 46

211   Karl Marx and Fredrick Engels, *Manifesto of the Communist Party*, February 1848, page 26

212   Gill Hands, *Marx: A Beginners Guide*, Hodder & Stoughton, London, 2000, page 48

213   David Held, *Introduction to Critical Theory*, Hutchinson & Co (Publishers) Ltd, London, 1980, page 190

214   Karl Marx and Fredrick Engels, *Manifesto of the Communist Party*, February 1848, page 16

215   Karl Marx and Fredrick Engels, *Manifesto of the Communist Party*, February 1848, page 24

216   Karl Marx and Fredrick Engels, *Manifesto of the Communist Party*, February 1848, page 52

217   Rick Roderick, *Habermas and the Foundations of Critical Theory*, MacMillan Publishers Ltd, London, 1986, page 32

218   Karl Marx and Fredrick Engels, *Manifesto of the Communist Party*, February 1848, page 34

219   Gill Hands, *Marx: A Beginners Guide*, Hodder & Stoughton, London, 2000, page 58

220   Robert Wistrich, *Trotsky*, Robson Books, London, 1979, page 87

221   Robert Wistrich, *Trotsky*, Robson Books, London, 1979, page 105

222   Robert Wistrich, *Trotsky*, Robson Books, London, 1979, page 108

223   Robert Wistrich, *Trotsky*, Robson Books, London, 1979, page 109

224   Robert Wistrich, *Trotsky*, Robson Books, London, 1979, page 113

225   Robert Wistrich, *Trotsky*, Robson Books, London, 1979, page 113

226   Robert Wistrich, *Trotsky*, Robson Books, London, 1979, page 114

227   Robert Wistrich, *Trotsky*, Robson Books, London, 1979, page 115

228   Robert Wistrich, *Trotsky*, Robson Books, London, 1979, page 51

229   Robert Wistrich, *Trotsky*, Robson Books, London, 1979, page 52

230   Stuart Schram, *The Thought of Mao Tse-Tung*, Cambridge University Press, Cambridge, 1989, page 110

231   Stuart Schram, *The Thought of Mao Tse-Tung*, Cambridge University Press, Cambridge, 1989, page 193

232   James Chieh Hsiung, *The Logic of Maoism*, Praeger Publishers, New York, 1974, page 89

233   James Chieh Hsiung, *The Logic of Maoism*, Praeger Publishers, New York, 1974, page 113

234   Stuart Schram, *The Thought of Mao Tse-Tung*, Cambridge University Press, Cambridge, 1989, page 169

235   Stuart Schram, *The Thought of Mao Tse-Tung*, Cambridge University Press, Cambridge, 1989, page 151

236   Stuart Schram, *The Thought of Mao Tse-Tung*, Cambridge University Press, Cambridge, 1989, page 164

237   James Chieh Hsiung, *The Logic of Maoism*, Praeger Publishers, New York, 1974, page 157

238   James Chieh Hsiung, *The Logic of Maoism*, Praeger Publishers, New York, 1974, page 158

239   James Chieh Hsiung, *The Logic of Maoism*, Praeger Publishers, New York, 1974, page 20

240   James Chieh Hsiung, *The Logic of Maoism*, Praeger Publishers, New York, 1974, page 20

241   James Chieh Hsiung, *The Logic of Maoism*, Praeger Publishers, New York, 1974, page 23

242   James Chieh Hsiung, *The Logic of Maoism*, Praeger Publishers, New York, 1974, page 44

243   James Chieh Hsiung, *The Logic of Maoism*, Praeger Publishers, New York, 1974, page 46

244   William Lind, *The Origins of Political Correctness*, speech, 2000, page 3

245   Martin Jay, *The Dialectical Imagination: A History of the Frankfurt School and The Institute of Social Research, 1923-1950*, page 11

246   Martin Jay, *The Dialectical Imagination: A History of the Frankfurt School and The Institute of Social Research, 1923-1950*, page 84

247   William S Lind, *'Political Correctness': A Short History of an Ideology*, edited by William S Lind, Free Congress Foundation, 2004, page 5

248   Raymond Marrow and David Brown, *Critical Theory and Methodology*, Sage Publication, London, 1994, page 15

249   William Lind, *The Origins of Political Correctness*, speech, 2000, page 4

250   Michael Minnicino, The New Dark Age, The Schiller Institute, Vol 1, No 1, 1992, page 8

251   Raymond V Raehn, *'Political Correctness': A Short History of an Ideology*, edited by William S Lind, Free Congress Foundation, 2004, page 9

252   Gerald L Atkinson, What Is The Frankfurt School (and its effect on America)?, *Western Voices World News*, 2009, page 4

253   Raymond V Raehn, *'Political Correctness': A Short History of an Ideology*, edited by William S Lind, Free Congress Foundation, 2004, page 10

254   Rick Roderick, *Habermas and the Foundations of Critical Theory*, MacMillan Publishers Ltd, London, 1986, page 137

255   Martin Jay, *The Dialectical Imagination: A History of the Frankfurt School and The Institute of Social Research, 1923-1950*, page 39

256   William Lind, *The Origins of Political Correctness*, speech, 2000, page 5

257   Douglas Kellner, *Herbert Marcuse and the Crisis of Marxism*, Macmillan Education Ltd, Basingstoke, 1984, page 122

258   Rick Roderick, *Habermas and the Foundations of Critical Theory*, MacMillan Publishers Ltd, London, 1986, page 148

259   Martin Jay, *The Dialectical Imagination: A History of the Frankfurt School and The Institute of Social Research, 1923-1950*, page 116

260   David Held, *Introduction to Critical Theory*, Hutchinson & Co (Publishers) Ltd, London, 1980, page 13

261   David Held, *Introduction to Critical Theory*, Hutchinson & Co (Publishers) Ltd, London, 1980, page 15

262   David Held, *Introduction to Critical Theory*, Hutchinson & Co (Publishers) Ltd, London, 1980, page 25

263   David Held, *Introduction to Critical Theory*, Hutchinson & Co (Publishers) Ltd, London, 1980, page 184

264   David Held, *Introduction to Critical Theory*, Hutchinson & Co (Publishers) Ltd, London, 1980, page 184

265   David Held, *Introduction to Critical Theory*, Hutchinson & Co (Publishers) Ltd, London, 1980, page 185

266   Raymond Marrow and David Brown, *Critical Theory and Methodology*, Sage Publication, London, 1994, page 95

267   Douglas Kellner, *Herbert Marcuse and the Crisis of Marxism*, Macmillan Education Ltd, Basingstoke, 1984, page 40

268   Raymond Marrow and David Brown, *Critical Theory and Methodology*, Sage Publication, London, 1994, page 97

269   Raymond Marrow and David Brown, *Critical Theory and Methodology*, Sage Publication, London, 1994, page 16

270   Raymond Marrow and David Brown, *Critical Theory and Methodology*, Sage Publication, London, 1994, page 151

271   Raymond Marrow and David Brown, *Critical Theory and Methodology*, Sage Publication, London, 1994, page 154

272   Rick Roderick, *Habermas and the Foundations of Critical Theory*, MacMillan Publishers Ltd, London, 1986, page 7

273   Rick Roderick, *Habermas and the Foundations of Critical Theory*, MacMillan Publishers Ltd, London, 1986, page 59

274   Rick Roderick, *Habermas and the Foundations of Critical Theory*, MacMillan Publishers Ltd, London, 1986, page 73

275   Rick Roderick, *Habermas and the Foundations of Critical Theory*, MacMillan Publishers Ltd, London, 1986, page 43

276   Rick Roderick, *Habermas and the Foundations of Critical Theory*, MacMillan Publishers Ltd, London, 1986, page 44

277   Rick Roderick, *Habermas and the Foundations of Critical Theory*, MacMillan Publishers Ltd, London, 1986, page 45

278   David Held, *Introduction to Critical Theory*, Hutchinson & Co (Publishers) Ltd, London, 1980, page 277

279   Douglas Kellner, *Herbert Marcuse and the Crisis of Marxism*, Macmillan Education Ltd, Basingstoke, 1984, page 93

280   Douglas Kellner, *Herbert Marcuse and the Crisis of Marxism*, Macmillan Education Ltd, Basingstoke, 1984, page 115

281   Martin Schoolman, *The Imaginary Witness*, The Free Press, New York, 1980, page 311

282   Gerald Atkinson, About the Frankfurt School, , August 1999, page 2

283   Raymond V Raehn, '*Political Correctness': A Short History of an Ideology*, edited by William S Lind, Free Congress Foundation, 2004, page 10

284   TW Adorno et al, *The Authoritarian Personality*, Harper & Brothers, New York, 1950, page vii

285   TW Adorno et al, *The Authoritarian Personality*, Harper & Brothers, New York, 1950, page 605

286   TW Adorno et al, *The Authoritarian Personality*, Harper & Brothers, New York, 1950, page 1

287   TW Adorno et al, *The Authoritarian Personality*, Harper & Brothers, New York, 1950, page 1

288   TW Adorno et al, *The Authoritarian Personality*, Harper & Brothers, New York, 1950, page 10

289   TW Adorno et al, *The Authoritarian Personality*, Harper & Brothers, New York, 1950, page 972

290   TW Adorno et al, *The Authoritarian Personality*, Harper & Brothers, New York, 1950, page 973

291   TW Adorno et al, *The Authoritarian Personality*, Harper & Brothers, New York, 1950, page 974

292   TW Adorno et al, *The Authoritarian Personality*, Harper & Brothers, New York, 1950, page 975

293   TW Adorno et al, *The Authoritarian Personality*, Harper & Brothers, New York, 1950, page 975

294   Martin Jay, *The Dialectical Imagination: A History of the Frankfurt School and The Institute of Social Research, 1923-1950*, page 240

295   *Studies in the Scope and Method of "The Authoritarian Personality"*, edited by Richard Christie and Marie Jahoda, The Free Press, Glencoe, Illinois, 1954, page 66

296   *Studies in the Scope and Method of "The Authoritarian Personality"*, edited by Richard Christie and Marie Jahoda, The Free Press, Glencoe, Illinois, 1954, page 119

297   TW Adorno et al, *The Authoritarian Personality*, Harper & Brothers, New York, 1950, page 23

298   TW Adorno et al, *The Authoritarian Personality*, Harper & Brothers, New York, 1950, page 24

299   TW Adorno et al, *The Authoritarian Personality*, Harper & Brothers, New York, 1950, page 26

300   TW Adorno et al, *The Authoritarian Personality*, Harper & Brothers, New York, 1950, page 31

301   TW Adorno et al, *The Authoritarian Personality*, Harper & Brothers, New York, 1950, page 31

302   TW Adorno et al, *The Authoritarian Personality*, Harper & Brothers, New York, 1950, page 57

303   TW Adorno et al, *The Authoritarian Personality*, Harper & Brothers, New York, 1950, page 60

304   TW Adorno et al, *The Authoritarian Personality*, Harper & Brothers, New York, 1950, page 60

305   TW Adorno et al, *The Authoritarian Personality*, Harper & Brothers, New York, 1950, page 60

306   TW Adorno et al, *The Authoritarian Personality*, Harper & Brothers, New York, 1950, page 61

307   Robert Wistrich, *Trotsky*, Robson Books, London, 1979, page 192

308   TW Adorno et al, *The Authoritarian Personality*, Harper & Brothers, New York, 1950, page 62

309   TW Adorno et al, *The Authoritarian Personality*, Harper & Brothers, New York, 1950, page 82

310   TW Adorno et al, *The Authoritarian Personality*, Harper & Brothers, New York, 1950, page 82

311   TW Adorno et al, *The Authoritarian Personality*, Harper & Brothers, New York, 1950, page 102

312   TW Adorno et al, *The Authoritarian Personality*, Harper & Brothers, New York, 1950, page 102

313   TW Adorno et al, *The Authoritarian Personality*, Harper & Brothers, New York, 1950, page 103

314   TW Adorno et al, *The Authoritarian Personality*, Harper & Brothers, New York, 1950, page 104

315   TW Adorno et al, *The Authoritarian Personality*, Harper & Brothers, New York, 1950, page 122

316   TW Adorno et al, *The Authoritarian Personality*, Harper & Brothers, New York, 1950, page 129

317   TW Adorno et al, *The Authoritarian Personality*, Harper & Brothers, New York, 1950, page 144

318   TW Adorno et al, *The Authoritarian Personality*, Harper & Brothers, New York, 1950, page 147

319   TW Adorno et al, *The Authoritarian Personality*, Harper & Brothers, New York, 1950, page 150

320   TW Adorno et al, *The Authoritarian Personality*, Harper & Brothers, New York, 1950, page 151

321   TW Adorno et al, *The Authoritarian Personality*, Harper & Brothers, New York, 1950, page 152

322   TW Adorno et al, *The Authoritarian Personality*, Harper & Brothers, New York, 1950, page 154

323   TW Adorno et al, *The Authoritarian Personality*, Harper & Brothers, New York, 1950, page 155

324   TW Adorno et al, *The Authoritarian Personality*, Harper & Brothers, New York, 1950, page 307

325   TW Adorno et al, *The Authoritarian Personality*, Harper & Brothers, New York, 1950, page 213

326   TW Adorno et al, *The Authoritarian Personality*, Harper & Brothers, New York, 1950, page 156

327   *Studies in the Scope and Method of "The Authoritarian Personality"*, edited by Richard Christie and Marie Jahoda, The Free Press, Glencoe, Illinois, 1954, page 25

328   *Studies in the Scope and Method of "The Authoritarian Personality"*, edited by Richard Christie and Marie Jahoda, The Free Press, Glencoe, Illinois, 1954, page 26

329   TW Adorno et al, *The Authoritarian Personality*, Harper & Brothers, New York, 1950, page 181

330   TW Adorno et al, *The Authoritarian Personality*, Harper & Brothers, New York, 1950, page 182

331   TW Adorno et al, *The Authoritarian Personality*, Harper & Brothers, New York, 1950, page 182

332   TW Adorno et al, *The Authoritarian Personality*, Harper & Brothers, New York, 1950, page 218

333   TW Adorno et al, *The Authoritarian Personality*, Harper & Brothers, New York, 1950, page 218

334   TW Adorno et al, *The Authoritarian Personality*, Harper & Brothers, New York, 1950, page 220

335   TW Adorno et al, *The Authoritarian Personality*, Harper & Brothers, New York, 1950, page 221

336   TW Adorno et al, *The Authoritarian Personality*, Harper & Brothers, New York, 1950, page 221

337   TW Adorno et al, *The Authoritarian Personality*, Harper & Brothers, New York, 1950, page 342

338   TW Adorno et al, *The Authoritarian Personality*, Harper & Brothers, New York, 1950, page 376

339   TW Adorno et al, *The Authoritarian Personality*, Harper & Brothers, New York, 1950, page 428

340   TW Adorno et al, *The Authoritarian Personality*, Harper & Brothers, New York, 1950, page 428

341   TW Adorno et al, *The Authoritarian Personality*, Harper & Brothers, New York, 1950, page 365

342   TW Adorno et al, *The Authoritarian Personality*, Harper & Brothers, New York, 1950, page 476

343   TW Adorno et al, *The Authoritarian Personality*, Harper & Brothers, New York, 1950, page 388

344   TW Adorno et al, *The Authoritarian Personality*, Harper & Brothers, New York, 1950, page 476

345   TW Adorno et al, *The Authoritarian Personality*, Harper & Brothers, New York, 1950, page 284

346   TW Adorno et al, *The Authoritarian Personality*, Harper & Brothers, New York, 1950, page 486

347   TW Adorno et al, *The Authoritarian Personality*, Harper & Brothers, New York, 1950, page 620

348   TW Adorno et al, *The Authoritarian Personality*, Harper & Brothers, New York, 1950, page 877

349   TW Adorno et al, *The Authoritarian Personality*, Harper & Brothers, New York, 1950, page 633

350   TW Adorno et al, *The Authoritarian Personality*, Harper & Brothers, New York, 1950, page 637

351   TW Adorno et al, *The Authoritarian Personality*, Harper & Brothers, New York, 1950, page 638

352   TW Adorno et al, *The Authoritarian Personality*, Harper & Brothers, New York, 1950, page 653

353   TW Adorno et al, *The Authoritarian Personality*, Harper & Brothers, New York, 1950, page 653

354   TW Adorno et al, *The Authoritarian Personality*, Harper & Brothers, New York, 1950, page 663

355   TW Adorno et al, *The Authoritarian Personality*, Harper & Brothers, New York, 1950, page 949

356   TW Adorno et al, *The Authoritarian Personality*, Harper & Brothers, New York, 1950, page 950

357   TW Adorno et al, *The Authoritarian Personality*, Harper & Brothers, New York, 1950, page 966

358   TW Adorno et al, *The Authoritarian Personality*, Harper & Brothers, New York, 1950, page 966

359   TW Adorno et al, *The Authoritarian Personality*, Harper & Brothers, New York, 1950, page 671

360   TW Adorno et al, *The Authoritarian Personality*, Harper & Brothers, New York, 1950, page 671

361   TW Adorno et al, *The Authoritarian Personality*, Harper & Brothers, New York, 1950, page 672

362   TW Adorno et al, *The Authoritarian Personality*, Harper & Brothers, New York, 1950, page 673

363   TW Adorno et al, *The Authoritarian Personality*, Harper & Brothers, New York, 1950, page 675

364   TW Adorno et al, *The Authoritarian Personality*, Harper & Brothers, New York, 1950, page 704

365   TW Adorno et al, *The Authoritarian Personality*, Harper & Brothers, New York, 1950, page 704

366   TW Adorno et al, *The Authoritarian Personality*, Harper & Brothers, New York, 1950, page 706

367   TW Adorno et al, *The Authoritarian Personality*, Harper & Brothers, New York, 1950, page 709

368   TW Adorno et al, *The Authoritarian Personality*, Harper & Brothers, New York, 1950, page 717

369   TW Adorno et al, *The Authoritarian Personality*, Harper & Brothers, New York, 1950, page 724

370   TW Adorno et al, *The Authoritarian Personality*, Harper & Brothers, New York, 1950, page 726

371   David Held, *Introduction to Critical Theory*, Hutchinson & Co (Publishers) Ltd, London, 1980, page 47

372   Martin Jay, *The Dialectical Imagination: A History of the Frankfurt School and The Institute of Social Research, 1923-1950*, page 228

373   Michael Minnicino, The New Dark Age, The Schiller Institute, Vol 1, No 1, 1992, page 4

374   TW Adorno et al, *The Authoritarian Personality*, Harper & Brothers, New York, 1950, page 753

375   TW Adorno et al, *The Authoritarian Personality*, Harper & Brothers, New York, 1950, page 759

376   TW Adorno et al, *The Authoritarian Personality*, Harper & Brothers, New York, 1950, page 971

377   TW Adorno et al, *The Authoritarian Personality*, Harper & Brothers, New York, 1950, page 797

378   TW Adorno et al, *The Authoritarian Personality*, Harper & Brothers, New York, 1950, page 806

379   TW Adorno et al, *The Authoritarian Personality*, Harper & Brothers, New York, 1950, page 858

380   TW Adorno et al, *The Authoritarian Personality*, Harper & Brothers, New York, 1950, page 872

381   TW Adorno et al, *The Authoritarian Personality*, Harper & Brothers, New York, 1950, page 873

382   TW Adorno et al, *The Authoritarian Personality*, Harper & Brothers, New York, 1950, page 878

383   TW Adorno et al, *The Authoritarian Personality*, Harper & Brothers, New York, 1950, page 882

384   TW Adorno et al, *The Authoritarian Personality*, Harper & Brothers, New York, 1950, page 888

385   TW Adorno et al, *The Authoritarian Personality*, Harper & Brothers, New York, 1950, page 889

386   TW Adorno et al, *The Authoritarian Personality*, Harper & Brothers, New York, 1950, page 889

387   TW Adorno et al, *The Authoritarian Personality*, Harper & Brothers, New York, 1950, page 890

388   David Held, *Introduction to Critical Theory*, Hutchinson & Co (Publishers) Ltd, London, 1980, page 128

389   Douglas Kellner, *Herbert Marcuse and the Crisis of Marxism*, Macmillan Education Ltd, Basingstoke, 1984, page 107

390   Douglas Kellner, *Herbert Marcuse and the Crisis of Marxism*, Macmillan Education Ltd, Basingstoke, 1984, page 108

391   Douglas Kellner, *Herbert Marcuse and the Crisis of Marxism*, Macmillan Education Ltd, Basingstoke, 1984, page 110

392   Martin Jay, *The Dialectical Imagination: A History of the Frankfurt School and The Institute of Social Research, 1923-1950*, page 92

393   Martin Schoolman, *The Imaginary Witness*, The Free Press, New York, 1980, page 80

394   Douglas Kellner, *Herbert Marcuse and the Crisis of Marxism*, Macmillan Education Ltd, Basingstoke, 1984, page 1

395   Martin Jay, *The Dialectical Imagination: A History of the Frankfurt School and the Institute of Social Research*, page 97

396   Martin Jay, *The Dialectical Imagination: A History of the Frankfurt School and The Institute of Social Research, 1923-1950*, page 97

397   Herbert Marcuse, *Repressive Tolerance*, essay, 1965, page 1

398   Herbert Marcuse, *Repressive Tolerance*, essay, 1965, page 2

399   Herbert Marcuse, *Repressive Tolerance*, essay, 1965, page 4

400   Herbert Marcuse, *Repressive Tolerance*, essay, 1965, page 4

401   Herbert Marcuse, One Dimensional Man, Routledge & Kegn Paul Ltd, London, 1964, page 8

402   Herbert Marcuse, *Repressive Tolerance*, essay, 1965, page 5

403   Herbert Marcuse, *Repressive Tolerance*, essay, 1965, page 5

404   Herbert Marcuse, *Repressive Tolerance*, essay, 1965, page 7

405   Herbert Marcuse, *Repressive Tolerance*, essay, 1965, page 8

406   Herbert Marcuse, *Repressive Tolerance*, essay, 1965, page 11

407   Herbert Marcuse, *Repressive Tolerance*, essay, 1965, page 11

408   Herbert Marcuse, *Repressive Tolerance*, essay, 1965, page 13

409   Herbert Marcuse, *Repressive Tolerance*, essay, 1965, page 14

410   Herbert Marcuse, *Repressive Tolerance*, essay, 1965, page 15

411   Raymond V Raehn, '*Political Correctness': A Short History of an Ideology*, edited by William S Lind, Free Congress Foundation, 2004, page 11

412   David Horowitz, The Origins of Political Correctness, William Lind, YouTube

413   Herbert Marcuse, *Repressive Tolerance*, essay, 1965, page 7

414   Herbert Marcuse, *Repressive Tolerance*, essay, 1965, page 7

415   Herbert Marcuse, *Repressive Tolerance*, essay, 1965, page 8

416   Douglas Kellner, *Herbert Marcuse and the Crisis of Marxism*, Macmillan Education Ltd, Basingstoke, 1984, page 95

417   Douglas Kellner, *Herbert Marcuse and the Crisis of Marxism*, Macmillan Education Ltd, Basingstoke, 1984, page 95

418   Martin Schoolman, *The Imaginary Witness*, The Free Press, New York, 1980, page 45

419   Douglas Kellner, *Herbert Marcuse and the Crisis of Marxism*, Macmillan Education Ltd, Basingstoke, 1984, page 96

420   Douglas Kellner, *Herbert Marcuse and the Crisis of Marxism*, Macmillan Education Ltd, Basingstoke, 1984, page 96

421   Douglas Kellner, *Herbert Marcuse and the Crisis of Marxism*, Macmillan Education Ltd, Basingstoke, 1984, page 231

422   Douglas Kellner, *Herbert Marcuse and the Crisis of Marxism*, Macmillan Education Ltd, Basingstoke, 1984, page 39

423   Douglas Kellner, *Herbert Marcuse and the Crisis of Marxism*, Macmillan Education Ltd, Basingstoke, 1984, page 85

424   Herbert Marcuse, *One Dimensional Man*, Routledge & Kegn Paul Ltd, London, 1964, page xii

425   Douglas Kellner, *Herbert Marcuse and the Crisis of Marxism*, Macmillan Education Ltd, Basingstoke, 1984, page 253

426   Herbert Marcuse, *One Dimensional Man*, Routledge & Kegn Paul Ltd, London, 1964, page 7

427   Martin Schoolman, *The Imaginary Witness*, The Free Press, New York, 1980, page 79

428   Herbert Marcuse, *One Dimensional Man*, Routledge & Kegn Paul Ltd, London, 1964, page 6

429   Martin Schoolman, *The Imaginary Witness*, The Free Press, New York, 1980, page 302

430   David Held, *Introduction to Critical Theory*, Hutchinson & Co (Publishers) Ltd, London, 1980, page 75

431   Martin Schoolman, *The Imaginary Witness*, The Free Press, New York, 1980, page 319

432   Douglas Kellner, *Herbert Marcuse and the Crisis of Marxism*, Macmillan Education Ltd, Basingstoke, 1984, page 289

433   Douglas Kellner, *Herbert Marcuse and the Crisis of Marxism*, Macmillan Education Ltd, Basingstoke, 1984, page 290

434   Martin Schoolman, *The Imaginary Witness*, The Free Press, New York, 1980, page 314

435   Martin Schoolman, *The Imaginary Witness*, The Free Press, New York, 1980, page 314

436   Herbert Marcuse, *Negations: essays in critical theory*, 1968, page 261

437   Douglas Kellner, *Herbert Marcuse and the Crisis of Marxism*, Macmillan Education Ltd, Basingstoke, 1984, page 303

438   Martin Schoolman, *The Imaginary Witness*, The Free Press, New York, 1980, page 303

439   Jurgen Habermas, Citizenship and National Identity: Some Reflections on the Future of Europe, *Theorizing Citizenship*, edited by Ronald Beiner, State University of New York, Albany, 1995, page 255

440   Jurgen Habermas, Citizenship and National Identity: Some Reflections on the Future of Europe, *Theorizing Citizenship*, edited by Ronald Beiner, State University of New York, Albany, 1995, page 256

441   Jurgen Habermas, Citizenship and National Identity: Some Reflections on the Future of Europe, *Theorizing Citizenship*, edited by Ronald Beiner, State University of New York, Albany, 1995, page 257

442   Jurgen Habermas, Citizenship and National Identity: Some Reflections on the Future of Europe, *Theorizing Citizenship*, edited by Ronald Beiner, State University of New York, Albany, 1995, page 258

443   Jurgen Habermas, Citizenship and National Identity: Some Reflections on the Future of Europe, *Theorizing Citizenship*, edited by Ronald Beiner, State University of New York, Albany, 1995, page 258

444   Jurgen Habermas, Citizenship and National Identity: Some Reflections on the Future of Europe, *Theorizing Citizenship*, edited by Ronald Beiner, State University of New York, Albany, 1995, page 258

445   Jurgen Habermas, Citizenship and National Identity: Some Reflections on the Future of Europe, *Theorizing Citizenship*, edited by Ronald Beiner, State University of New York, Albany, 1995, page 259

446   Jurgen Habermas, Citizenship and National Identity: Some Reflections on the Future of Europe, *Theorizing Citizenship*, edited by Ronald Beiner, State University of New York, Albany, 1995, page 259

447   Jurgen Habermas, Citizenship and National Identity: Some Reflections on the Future of Europe, *Theorizing Citizenship*, edited by Ronald Beiner, State University of New York, Albany, 1995, page 259

448   Jurgen Habermas, Citizenship and National Identity: Some Reflections on the Future of Europe, *Theorizing Citizenship*, edited by Ronald Beiner, State University of New York, Albany, 1995, page 260

449   Jurgen Habermas, Citizenship and National Identity: Some Reflections on the Future of Europe, *Theorizing Citizenship*, edited by Ronald Beiner, State University of New York, Albany, 1995, page 261

450   Jurgen Habermas, Citizenship and National Identity: Some Reflections on the Future of Europe, *Theorizing Citizenship*, edited by Ronald Beiner, State University of New York, Albany, 1995, page 264

451   Jurgen Habermas, Citizenship and National Identity: Some Reflections on the Future of Europe, *Theorizing Citizenship*, edited by Ronald Beiner, State University of New York, Albany, 1995, page 265

452   Jurgen Habermas, Citizenship and National Identity: Some Reflections on the Future of Europe, *Theorizing Citizenship*, edited by Ronald Beiner, State University of New York, Albany, 1995, page 266

453   Jurgen Habermas, Citizenship and National Identity: Some Reflections on the Future of Europe, *Theorizing Citizenship*, edited by Ronald Beiner, State University of New York, Albany, 1995, page 267

454   Jurgen Habermas, Citizenship and National Identity: Some Reflections on the Future of Europe, *Theorizing Citizenship*, edited by Ronald Beiner, State University of New York, Albany, 1995, page 270

455   Jurgen Habermas, Citizenship and National Identity: Some Reflections on the Future of Europe, *Theorizing Citizenship*, edited by Ronald Beiner, State University of New York, Albany, 1995, page 272

456   Jurgen Habermas, Citizenship and National Identity: Some Reflections on the Future of Europe, *Theorizing Citizenship*, edited by Ronald Beiner, State University of New York, Albany, 1995, page 278

457   Jurgen Habermas, Opening Up Fortress Europe, *Kolner Stadtanzeiger*, 8 November 2006, page 1

458   Jurgen Habermas, Opening Up Fortress Europe, *Kolner Stadtanzeiger*, 8 November 2006, page 2

459   Jurgen Habermas, Opening Up Fortress Europe, *Kolner Stadtanzeiger*, 8 November 2006, page 2

460   *Collins English Dictionary*, Second Edition, Collins, Glasgow, 1986

461   *Collins English Dictionary*, Second Edition, Collins, Glasgow, 1986

462   *Collins English Dictionary*, Second Edition, Collins, Glasgow, 1986

463   *Collins English Dictionary*, Second Edition, Collins, Glasgow, 1986

464   *Collins English Dictionary*, Second Edition, Collins, Glasgow, 1986

465   *Collins English Dictionary*, Second Edition, Collins, Glasgow, 1986

466   *Collins English Dictionary*, Second Edition, Collins, Glasgow, 1986

467   *Collins English Dictionary*, Second Edition, Collins, Glasgow, 1986

468   Patriotism, *Stanford Encylcopedia of Philosophy*, 2009, page 2

469   Patriotism, *Stanford Encylcopedia of Philosophy*, 2009, page 3

470   Patriotism, *Stanford Encylcopedia of Philosophy*, 2009, page 12

471   Jan-Werner Muller, On the Origins of Constitutional Patriotism, *Contemporary Political Theory*, 2006, 5, page 281

472   Jan-Werner Muller, On the Origins of Constitutional Patriotism, *Contemporary Political Theory*, 2006, 5, page 282

473   Jan-Werner Muller, On the Origins of Constitutional Patriotism, *Contemporary Political Theory*, 2006, 5, page 283

474   Jan-Werner Muller, On the Origins of Constitutional Patriotism, *Contemporary Political Theory*, 2006, 5, page 284

475   Jan-Werner Muller, On the Origins of Constitutional Patriotism, *Contemporary Political Theory*, 2006, 5, page 287

476   Jan-Werner Muller, On the Origins of Constitutional Patriotism, *Contemporary Political Theory*, 2006, 5, page 289

477   Jan-Werner Muller, On the Origins of Constitutional Patriotism, *Contemporary Political Theory*, 2006, 5, page 289

478   Jan-Werner Muller, On the Origins of Constitutional Patriotism, *Contemporary Political Theory*, 2006, 5, page 292

479   Habermas, cited by Clarissa Rile Hayward, *Democracy's Identity Problem: Is "Constitutional Patriotism" the Answer?*, Ohio State University, 2006, page 5

480   Cecile Laborde, *From Constitutional to Civic Patriotism*, 32 BJ Pol S, Cambridge University Press, 2002, page 591

481   Clarissa Rile Hayward, *Democracy's Identity Problem: Is "Constitutional Patriotism" the Answer?*, Ohio State University, 2006, page 8

482   Cecile Laborde, *From Constitutional to Civic Patriotism*, 32 BJ Pol S, Cambridge University Press, 2002, page 595

483   P Markell, Making Affect Safe For Democracy? On "Constitutional Patriotism", *Political Theory,* 28, 2000, page 54

484   Cecile Laborde, *From Constitutional to Civic Patriotism*, 32 BJ Pol S, Cambridge University Press, 2002, page 596

485   Cecile Laborde, *From Constitutional to Civic Patriotism*, 32 BJ Pol S, Cambridge University Press, 2002, page 597

486   Patriotism, *Stanford Encyclopedia of Philosophy*, 2009, page 18

487   Roger Scruton, In Defence of the Nation, *The Philosopher on Dover Beech*, Manchester, 1990, page 319

488   John Eric Fossum, *On the Prospects for a Viable Constitutional Patriotism in Complex Multinational Entities, Canada and the European Union Compared*, Arena, University of Oslo, Norway, 2007, page 2

489   Andrea Baumeister, *Diversity and Unity: The Problem with Constitutional Patriotism*, University of Sterling, page 2

490   Habermas cited by Clarissa Rile Hayward, *Democracy's Identity Problem: Is "Constitutional Patriotism" the Answer?*, Ohio State University, 2006, page 8

491   John Eric Fossum, *On the Prospects for a Viable Constitutional Patriotism in Complex Multinational Entities, Canada and the European Union Compared*, Arena, University of Oslo, Norway, 2007, page 9

492   Cecile Laborde, *From Constitutional to Civic Patriotism*, 32 BJ Pol S, Cambridge University Press, 2002, page 600

493   Clarissa Rile Hayward, *Democracy's Identity Problem: Is "Constitutional Patriotism" the Answer?*, Ohio State University, 2006, page 4

494   Simon Hix, The Study of the European Union II: the 'new governance' agenda and its rival, *Journal of European Public Policy,*

5:1, March 1998, page 41

495   Andreas Follesdal and Simon Hix, Why There is a Democratic Deficit in the EU: A Response to Majone and Moravcsik, *JCMS*, 2006, Volume 44, Number 3, page 552

496   Simon Hix, The Study of the European Union II: the 'new governance' agenda and its rival, *Journal of European Public Policy*, 5:1, March 1998, page 51

497   Simon Hix, The Study of the European Union II: the 'new governance' agenda and its rival, *Journal of European Public Policy*, 5:1, March 1998, page 53

498   Kevin Featherstone, Jean Monnet and the 'Democratic Deficit' in the European Union, *Journal of Common Market Studies*, volume 32, number 2, June 1994, page 150

499   Kevin Featherstone, Jean Monnet and the 'Democratic Deficit' in the European Union, *Journal of Common Market Studies*, volume 32, number 2, June 1994, page 164

500   Derek Unwin, The European Community: From 1945 to 1985, *European Union Politics*, edited by Michelle Cini, Oxford University Press, Oxford, 2003, page 17

501   Andreas Follesdal and Simon Hix, Why There is a Democratic Deficit in the EU: A Response to Majone and Moravcsik, *JCMS*, 2006, Volume 44, Number 3, page 538

502   Andreas Follesdal and Simon Hix, Why There is a Democratic Deficit in the EU: A Response to Majone and Moravcsik, *JCMS*, 2006, Volume 44, Number 3, page 541

503   Lene Hansen and Michael C Williams, The Myths of Europe: Legitimacy, Community and the 'Crisis' of the EU, Journal of Common Market Studies, volume 37, number 2, June 1999, page 236

504   Cecile Laborde, *From Constitutional to Civic Patriotism*, 32 BJ Pol S, Cambridge University Press, 2002, page 607

505   John Eric Fossum, *On the Prospects for a Viable Constitutional Patriotism in Complex Multinational Entities, Canada and the*

European Union Compared, Arena, University of Oslo, Norway, 2007, page 14

506   *Collins English Dictionary*, Second Edition, Collins, Glasgow, 1986

507   Bhikhu Parekh, Cultural Diversity and Liberal Democracy, in David Beetham (editor), *Defining and Measuring Democracy*, Sage Publications, London, 1994, pages 200-201

508   Bhikhu Parekh, Cultural Diversity and Liberal Democracy, in David Beetham (editor), *Defining and Measuring Democracy*, Sage Publications, London, 1994, page 201

509   Bhikhu Parekh, Cultural Diversity and Liberal Democracy, in David Beetham (editor), *Defining and Measuring Democracy*, Sage Publications, London, 1994, page 201

510   Bhikhu Parekh, Cultural Diversity and Liberal Democracy, in David Beetham (editor), *Defining and Measuring Democracy*, Sage Publications, London, 1994, page 201

511   Bhikhu Parekh, Cultural Diversity and Liberal Democracy, in David Beetham (editor), *Defining and Measuring Democracy*, Sage Publications, London, 1994, page 202

512   Bhikhu Parekh, Cultural Diversity and Liberal Democracy, in David Beetham (editor), *Defining and Measuring Democracy*, Sage Publications, London, 1994, page 202

513   Bhikhu Parekh, Cultural Diversity and Liberal Democracy, in David Beetham (editor), *Defining and Measuring Democracy*, Sage Publications, London, 1994, page 203

514   Bhikhu Parekh, Cultural Diversity and Liberal Democracy, in David Beetham (editor), *Defining and Measuring Democracy*, Sage Publications, London, 1994, page 204

515   Bhikhu Parekh, Cultural Diversity and Liberal Democracy, in David Beetham (editor), *Defining and Measuring Democracy*, Sage Publications, London, 1994, page 205

516   Bhikhu Parekh, Cultural Diversity and Liberal Democracy, in David Beetham (editor), *Defining and Measuring Democracy*, Sage Publications, London, 1994, page 205

517   Bhikhu Parekh, Cultural Diversity and Liberal Democracy, in David Beetham (editor), *Defining and Measuring Democracy*, Sage Publications, London, 1994, page205

518   Bhikhu Parekh, Cultural Diversity and Liberal Democracy, in David Beetham (editor), *Defining and Measuring Democracy*, Sage Publications, London, 1994, page 206

519   Bhikhu Parekh, Cultural Diversity and Liberal Democracy, in David Beetham (editor), *Defining and Measuring Democracy*, Sage Publications, London, 1994, page 206

520   Bhikhu Parekh, Cultural Diversity and Liberal Democracy, in David Beetham (editor), *Defining and Measuring Democracy*, Sage Publications, London, 1994, page 206

521   Bhikhu Parekh, Cultural Diversity and Liberal Democracy, in David Beetham (editor), *Defining and Measuring Democracy*, Sage Publications, London, 1994, page 207

522   Bhikhu Parekh, Cultural Diversity and Liberal Democracy, in David Beetham (editor), *Defining and Measuring Democracy*, Sage Publications, London, 1994, page 207

523   Bhikhu Parekh, Cultural Diversity and Liberal Democracy, in David Beetham (editor), *Defining and Measuring Democracy*, Sage Publications, London, 1994, page 207

524   Bhikhu Parekh, Cultural Diversity and Liberal Democracy, in David Beetham (editor), *Defining and Measuring Democracy*, Sage Publications, London, 1994, page 208

525   Bhikhu Parekh, Cultural Diversity and Liberal Democracy, in David Beetham (editor), *Defining and Measuring Democracy*, Sage Publications, London, 1994, page 208

526   Bhikhu Parekh, Cultural Diversity and Liberal Democracy, in David Beetham (editor), *Defining and Measuring Democracy*, Sage Publications, London, 1994, page 210

527   Bhikhu Parekh, Cultural Diversity and Liberal Democracy, in David Beetham (editor), *Defining and Measuring Democracy*, Sage Publications, London, 1994, page 211

528   Bhikhu Parekh, Cultural Diversity and Liberal Democracy, in David Beetham (editor), *Defining and Measuring Democracy*, Sage Publications, London, 1994, page 212

529   Bhikhu Parekh, Cultural Diversity and Liberal Democracy, in David Beetham (editor), *Defining and Measuring Democracy*, Sage Publications, London, 1994, page 213

530   Bhikhu Parekh, Cultural Diversity and Liberal Democracy, in David Beetham (editor), *Defining and Measuring Democracy*, Sage Publications, London, 1994, page 216

531   Bhikhu Parekh, Cultural Diversity and Liberal Democracy, in David Beetham (editor), *Defining and Measuring Democracy*, Sage Publications, London, 1994, page 217

532   Edmund Burke, *Reflections on the Revolution in France*, 1790, Harvard Classics, Volume 2, Part 3, paragraph 279

533   JS Mill, *Dissertations and Discussions*, volume 1, second edition, Longmans, Green, Reader, and Dyer, London, page 162

534   Beate Jahn, Barbarian Thoughts: Imperialism in the Philosophy of John Stuart Mill, *Review of International Studies*, 31:3 (2005), page 188

535   Bhikhu Parekh, Cultural Diversity and Liberal Democracy, in David Beetham (editor), *Defining and Measuring Democracy*, Sage Publications, London, 1994, page 218

536   Bhikhu Parekh, Cultural Diversity and Liberal Democracy, in David Beetham (editor), *Defining and Measuring Democracy*, Sage Publications, London, 1994, page 218

537   Bhikhu Parekh, Cultural Diversity and Liberal Democracy, in David Beetham (editor), *Defining and Measuring Democracy*, Sage Publications, London, 1994, page 219

538   Brian Barry, *Culture and Equality*, Harvard University Press, USA, 2001, page 23

539   Colin Tyler, Strangers and Compatriots: The Political Theory of Cultural Diversity, *Governance in Multicultural Societies*, Ashgate, Aldershot 2004

540   Bhikhu Parekh, *Rethinking Multiculturalism: Cultural Diversity and Political Theory*, London, Macmillan, 2000, page 6

541   RG Collingwood, *The New Leviathan*, Oxford Univeristy Press, New York, 1992, page 485

542   RG Collingwood, *The New Leviathan*, Oxford Univeristy Press, New York, 1992, paragraphs 41.53 and 41.54

543   Brian Barry, *Culture and Equality*, Harvard University Press, USA, 2001, page 22

544   Brian Barry, *Culture and Equality*, Harvard University Press, USA, 2001, page 72

545   Brian Barry, *Culture and Equality*, Harvard University Press, USA, 2001, page 72

546   Brian Barry, *Culture and Equality*, Harvard University Press, USA, 2001, page 89

547   Brian Barry, *Culture and Equality*, Harvard University Press, USA, 2001, page 88

548   Uri Ra'anan, State and Nation in Multiethnic Societies, Manchester University Press, Manchester, 1991, page 10

549   Uri Ra'anan, State and Nation in Multiethnic Societies, Manchester University Press, Manchester, 1991, page 5

550   Bhikhu Parekh, *Rethinking Multiculturalism: Cultural Diversity and Political Theory*, London, Macmillan, 2000, page 235

551   Uri Ra'anan, State and Nation in Multiethnic Societies, Manchester University Press, Manchester, 1991, page 11

552   Brian Barry, *Culture and Equality*, Harvard University Press, USA, 2001, page 77

553   Brian Barry, *Culture and Equality*, Harvard University Press, USA, 2001, page 77

554   Brian Barry, *Culture and Equality*, Harvard University Press, USA, 2001, page 124

555   Brian Barry, *Culture and Equality*, Harvard University Press, USA, 2001, page 127

556   Brian Barry, *Culture and Equality*, Harvard University Press, USA, 2001, page 135

557   Jeremy Waldron, Minority Cultures and the Cosmopolitan Alternative, *The Rights of Minority Cultures*, Will Kymlicka (editor), Oxford University Press, USA, 1995, page 109

558   Brian Barry, *Culture and Equality*, Harvard University Press, USA, 2001, page 253

559   Bhikhu Parekh, *Rethinking Multiculturalism: Cultural Diversity and Political Theory*, London, Macmillan, 2000, page 104

560   Bhikhu Parekh, Cultural Particularity of Liberal Democracy, in *Prospects for Democracy*, David Held (editor), Polity Press, Cambridge, 1993, page 158

561   Bhikhu Parekh, *Rethinking Multiculturalism: Cultural Diversity and Political Theory*, London, Macmillan, 2000, page 97

562   Bhikhu Parekh, *Rethinking Multiculturalism: Cultural Diversity and Political Theory*, London, Macmillan, 2000, page 343

563   Bhikhu Parekh, *Rethinking Multiculturalism: Cultural Diversity and Political Theory*, London, Macmillan, 2000, page 194

564   JA Scholte, *Globalization and Governance: From Statism to Polycentrism*, Centre for the Study of Globalization and Regionalization, February 2004, page 6; and Vince Cable MP, *Multiple Identities: Living with the New Politics of Identity*, Demos, 2005

565   Richard Body, *England for the English*, New European Publications, London, 2001, page 11

566   Gianfranco Poggi, *The Development of the Modern State*, Hutchinson & Co (Publishers) Ltd, London, 1978, pages 6, 8 and 90

567   Hagen Schulze, States, *Nations and Nationalism*, Blackwell Publishers, Oxford, 1996, page 97

568   Parekh Report, London, Profile, 2000, paragraphs 3.28-3.30

569   Brian Barry, *Culture and Equality*, Harvard University Press, USA, 2001, page 292

570   Tony Linsell, *An English Nationalism*, Athelney, King's Lynn, 2001, page 62

571   Tony Linsell, *An English Nationalism*, Athelney, King's Lynn, 2001, page 64

572   Richard Body, *England for the English*, New European Publications, London, 2001, page 64

573   Cecile Laborde, *From Constitutional to Civic Patriotism*, 32 BJ Pol S, Cambridge University Press, 2002, page 611

574   Jan-Werner Muller, *A General Theory of Constitutional Patriotism*, page 12

575   Jan-Werner Muller, *A General Theory of Constitutional Patriotism*, page 22

576   Jan-Werner Muller, *A General Theory of Constitutional Patriotism*, page 15

577   Jan-Werner Muller, *A General Theory of Constitutional Patriotism*, page 29

578   Clarissa Rile Hayward, *Democracy's Identity Problem: Is "Constitutional Patriotism" the Answer?*, Ohio State University, 2006, page 2

579   Andrea Baumeister, *Diversity and Unity: The Problem with Constitutional Patriotism*, University of Sterling, page 4

580   Andrea Baumeister, *Diversity and Unity: The Problem with Constitutional Patriotism*, University of Sterling, page 5

581   Andrea Baumeister, *Diversity and Unity: The Problem with Constitutional Patriotism*, University of Sterling, page 22

582   Ann Coulter, *Adios America*, Regency Publishing, Washington, 2015, page 94

583   Melanie Phillips, *Londonistan*, Gibson Square, London, 2006, page 70

584   Simon Jenkins, *Daily Mail*, 12th September 2015

585   Melanie Phillips, *Londonistan*, Gibson Square, London, 2006, page 57

586   Fjordman, Stupidity Without Borders – The Alliance of Utopias, The Brussels Journal, 17th July 2006

587   Ann Coulter, *Adios America*, Regency Publishing, Washington, 2015 (a long and detailed set of examples are given throughout the book)

Printed in Great Britain
by Amazon